for Jo (Mi Dandas

... I hope this book will illuminate your ideas about how we could move forward.

With respect + affection,

(Mark (Bush Doctor II))

THE STATE, VIOLENCE AND DEVELOPMENT

To my mother, for her great warmth,
and for teaching me to care and persevere

The State, Violence and Development

The Political Economy of War in Mozambique, 1975-1992

MARK F. CHINGONO

Avebury

Aldershot • Brookfield USA • Hong Kong • Singapore • Sydney

© Mark F. Chingono 1996

Published by
Avebury
Ashgate Publishing Limited
Gower House
Croft Road
Aldershot
Hants GU11 3HR
England

Ashgate Publishing Company
Old Post Road
Brookfield
Vermont 05036
USA

British Library Cataloguing in Publication Data

Chingono, Mark F.
   The state,violence and development : the political economy
   of war in Mozambique, 1975-1992. - (The making of modern
   Africa)
   1. Mozambique - History - 1975- 2.Mozambique - Economic
   conditions - 1975- 3.Mozambique - Politics and government -
   1975-
   I. Title
   967 . 9 ' 05

   ISBN 1 85972 077 3

Library of Congress Catalog Card Number: 96-84017

Printed and bound in Great Britain by
Ipswich Book Co. Ltd., Ipswich, Suffolk

Contents

Tables   *vii*

Acknowledgements   *viii*

Foreword   *x*

Preface   *xii*

Abbreviations   *xv*

1   Introduction   1

2   The local dynamics of the war:
     From banditry to civil war   25

3   War, economic crisis and the emergence of
     the grass-roots war economy   71

4   War and political change: Issues and perspectives   127

5   Religion, war and politics: Religious ideology and
     power in a changing society   161

6   Women, war and change: An ambiguous legacy   209

7   Elements of a critical social theory of
     the state, violence and development   244

Conclusion   276

Selected bibliography   282

Appendix   288

Name index   290

Tables

Table 3.1   Changes in grassroots war economy exchange
             rates in Manica Province   103

Table 4.1   Reasons for the war as perceived by the dispossessed 139

Table 4.2   Proportion of people who wanted to vote   139

Table 7.1   Projected population data for 2000   257

Table I   Impact of insecurity on population distribution   288

Table II   Data on displaced and affected populations in
             Manica Province   289

Acknowledgements

The thoughts, comments and even life experiences of many people have, to varying degrees and in different ways, shaped the evolution of this work; they will be found on the following pages. Let me acknowledge with gratitude the friends and colleagues who solicited, encouraged, criticized, occasionally resisted, and yet somehow always managed to improve one or more of the themes touched in the study: David Lehmann, for invaluable help from the initiation to the completion of this study; Ken Wilson, a seasoned researcher on Mozambique, for advice on conducting research in a war situation, for giving me access to his work, and for encouragement as well as critical comments on an early draft; Peter Fry for his useful criticisms and comments during the early phase of the research; Jean Claude-Legrand for providing the much needed critical intellectual associate in the field; the late Otto Roesch for useful comments on Chapter Five; and John Illiffe and John Lonsdale, for their critical comments. Among those who also deserve special thanks for encouraging comments on various chapters of the book are: Patricia Hayes, Joanna Lewis, Marella Buckley, Alissa Trotz, Ato Quayson and Sam Kostmayer. The detailed constructive criticisms of Keith Hart have, however, made a special contribution. I would like to thank Sam Akech for assistance in the daunting task of data processing and type-setting the manuscript and Consolata Dengu for typing the Bibliography.

I am also grateful to the Cambridge Commonwealth Trust and King's College for sponsorship which made this research possible. The Mozambican authorities, in particular the National Commission for Emergencies (CENE), must be thanked for their cooperation and permission to conduct the research. Heartfelt thanks go to my research guides, Anselmo Kampira, Anabella Tome and Adjuni Albasini for risking their lives during our frequent 'quick road marches' - to use Kampira's phrase - into the danger zones. Most especially, I am grateful to the ordinary Mozambicans who have had more than their quotient of misery, but whose warmth and love made my stay with them an ever memorable experience. Last, but not least, 'enough respect' to all the unacknowledged heroes and heroines who have kept our afflicted communities 'well-charged', lively and dynamic.

All the errors, of omission or commission, are, however, my sole responsibility.

Mark F. Chingono, Cambridge, January 1996.

Foreword

Our twentieth century world has been a world of war and revolution - and of counter-revolution. The pattern was inaugurated by the French revolution, a popular uprising whose attempt to establish democracy was subverted by Napoleon's restoration of privilege and inequality. In this century there have been two periods of unparalleled social upheaval on a global scale. We call them the first and second world wars. Each provoked a distinctive phase in the ongoing transformation of world society: the Russian revolution and the anti-colonial revolution. And, sure enough, each revolution was subverted by a counter-revolution, the assertion of reactionary power from the top.

After the first world war, this took the form of powerful bureaucratic states - fascist, communist and welfare states, including Stalin's "socialism in one country". The second world war, having undermined European empire in Asia and then in Africa, launched America to a position of world dominance which it used to sustain the counter-revolution, confronting the communist alliance in what became the Cold war and supporting dictatorship against democracy wherever it emerged in the former colonies.

Portugal's empire took longer than most to collapse. It was overthrown by a genuine popular movement, the anti-colonial revolution of the peoples of Mozambique, Angola and the other African territories. In Southern Africa, the independent government of Mozambique, formed by Frelimo, was aligned with the Russian bloc; and its Stalinist bureaucracy soon turned against many of the people who had fought for liberation. To this counter-revolutionary tendency was added a regional variant of America's strategy for containing Third World democratic movements, this time allied to the white settler regimes of Southern Africa. Renamo was the instrument of this counter-revolution, the protracted war in Mozambique its disastrous consequence.

Mark Chingono's path-breaking study looks back at this confusion from the standpoint of an end to the Cold War and the cessation of fighting in

Mozambique. He recognises that, at one level, Frelimo and Renamo are two sides of the counter-revolutionary coin. Moreover, he is open to the new social possibilities entailed in the wreckage left by the war. He finds in the grass-roots market economy, in the violence of everyday life, in the new religious movements and in the freedom of women and youth the stuff of an emergent civil society capable of restoring the momentum lost so tragically soon after the achievement of independence.

It is too early to say whether Africa's stalled anti-colonial revolution can be revived at this time. America's global posture will be decisive; but South Africa's transition to non-racial democracy has removed the single largest obstacle in Mozambique's immediate hinterland. Chingono rests his case with demonstrating the sheer resilience of the people of Chimoio. Their efforts of social reconstruction link them inexorably to the general movement of world society in the 1990s. They know this and their awareness is reflected in the forms of religious and political experiment they are now generating in the aftermath of decades of war. There was a time when misguided western left-wingers looked to Mozambique as a model of socialist development. They would be well-advised to look to Mozambique today through the lens provided by Mark Chingono in this innovative book.

Keith Hart
Director
African Studies Centre
University of Cambridge

Preface

The motivation for this study was threefold. First, I felt that the prevailing accounts of Mozambique's recently ended conflict, in particular its impact on state-society relationships, were theoretically inadequate. Left largely to either ideologically partisan analyses or analyses that highlight and dramatize the enormity of the conflict's destruction, the study of Mozambique seemed in need of a critical and refreshing analysis of the complex relationships between the state, violence and social change. Second, by virtue of being a spring-board for revolutionary transformation in Southern Africa, initially by supporting liberation movements in the region, and now by making radical break-throughs (or a break with the past) in the relationship between the state and society, Mozambique assumes a general significance for development and policy and offers an opportunity to critically examine some popular assumptions about the state and the war-society interface. Third, and a fact that all too many scholars omit, by accident or design, the dispossessed's innovative response to war and economic crisis offers some useful insights into the beautiful simplicity and emancipatory potential of discovering elements of the solution in the problem itself; remarkably, the dispossessed did this by inventing a dynamic grass-roots war economy in response to economic crisis.

Motivated by the above concerns, this work is a modest attempt at conceptually capturing the essence of this important historical moment in the transformation of Mozambique's political economy. As we shall see in the pages to come, not only did war cause considerable destruction of the economy, the break-down of the basic institutional fabric of society, but it also accelerated and intensified processes of social transformation. These processes, characterised by social decomposition, political recomposition and economic re-organisation, have resulted in a fundamental alteration of the relationship between the state and the civil society and a change in the power configuration between and among various social groups. The disintegration of the state and other traditional structures of domination, for instance, resulted in a power vacuum which has been filled by newly emergent social groups and movements. These 'unintended consequences' of the war, in particular the subversion of established norms and values and a challenge to the dominant power structures, in some ways constitutes a 'social revolt within a rebellion'. This book seeks to explore the dynamics of this complex process.

The overriding concern is to identify the major forces - and their articulation - shaping the unfolding processes of change, and to delineate elements of a critical social theory of violence and development. The thrust of the analysis will be on highlighting the regenerative potential of violence and the resilience and resourcefulness of the dispossessed; far from being mere victims of war, the dispossessed have been active agents shaping their lives and societies, and in their political engagement in a context of anarchy and disorder, they have transformed adversity into advantage. In an attempt to anticipate what the future holds, the study will also try to understand the significance of these changes to the ordinary people and their implications for post-war economic and socio-political reconstruction.

Situated within a dynamic historical analytical framework that emphasises systems of control, domination and accumulation as central to historical change, the study will examine the 'weapons' (economic, cultural, religious, ideological, overt resistance, etc.) the weak use in their political struggle against domination.[1] This holistic framework, which is based on a contextualization of interactions and happenings at both micro and macro, local and global levels, illuminate the dynamics of social change and demystify some of the assumptions about the war-society interface. The fundamental conclusion is that war has to be understood as an historical process with multiple consequences, some of them positive in the long-run. If the analysis appears too negative/critical, then it would have achieved its objectives, for it is only through such criticism and self-criticism that we can discover our weaknesses and move forward - criticism is a negative task that seeks to achieve positive results. Indeed the ideas which are articulated here are extremely simple and should be obvious. The difficulty lies, as Keynes once put it, "not in the new ideas, but in escaping from the old ones, which ramify, for those brought up as most of us have been, into every corner of our minds."[2] Needless to say, the book only provides only an introduction to its subject, and it should be followed by a number of related works by a variety of authors.

Empirically, the study is based on data obtained from a critical historical survey conducted in Manica Province between March and October 1992. During this period the war was at its height as each side in the conflict tried to gain more ground in the battlefield so as to bargain from a position of strength in the negotiation process, which resulted in the cease-fire agreement signed in October 1992. It therefore need not be emphasized how such a military situation presented considerable constraints that made the use of highly structured research techniques an impossibility; the researcher in a war situation, just as with combatants and non-combatants, is governed by a multitude of unpredictable forces and events that necessitate a high degree of flexibility, innovativeness and resilience. The observations and generalizations in this work should therefore be treated as tentative rather than definitive. But the point is, as Ellis and Barakat put it, "there is no legitimacy to war research conducted in peacetime".[3] Finally, the merging of the past, present and future in the change-continuity nexus, both in social discourses and reality, posed philosophical and semantic problems about the appropriate tense to use; I chose to use all the tenses interchangeably as and when it seems appropriate.

Notes

1. See James Scott, *Weapons of the Weak*, New Haven, Yale University Press, 1985.

2. John Maynard Keynes, Preface to *The General Theory of Employment, Interest and Money*, London, 1961.

3. Sultan Barakat and Sue Ellis, "Researching Under Fire: Issues for consideration when collecting data and information in war circumstances, with specific reference to relief and reconstruction projects", in *Disasters* (forthcoming)

Abbreviations

ANC	African National Congress (of South Africa)
BBC	British Broadcasting Corporation
CENE	National Commission for the Emergence
COREMO	Mozambican Revolutionary Committee
FRELIMO	Front for the Liberation of Mozambique
FLS	Frontline States
FPLM	Popular Front for the Liberation of Mozambique
ILO	International Labour Organization
IMF	International Monetary Fund
GDP	Gross Domestic Product
GPA	General Peace Accord
MANU	Makonde African National Union
MNR/Renamo	Mozambique National Resistance
NEP	New Economic Plan
NGOs	Non-governmental Organizations
OMM	Mozambique Women's Organization
PAFEMO-DF	Federal Party of Mozambique-Democratic Federalist
PRE	Economic Reform Programme
UDENAMO	Mozambique National Democratic Union
UN	United Nations
UNAMI	National Union for the Independence of Mozambique
UNAMO	Mozambique National Union
UNAR	Rombezia African National Union
UNDP	United Nations Development Programme
UNICEF	United Nations Children Fund
UNHCR	United Nations High Commissioner for Refugees
UNUMOZ	United Nations Mission in Mozambique
ZANU-PF	Zimbabwe African National Union

| ZNA | Zimbabwe National Army |
| ZTV | Zimbabwe Television |

1 Introduction

For nearly three decades, since 1964 when the independence war led by the Front for the Liberation of Mozambique (FRELIMO)[1] started, Mozambique has been a theatre of turmoil and violent transformation. An entire generation was to know nothing but war, the single and most salient factor to condition the political, economic, social and cultural life during this period, and which represented the struggle for food, shelter, space, security, power and self-justification. The ten-year war which led to independence in 1975 was followed in 1976 by undeclared war, which targeted economic installations, waged against Mozambique by the Rhodesian racist regime in retaliation for the former's support of Zimbabwean guerrillas. After the formation of the Mozambique National Resistance (MNR, also known by its Portuguese acronym, Renamo) in 1977 in Harare (then Salisbury), the country entered into another more vicious war which lasted for sixteen years. In the last war, the reciprocal destruction of the conflicting forces took place with the establishment of the peace of the graveyard, and yielded considerable social, economic and political damage. Reversing Frelimo's successes, the war undermined the state and heralded the demise of authoritarian populism.

The immediate negative effects of the war have been dramatic: the whole social fabric of the Mozambican society has been disrupted, the economy has been brought to a standstill, with the limited benefits of growth concentrated in elite hands. By 1990 the death rate had reached 30 people per day, one million dead[2], and US$18 billion in economic losses[3], which, according to Saferworld was equivalent to four times the 1988 GDP. The modest economic growth achieved between 1977 and 1981, in which Gross Domestic Product (GDP) rose by 2.8 per cent per annum, that of industrial output by 13.7 per cent, while export production doubled and textile production tripled[4], has been reversed. This has resulted in an economic crisis of vast proportions

1

which has made the country the "world's poorest, hungriest, most indebted and, most aid-dependent".[5]

Although the war intensified this crisis, it is hard to distinguish its effects from those of the government's 'socialist' policies; over-centralisation, violent agrarian 'modernisation', and the regimentation/militarization of society. For instance when Frelimo revised its strategy for the countryside, favouring small family production units and moving away from the collectivist model, the war was already fanning out throughout the countryside, and a severe drought had the country in its grip.[6] The war and the economic crisis fuelled each other.

In an attempt to stop MNR economic sabotage, Frelimo entered into a non-aggression pact with South Africa in 1984.[7] In the mid 1980s, hoping to bring the MNR out of the bush into peaceful electoral confrontation, it also abandoned its radical development strategy and instead, adopted liberal economic and political reforms, with far reaching implications. Despite this, and building on pre-existing ethnic, class, religious and ideological tensions, the war continued unabated until the signing of a cease-fire agreement in October 1992. The cease-fire paved the way for the December 1994 elections which returned Frelimo to power, albeit with a narrow margin. With the euphoria surrounding the cease-fire and the elections fizzling out, the future of the country is much blurred, the present volatile and fluid.

Indeed the post-election period has been characterized by occasional outbursts of dissent by striking workers, women and soldiers as well as blame and counter-blame by the major political protagonists in an attempt to shore up their hegemony. With concerted propaganda campaign by the major protagonists in the conflict truth, as in any war, has become the first casualty. This has made sifting through the mass of conflicting information a daunting task. Macksey correctly warns us:

> The justification of war, for political or personal purposes, is frequently the glorification of a lie, the purveying of distortions carried forward in the guise of historic fact. A victor's tale is unlikely to coincide with that of the defeated. The unravelling of the facts about war is a feat in itself.[8]

In the case of Mozambique, as shall become clear, whatever the intentions or justifications of both Frelimo and Renamo in waging the war, the outcome has, if anything, belied their claim to a just cause to promote the common interest; the former is increasingly getting alienated from the population while the demands of the ordinary people go beyond the parochialism of the latter. This study attempts to 'unravel' some of the oft neglected facts about the Mozambican civil war, and focuses in particular on the interrelationships

2

between major political and socio-economic developments of the time. It is based on a premise that, to understand the range of possible relationships between war and socio-political development, war has to be viewed as a dialectical and historical process capable of multiple consequences, positive as well as negative.

This premise, although it provided a useful critical point of departure, simply pointed a way into a fairly uncharted territory. Precisely because war is a dynamic, extremist activity it has lent itself to description by means of the dramatic, the eulogisation of superlative feats and the creation of an heroic image.[9] Heart-rending works that dramatise suffering now abound in the literature.[10]Other scholars have focused on the problems associated with the management of a war economy[11], in a context of agrarian failures[12] and structural adjustment conditionalities.[13] Yet others still have tried to explore the internal dynamics of the MNR, and its evolving relationship with the peasantry.[14]All these are fruitful lines of enquiry that add to the increasing diversity and richness of literature on Mozambique. However, in spite of this impressive burgeoning of research on Mozambique - 'a virgin area of research' is a common euphemism among scholars in the region - a comprehensive sociological study of war, society and change has yet to be written. Such a comprehensive understanding of the war-society interface requires a deeper and detailed probing of the historical record of large-scale processes of economic and socio-political change than the descriptive recounting of the war's destructive impact characteristic of much recent journalistic (for example Bredin, Finnegan and Middleton), NGO-sponsored and official research.[15] This book constitutes a preliminary attempt towards that quest.

The causes and effects of the conflict

The interpretation of the causes and effects of the conflict has been a subject of much controversy in the literature. With respect to the causes, two broad schools of thought, if not paradigms, can be identified;one that blames Frelimo or focuses on internal dynamics, and the other, its anti-thesis, that blames external forces. Hoile, for example, in an openly ideological analysis, argues that the conflict was a civil war of Frelimo's own making and that the attempted socialist transformation could not succeed.[16] He concludes that the MNR is a 'genuine popular movement' and its war a 'bona fide civil war'. His review of 'The 1992 Africa Watch Report on Mozambique'[17] is, however, a refreshing antidote to the standard, "stereotyped and fragmentary" accounts of war in Mozambique.[18] The review highlights the deficiencies of politically partisan research, as well as suggests that it was not only Renamo

3

that was responsible for human rights abuse in Mozambique. Although illuminating, the review ignores the impact of global and structural processes, and in fact remains an ideological defence of Renamo and of private property.

Similarly, Geffray's anthropological study of the causes of war in Erati district of the northern province of Nampula emphasized internal weaknesses and contradictions, in particular the marginalization of local traditions, as central to the genesis of the conflict.[19] Although proffering invaluable insights, however, these approaches' neglect of the international structures, the place of Mozambique in the international division of labour and the changes in the global economy, lead into an equally misleading conclusion that the rural people rebelled in order to restore their traditions which had been marginalised by Frelimo.

Out of sympathy and commitment to 'defend the revolution', the second approach equally distorts and idealises the reality of Mozambican history by blaming external forces for all the ills in Mozambique. From this perspective, whose main advocates are Hanlon and Nilsson, it is contented that the conflict in Mozambique was caused principally by western political, economic and strategic interests in Southern Africa.[20] As with the nineteenth century wars of conquest, external forces resorted to divide and rule tactics in order to influence internal processes. While Renamo would not have survived without external support, exclusive focus on external factors equally distorts the reality and denies the Mozambicans their own history; they are reduced to mere passive victims of manipulations and machinations by powerful external forces, yet as we shall see in the following pages, they have been active agents shaping their histories and society. Consequently, as with the perspective represented by Hoile this approach also obscures understanding of "the contradictions that took Frelimo from victory to the verge of defeat"[21], as well as the inexorable and enduring processes of social change occasioned by the war.

Ironically, neo-marxisant thinkers such as Hanlon, Saul and Mittleman[22], for whom internal contradictions should take primacy over external factors, have been the first to point to external forces. Class conflict and economic contradiction seem to have been overshadowed by the external, in particular South Africa destabilisation. As we shall see, internal and external factors, the war and economic crisis, mutually reinforced each other in fuelling the war, and shaping its consequences. The question of primacy does therefore not arise, rather it is the dialectic between these forces that should be stressed. Thus, whatever the merits of these perspectives, it is important to shift the terms of the debate about the conflict in a new direction, which would illuminate the possible range of the complex relationship between war and society.

Whereas these perspectives remained locked in an ideological battle of blame and counter-blame, with their conceptual representations never fully adequate to their objects, this study focuses instead on relations between and among people, their economic and political engagement, and their changing relationship with the state. It stresses that, the war fuelled by many determinations as it were, gave rise to multiple unintended consequences with fundamental significance for post-war reconstruction and development. The end of the war has naturally resulted in a paradigmic shift in intellectual focus from an analysis of the causes of the war to an analysis of its effects and implications for post war reconstruction and 'integration'.

With increasing desperation, if heroically, local and international officialdom, as well as scholars, have jumped onto the band-wagon of the redemptive post-war reconstruction project. Indeed there has been a remarkable fusion of horizons and dialogic interaction between erstwhile foes of yesteryear as the focus has shifted from *who* is to blame to *how* to deal with the immediate manifestations of the crisis. This endeavour to grapple with the vexing question of post-war reconstruction has, unfortunately, led to an exclusive focus on surface or dramatic events, and to expound as directly operative causes which instead operate indirectly. Most of this current research, especially non-governmental (NGO)-sponsored research, has tended to concentrate on the technicalities of economic rehabilitation, repatriation, demobilization and resettlement. In the authoritative reports by Brochmann and Ratilal, for example, people as they live their daily lives are simply invisible, while in Saferworld's influential report, it is statistics that take the pride of place. Yet it is precisely people and their dynamic social relations and processes that will determine the success or otherwise of the reconstruction project. As shall become clear, identifying direct causes and consequences as the only effective causes and consequences, hampers understanding of long-term structural and ideological causes and effects of the war. That war inflicted enormous suffering and that it was immoral cannot be overstated, but this alone does not broaden our understanding of what is a complex historical process.

In contrast to most contemporary scholarly work on the war and post-war reconstruction, which dwells too well upon the wounds inflicted upon society by war, this work looks at war in terms of its impact, good or bad. Rather than agonize about a passive society being systematically destroyed by war, the study instead highlights the resilience and resourcefulness of people in responding to war and economic crisis. It also refutes certain underlying assumptions of the dominant approaches, such as, for example, those which make the nation-state the inevitable end of development, or stress the sanctity of market fundamentalism, and unchanging African traditions and customs. It shows that the changing parameters of political and social life point to the

5

development and potential existence of a civil society in Mozambique, and emphasizes the basic experiences of individuals living in societies. A discussion of such transitions, as Campbell urges us, "should not lead to despair but to a more rigorous analysis of the forms of struggle, political organization and the role of the popular masses in the struggle to transform Africa".[23]

Through the anatomy of the embryonic civil society and its relation to the state the following chapters will dialectically look backwards to provide explanations of why private individuals are increasingly involving themselves in voluntary associations but at the same time accepting the legitimacy of authorities external to themselves; confront the present to see if the bonds between individuals, associations and authorities are sustainable and acceptable; and look forward to ask whether new sources of authority and different associations are at all likely. Focusing specifically on the 'unintended consequences of the war' on state-society relationships, this undertaking seeks to 'decolonise' the theorization of the war-society interface as it has manifested itself in Mozambique.

The state, civil society and violence

The relationship between the state, society and violence is indeed complex, and has been a subject of much contestation in the literature. Vojin, in his critical and polemical *Anticapital*, asserts:

> Until yesterday the state was considered to be an irreplaceable instrument for safeguarding society against chaos and anarchy. Today it is the state that is the main cause of growing chaos and anarchy ...The state invented war in order to plunder and to protect itself from being plundered. The end of the state will mean the end of war ... With the elimination of the state, society will not be risking chaos. On the contrary, for the first time in history it will emerge from chaos, never to return.[24]

To argue that the state has played a role in the production of chaos, anarchy and violence, and in this case in Mozambique, is not novel. It is commonplace knowledge, especially in Mozambique, that Renamo anti-state insurgency and, what Wilson calls, 'cults of violence and counter-violence' were largely attempts to challenge and subvert the state's monopoly of violence. In other words, as everywhere in the world, state violence generated anti-state violence, and as we shall see, in Mozambique, it set in motion a process with diverse trajectories. However, the contention that the 'end of the state will mean the end of war', is provocative, and raises important questions about the conception of the state, and its evolving relationship with society.

The state versus civil society debate is itself "an arena where competing class projects confront each other, each seeking to ensure a social basis for its control over the state".[25] A central debate has focused on the African state's 'relative autonomy' vis-a-vis society. Mamdhani, modifying Alavi's model of the Pakistan state, depicts the state in Africa as 'overdeveloped' in relation to the society that it sits atop, and this is because it is a transplant from a developed European society. In contrast, but interestingly for the same reasons, Hyden portrays the African state as 'weak' and as suspended in thin air like a balloon, and lacking organic roots in society.[26]Yet vulgar Marxists have simply dismissed the state as an instrument of class domination and capital accumulation. These diverse and contradictory interpretations of the state in Africa indicate, not only the ideological assumptions of the scholars concerned, but the also the diversity and uniqueness of the state in Africa.

That the African state is a European graft, and imposed from above, is beyond dispute. But nonetheless, and perhaps more important, societal interests permeated its structures, and shaped its evolution. For instance, as in the rest of Africa, in Mozambique the institutions of the colonial state, which later formed the basis of the post-colonial state, emerged largely as a response to local resistance to colonial conquest. Thus none of the three perspectives are entirely satisfactory, and in fact they misrepresent the relationship between the state, society and violence. As the evidence of Mozambique suggests, the specific nature of a state's strength and weakness in relation to society.cannot be ascertained in abstract or a priori; it is instead shaped by historical probabilities that derive from the productive logic of social organization, and the conflicts of interests that it gives rise to.

The analysis in this book challenges the partial and inadequate treatment of the state-society relation by writers informed by these approaches. In this analysis, the state-society relationship is presented as a dialectical one, and as constantly being redefined. As shall become clear, the dialectic of the state-society relationship is an historical outcome of largely unconscious and contradictory historical processes of conflicts, compromises and cooptations between diverse groups whose self-serving actions, in the case of Mozambique, resulted in the degeneration of politics into warfare. The state is viewed not merely as a coercive instrument of the dominant class as in the orthodox Marxist conception. Nor is it viewed as a neutral arbiter between divergent interests in society as in liberal theory.

On the contrary, the state, as it has manifested itself in Southern Africa in general and Mozambique in particular, has been at one and the same time, the primary instrument for the expansion of dominant group power, and a coercive force that keeps subordinate groups weak and disorganised. It has also been an arena of struggle and an effective weapon in that struggle worth fighting for.[27] It's relationship to civil society has been complex, simultaneously responding to pressure from some civil society organisations, supporting others and yet still undermining others.

The idea of civil society itself has, indeed, continued to be subjected to considerable variation and used in a variety of contexts.[28] It has been used both as an analytical category and as a standard point of reference in political debates which accept it in one way or another without really asking what the acceptance actually involves. For purposes of this discussion, civil society is conceived of as composed of all those social relationships that involve the voluntary association and participation of individuals acting in their private capacities. It is about basic social relationships, experiences and the coming together of private individuals, and is inevitably characterised by conflict and struggle between its various elements.

The anatomy of civil society itself needs to be questioned. With respect to Mozambique this involves examining how various social groups have attempted to penetrate, influence, or capture and control the state, and how in response to these pressures the state itself has developed and its relationship with civil society re-defined. As shall become clear, civil society is clearly distinct, but not independent, from the state.[29] Their relationship, mediated by the operation of the 'dialectic of control', is dynamic and always changing. It is therefore important to go beyond mere polarisation of the state and civil society. The introduction of a third dimension, war, by virtue of its destructiveness, inevitably alters both the relationship of the state to civil society as well as that of the constitutive elements of civil society. It is the contingent outcomes of war on these contested processes that is of prime concern to this study and we shall explore them in some detail in the following chapters.

The paradox of the state in Mozambique: War and the transformation of state-society relationships

As in most of sub-Saharan Africa, the post-colonial state in Mozambique has exhibited a paradox in which both strong and weak components simultaneously co-existed. On the one hand, as the testimonies of ordinary people interviewed in Manica Province suggest, in its authoritarian modernisation project the state became the dominant power over civil society. In the construction of this hegemonic project Frelimo established a centralised bureaucracy that intervened in nearly all facets of economic, social and political life. In what amounted to a violent transformation of society from

8

above, the civic arena was delimited and legitimacy was achieved through order, cooptation/assimilation and/or punishment of dissenters.

The state's predominance in society was inevitable given the absence of an entrepreneurial class to initiate the much needed 'development'.[30] Unlike in Western Europe where the development of liberal democracy and the state was supported by a rising entrepreneurial class, in Mozambique, as in many other 'Third World' countries, economic development is itself a political task. Politics and the state thus became the primary source of economic dynamism. In addition, the new political elite which controlled state power after independence faced competing imperatives that were not easy to reconcile.

On the one hand, and to enhance regime legitimacy, the ruling elite had to incorporate the demands of diverse social groups. On the other, conditions of economic scarcity and the weak position of the country in the global political economy placed considerable constraints on the state's ability to meet its people's demands. To reconcile these competing impulses, Frelimo adopted a command approach in its management of the national economy. As in other 'socialist' countries, especially the Soviet Union after Stalin[31] and before its collapse, a planned economy, in which the overall interests of the state were uppermost, was seen as vital in creating conditions for acquiring surplus value and expanding the process of production. As Lenin had warned with respect to the Soviet Union in his well-known New Economic Policy (NEP),[32] this Stalinist counterrevolution made the state's responsiveness to society inherently difficult. As a result, competition among and between various groups became fierce, and ultimately resulting in the degeneration of politics into warfare.

While the state appeared strong, in another sense it was also a weak state. The state's weakness was manifested in its inability to translate policy into practice, and later, to defeat the rebels. This weakness was partly due to lack of administrative capacity and financial resources, as well as to the permeation of the state by societal interests, domestic or foreign. In short, the relationship between the state and society was complex: as an actor the state had its own strengths and preferences, yet it was also contextually bound by specific issue areas that prevailed at one time in its relation to societal actors. The added dimension of war has complicated this situation, simultaneously amplifying the weakness of the state and strengthening some its institutions, especially its coercive apparatus.

Paradoxically, the most remarkable unintended consequence of Renamo counterrevolution (to restore the capitalist and traditional status quo ante) has been the revolutionizing of Frelimo itself, and a redefinition of its relationship with society. With far reaching consequences, in response to the contradictory impulses from various segments of society and the increasing difficulty of managing a war economy Frelimo embarked on a democratic project to

9

devolve power and decentralize administration from the centre to provincial and local governments.[33] Such enforced political reforms have made the Frelimo government one of the most flexible and open regimes in the region, thus allowing the flourishing of new ideas and diversity.Related to this, the requirements of fighting the war forced the government to be more efficient with the management of scarce resources, and to be flexible and innovative in policy formulation and implementation. These developments' significance for democratic post-war reconstruction need not be overemphasized.

However, as is well documented in the literature, the most direct impact of the war on the state been to undermine its capacity to manage the economy. As state survival itself was at stake security, and not development, became the overriding policy concern. The maxim that 'production is the best defence' was ignored, as resources were diverted to the war effort. With the productive sector starved of capital investment, the official economy almost ground to a standstill, forcing the country to embark on a rapid economic reform in the mid 1980s. This, as we shall see, had fundamental implications for the state-civil society relationship.

First, the erosion of the economic basis of state power fuelled the break-up of its legitimacy and its ruling ideology in the eyes of the ruled. Consequently, with demoralisation rising high, even among sections of the state apparatus, and resources diminishing the Frelimo regime increasingly resorted to coercion to contain popular discontent, leading to further popular alienation. Second, the erosion of state power and the breakdown of censorship allowed the expansion of politics through society, enabling traditional and religious authorities and other agents of society to consolidate their power. In other words, the weakening of the state by the war created a political power vacuum, which has been filled by the ever increasing non-governmental organizations, social and religious movements. The consequent political and religious toleration let loose a flood of speculation, and open criticism of the establishment, that hitherto had only been muttered in secret. These new social movements have not only asked sceptical questions about all the institutions and beliefs of their society, but have also taken the initiative to set up alternative socio-economic arrangements.

For example, and third, in response to the state's inability to provide security and to deliver the goods, the dispossessed invented the grass-roots war economy. The grass-roots war economy has not only been a source of livelihood for most of the people who have been violently separated from their means of sustenance by war, the dispossessed, but has also been the vehicle for capital accumulation by the nascent bourgeoisie as well as social differentiation and class formation. Based on a hybrid economic system combining elements of traditional kinship (the economy of affection), socialist ethics, and market fundamentalism, the grass-roots war economy has provided

10

the basis for an independent and strengthened civil society. Wealth generated within this economy has been translated into political power, altering the overall distribution of power.

In addition, the grass-roots war economy, especially the values and norms it embodies, presents a challenge to the modern secular state in several ways. For instance, some of the survival strategies within the grass-roots war economy, such as violent piracy, dealings in foreign currency and precious stones and minerals and smuggling etc, threatened to undermine the very basis of the nation-state as well as to subvert the hegemony of the dominant groups. In many instances, the survival strategies adopted the by dispossessed were in opposition to the wishes of the dominant groups who control the institution of war. For example, in spite of the elite's contempt for traditional ritual as a feudal anachronism, people did invoke traditional religion and practised the rituals - and even set up their own defence militias, such as the Naprama movement - to resist Renamo and Frelimo hegemony. In short, violence generated social revolt and protest in ideas, values and behaviours which took many forms; innovative economic enterprising; increased political activism and militancy; religious revivalism; unorthodox feminine politics and youth sub-culture(s). In doing so the dispossessed have indeed been active agents shaping the institutional structure of their society and strengthening the embryonic civil society, and weakening the state.

These developments reflected the extent to which Frelimo's traditional approach to the politics of the state had become inadequate to meet the demands of a war economy; the economic and social conditions it was designed to address were being transformed by the war. The interaction of these movements, which on the surface are apparently spontaneous and unrelated, has produced the dynamic of, and for, the 'movement of the social whole'. Such changing parameters of political and social life point to the development and potential existence of a civil society in Mozambique. In this study we explore the anatomy of this civil society, focusing in particular on how the contradictions of a violently changing political economy impacted upon state-society relationships.

The underlying objective of this exploration is therefore to understand the nature of this movement of society, and its ambiguous legacy, the contradictions and conflicts, and the forms they have taken, that produced it. Without under-playing the negative impact of the war, it shows that the war has also set in motion a multifaceted process of social restructuring and political recomposition and economic reorganization. The aim is to highlight what might be considered subsidiary episodes in the Mozambican civil war: the experiences and activities of the obscure women and men who are invisible in the dominant literature, but whose remarkable resilience leads us to conclude that what is emerging is not total catastrophe but is instead a different set of arrangements; in this study their responses, survival and transformation strategies will receive pride of place. Building on themes touched on by Lundin, Numes and Wilson[34], the study emphasises the dispossessed's 'political activism', rather than passive submission to fate, as central to the on-going processes of change.

Analytical framework

The controversy on the impact of war on society is as old as the history of war itself. In the historical study of war three distinct perspectives can be identified. First, there is the commonsensical view best represented by Nef, and recently by Saferworld and Rimmer which stresses the dysfunctional aspects of war, and considers it as 'inimical to human progress'. A second view, most well articulated by Hall and by Bayart with regard to Western Europe and Africa respectively, views war as a catalyst for positive growth and change and an agent for introducing modernization. As will become clear from the evidence presented in the following chapters, neither of these views is false; rather their vantage points do not offer a complete overview of the whole picture. The first, which has informed most analysis on Mozambique, underplays the resilience of communities at war and their capacity to 'progress' through war, while the latter ignores the destructive aspect of war. A third view, which informs much of Marxist scholarship, focuses on the question of whether or not specific modes of production give rise to warfare, and vice versa.

A more complex variation of this perspective, and perhaps more illuminating, is articulated by Kaldor, who stresses a Clauewitzian analogy between 'mode of warfare' and 'mode of production'. Here, as in this study, the emphasis is on the dialectical relationship between war and historical and economic processes. In a similar vein, Goody in his *Technology, Tradition and the State in Africa,*[35] made observations that bear directly to the phenomena under consideration here and upon current problems. As he stresses, "[t]he analysis of a political system needs to be related to its economic possibilities and these in turn are linked to technology".[36] As we shall see in the case of Mozambique, war brought, directly and indirectly (for example through international aid), in new technology, as a means of both destruction and production, and this new technology has been one major factor in the process of social change.

By emphasizing this *dialectic,* rather than monocausality, the study seeks to contribute towards correcting the 'fallacy of misplaced emphasis' characteristic of the literature on Mozambique. It seeks to do so by developing an alternative framework that integrates the particular and the

12

universal, the specific and the general as well as economics and politics. The framework emphasizes systems of control and domination, accumulation and distribution as central to historical development. In this framework, apparent 'oppositions' and 'spontaneous' activities are viewed as dialectically interrelated and mutually reinforcing. None of these forces are considered primary or determinant: instead it is their dialectical articulation that is emphasized. (see Chapter Six for a detailed elaboration of this framework).

The critical concepts of this framework pertinent to this analysis are the 'dialectic of control' and 'unintended consequences'. According to Giddens, in all social systems there is a 'dialectic of control', which means that the apparently weak, by mobilizing resources at their disposal can carve out a social space for themselves. This is because, as the case of Manica amply demonstrates, power relations are relations of autonomy and independence. As we shall see, in the war political of Mozambique the operation of such a dialectic of control has been such that the balances of resources have continuously shifted, reconfiguring the overall distribution of power. The weak of Chimoio, for example, have been able to alter the distribution of power precisely because the powerful are also dependent on the weak, and vice-versa. With remarkable ingenuity and skill, they have exploited the resources of a dependence which are astutely fabricated as much as predetermined. The unintended consequences of the weak's participation in the dialectic of control have been diverse, contradictory and ambiguous.

As Manica's experience suggests, 'unintended consequences' occur precisely because, when human beings act and interact there are so many variables, or what Giddens calls 'unacknowledged conditions of action', that come into play in shaping the outcome.[37] As Giddens points out; "[t]he knowledgeability of human agents and their actions, in specific historical circumstances, is always bounded by the unacknowledged conditions of action on 'one side', and its unintended consequences on the other".[38] War, which according to Clausewitz is governed by "the play of probability and chance",[39] amplified the significance of these variables.

More important, in so far as unintended consequence were systematically involved in social reproduction, they became objective conditions of action and further change. In other words, the consequences of war (intended and unintended), displacement, the disruption of the social fabric of society and the weakening of the state, have become objective conditions in which the dispossessed have continued to make their histories. The outcome of these struggles for hegemony - in which all the major forces in the conflict have resorted to blame, self-justification and moral and counter-moral argument - is less predictable and their implications for post-peace democratic reconstruction and the theorization of the relationship between the state, violence and development are rather ambiguous. In some ways, such unintended consequences of war constitute an 'invisible revolution' which has set the stage for further change, development and strengthening of civil society.

The emergent civil society derives its dynamism from the participation of the dispossessed in the dialectic of control. By participating in the dialectic of control, the dispossessed have expanded their political space, subverted traditional values and norms, and especially through some of their survival strategies, have even challenged the sanctity of the nation-state. This remarkable capacity of the dispossessed to change some of the institutions, social relations and structures of their society in a war political economy necessitates the adaptation of an approach that transcends the fruitless polarization of positions between advocates of structural determinism and of political voluntarism, most well represented by Althusser and Gramsci respectively. Instead, one needs to find a conceptual space between systematic structuralism and wilful instrumentality, and to stress the dialectic between them. However, the latter's critical concepts of 'crisis of hegemony' 'war of position' and 'organic intellectuals',[40] which he developed to specify the dynamics of change in the development of capitalism in Western Europe should guide this analysis.

In the following chapters, and within a framework that treats structural constraint and human agency as dialectical components of historical experience, an attempt will be made to identify factors /forces, both universal and local, within the context of a war political economy that interact to produce diverse outcomes. It explores the connections between structural changes and changing forms of social and political organisation, and the extent to which superstructures react on the structure, politics and economics, and vice versa.It will highlight how, for instance, changes in the modes and relations of production, for example 'depeasantisation' through displacement, have prompted changes in behaviour and attitudes; the difference in social and organizational requirements of living in an urban milieu, Chimoio city, often as barefoot-entrepreneurs, and those of survival in the country-side, as peasants, accounts for the disintegration of traditional norms and values.

Apart from our own limitations (lack of data due to the war, for instance) and from those imposed by the vastness and complexity of the subject, the task is made more difficult by the absence of a proper theory of war and social change. A number of issues will have to be ignored, while others, often very important will only be brought in to illuminate the argument. While a narrower focus on any specific issue would have yielded deeper insights into the problem, the danger is that the category under examination could easily be taken as a self-contained element rather than in its relation with other groups or elements in the global political economy. Consequently, one ends up with the impression that society is some kind of jigsaw, in which, if we study the individual components then we need simply fit the pieces together to see how the whole functions. But here we are dealing with a dynamic process, a 'social whole in movement', in which 'the whole is more than the sum of its parts'.

The need for a holistic perspective has, however, resulted in the dilemma of trying to capture a picture of the whole while at the same time not suppressing the specificities of particular situations. This tension between the universal and the particular reverberates throughout this study. To reconcile the general thrust of the argument and specific events or issues, I chose a route which emphasises issues of change and continuity, as well as accumulation and domination. Both are winding and criss-crossed by other paths, but they seem to provide the best vantage points from which to view the rest of the terrain.

The specific forms of organization, resistance or domination and control which are derived from and facilitate the accumulation process adopted by various social groups are considered insofar as they are relevant to our main object of analysis. This selective but qualitative multiple engagement will obviously be unsatisfying to specialists in particular areas/issues which the study touches. But the point is that, to exhaustively discuss these diverse issues would require 'whole other books'. This is beyond the scope of this study's objective to conceptually capture this important historical moment in the political economy of Mozambique. Basing its evidence on Manica province, the province that had the longest war experience, this book seeks to provide a synoptic overview of the unfolding contradictory reality.

The context: Manica Province and its people

Fieldwork for this study was done in the central western Province of Manica and primarily in Chimoio city, the Provincial capital. Unless stated otherwise, all the interviews were conducted in this area between April and October 1992. Focus on Manica Province was not arbitrary. In addition to the fact that I speak the major local language, Shona, and the fact that I had lived in the province as a teenager from 1976-1980, the choice was influenced by a consideration of two important factors. First, as already pointed out, the province has had the longest experience of war: the civil-war started in this province as 'banditry' in 1976. Second, the partial cease-fire signed in December 1990 resulted in the emergence of relatively stable communities in areas of the Province along the Beira Corridor from Inchope to the Machipanda border with Zimbabwe.

Even before the signing of the partial cease-fire hundreds of thousands of dislocated people had fled their homes to the safety of the Provincial towns,

Chimoio, Gondola in the east and Manica in the west. By the early 1980s, when dirty war tactics based on a culture of terror were elevated to a common strategy by both belligerents, about 600, 000 people were forced to leave their homes. Of these, nearly 200, 000 found refuge in the peri-urban slums of Chimoio city[41], more than quadrupling the original capacity the city was built to carry. Longest war experience and relative security, which allowed the emergence of comparatively stable communities, make the experience of the province historically significant. It can offer us deeper insights into the possible post-war arrangements. It is hoped that by understanding the nature of the evolving social organisation in Chimoio it would be possible to identify the major elements of the post-war civil society and its possible trajectory. Nonetheless the conclusions from Manica may not be generalisable to the whole country, which is diverse.

Five interrelated factors make the province a special case: the impact of the Rhodesian war on the local economy; the 'Ndau factor'; the strength of traditional ideologies, as evidenced by the legitimacy Renamo has won itself by claiming to be fighting a 'war of spirits'; as a result of all the above, the substantial popularity of Renamo in the province; and finally, the high degree of urbanisation in the region.

First, during the Rhodesian war Mozambique imposed sanctions on the former and offered rear bases to Zimbabwean guerrillas. In response Rhodesia air-raided bases in Manica Province in hot-pursuit of Zimbabwean guerrillas. The attacks, which included commando attacks on rail lines, refineries and other vital installations, destroyed rural commerce.[42] By the early 1980s, especially after the adoption of the insurgent movement by South Africa, much of rural Mozambique was discontented and restless.[43]

Second, there is also a background of historical hostility between the Ndaus (who inhabit southern Manica and Sofala provinces) and the 'Southerners' (Gaza, Maputo and Inhambane). The former are accused of superstition and witchcraft by the latter, who are in turn accused of a superiority complex by the former. This hostility has translated itself, though not explicitly, into Renamo/Frelimo conflict with the top leadership of Renamo coming from the province, just as Frelimo's, at least during the early years of independence, came from the south. The first leader of Renamo, Andrea Matada Matsangaissa, came from the province, and in the province the movement is known by his name as 'Matsanga'.

Third, in rural communities deeply immersed in superstition and mysticism, the slogans 'war of spirits' and 'our traditions' have appealed to many who see Renamo as their liberator from an insensitive state. All these factors have shaped the changing political perspectives of the local communities, in particular their relationship with Renamo. Finally, rapid urbanisation, itself a result of the above factors, has further complicated the picture: some of the

16

values, norms and practices it embodies conflict with those celebrated in traditional society.

The central region, precisely because of economic activity in the Beira Corridor and the war itself which has pushed many people into the corridor, is now one of the most urbanised regions in Mozambique. Thus the contemporary actor in the periphery of Chimoio straddles both the arbitrary boundaries of tradition and modernity; the communities under study are transitional communities of former peasants trying to negotiate for an existence in an urban milieu. This partly explains Renamo's failure, with its 'neo-traditionalist, quasi-nationalist and anti-Marxist ideology, to penetrate the cities ideologically. These particular factors make the experience of the province unique, and hence cautions us against the dangers of generalizations.

Based on a critical historical survey method, the research combined various tools of data gathering such as in-depth interviews and open-ended questions, tape-recorded life histories, and collection of quantitative data on economic activities as well as participant observation. Open-ended questions were used in the main interview schedule to glean insights into the ordinary people's changing perspectives on war, politics and society. Quantitative data was gathered on barefoot-entrepreneurs in specific markets/localities to assess the level of their profits and to evaluate their capacity to reproduce themselves (as entrepreneurs) at an extended scale by re-investing their surplus. The life-history approach was used mainly to explore women's changing status, priorities and their aspirations. In addition, participant observation techniques were employed. At one point, for example, I taught English at a newly established college of international languages in Chimoio city.

For security considerations, it was not possible to follow the proper procedures for random sampling. Crude geographic methods were instead used in the sampling of respondents. This involved selecting a number of interviewees in a specific locality on the basis of the population density in relation to the overall target population, the displaced peoples. Figures on population density and movement were obtained from the Provincial department of Planning, but they were unavoidably unreliable as people continued moving. The sampling task was made easier by the fact that most of the target population lived in crowded 'new accommodation centres', a euphemism for the peri-urban slums.

My presence was not unfelt and this influenced the kind of information that was proffered to me. The unequal power relation between the researcher and the subjects, a central problem in the politics and ethics of field research, in many instances operated in such a way as to prejudice the kind of information that was proffered. Moreover, the security situation, in particular the fear of the state coercive apparatus as well as the rebels, meant that many people

17

were unwilling to comment on sensitive political questions. Much time was therefore spent trying to build a good rapport with the interviewees.

Cross-checking was also used as a built-in mechanism to counter the respondents' tendency to say what they thought the researcher wanted to hear, or to offer a standard response. Even then it is not possible to legitimate the findings by faultless technique or precise calculation. The testimonies of the ordinary people in this study should therefore be taken with caution and in their context. Basing its evidence on the voices of the 'obscure man' this study is therefore largely qualitative and its conclusions reflect the subjectivities of both the interpreter and the interpreted.

Analyzing the enormous amount of data gathered from the field and to make sense out of it proved difficult. The multiplicity of the interacting variables made establishing correlationships of cause and effect, and explaining them particularly difficult. Consequently I have had to adopt a number of complementary approaches to data analysis. The first involved classifying/categorising, coding the responses and then entering and processing them in a Software Package for Social Sciences (SPSS) programme. Frequencies and crosstabulations were used to display relationships between variables and to inductively develop explanations.

Some tentative, and often ambiguous, links could be established. But these could not be explained solely on the basis of the data available. For instance, while it was clear that there was a link between people's age and their political attitudes - conservative, radical or moderate - conservatism could not be explained only by reference to age. Other variables, class, education, sex, ethnicity and the specific histories of the people concerned, all combined in shaping their political orientation. The question of which of these factors should be given more weight was almost an impossible task. Moreover, people's political consciousness and allegiances have been shifting over time. The pattern of this movement could not be established on the basis of the data gathered. Also, the condensation or compression of diverse responses into codifiable variables during the process of classification of responses, an unavoidably arbitrary process, meant that some of the richness of the qualitative data was lost.

These problems led me to explore the use of a comparative analysis with countries in similar as well as different situations. The comparison with Zimbabwe, the western neighbour, will be used to demonstrate that the war has forced Mozambicans to be far more innovative and enterprising than Zimbabweans, and that it has fundamentally altered the position of women. Parallels will also be drawn between the experiences of the Zimbabwean war of independence and Mozambican civil-war, especially with reference to the role of traditional religion and guerrilla mobilisation. Colonial and post-colonial history and social structure will be briefly examined in order to ascertain which of the changes have merely been accelerated by the war or are changes which would not have occurred had it not been for the war. In short, the analysis is based on a combination of complementary approaches, and operates at basically three levels: narrative, conceptualisation and analysis.

The obscure men and women, who have lived their lives outside official history, will be allowed to speak for themselves. But what they say about their experiences of violence and warfare has to be simultaneously located in its historical and material context, as well as critically analyzed at a theoretical level. This way, it is hoped, the gap between the outsider's view and the insider's experience, past, present and future, might be narrowed. Nonetheless, despite this effort, what is offered in this study is not a definitive account of the history of war in Mozambique. It is instead an invitation that scholars might consider the problems of other people and other groups in other societies from the latter's position.

To sum up, past studies on the Mozambican conflict highlighted the role of external aggression as the decisive factor in the demise of Frelimo's socialist experiment. The later wave of scholarly production emphasised Frelimo's own weaknesses, namely its agrarian reform programme, overcentralisation and insensitivity to peasant aspirations. Current studies concentrate on the technicalities of the post-war reconstruction project. This book will concentrate its attention chiefly on one subject, namely, the contingent outcomes of war. It focuses on two interrelated levels of analysis, the state/civil society relationship and the relationship between the constitutive elements of civil society itself.

It is organized into seven chapters, and each moves from the abstract to the concrete, and the general to the particular, and back again. The next chapter analyses the local dynamics of the war. The focus is on 'how' and 'why' mere 'banditry' developed into a fully fledged civil-war engulfing the whole country. It emphasises that although the MNR was created by the Rhodesians, as a result of a historical coincidence of interests between internal and external forces, the war built on pre-existing contradictions in Mozambique. Chapter three examines the dispossessed's responses to the economic crisis. It shows how, through their survival strategies they have created a dynamic alternative grass-roots economy, an economy which could form the foundation of post-war society. Chapter four, an opinion survey, documents the changing political perspectives of the ordinary people. It assesses the implications of this changing political consciousness for power configuration, control and domination.

Chapter five looks at religious revivalism, paying particular attention to its impact on the state-civil society relationship, emancipation and subjugation. Chapter six, explores the varied impact of war on women, and concludes that the legacy of war has been ambiguous for women. Chapter seven is an attempt at pulling together the various elements of the theoretical approach that have been developed in throughout the study, and to identify elements of a critical theory of war in Southern in general, and Mozambique in particular. It attempts to develop a framework that links war and social change, within a historical context. Finally, the conclusion ties up issues raised in the study and stresses the need for a sociological theory of war in Southern Africa that views war as a historical process capable of multiple consequences.

Notes

1. In accordance with the tradition in Mozambique, FRELIMO (uppercase) will be used to denote the front which was later transformed at the movement's Third Congress in 1977 into Frelimo (lowercase), the Marxist-Leninist vanguard party.

2. British Broadcasting Corporation (BBC) World service, *Focus on Africa*, 27 April, 1990.

3. Joseph Hanlon, *Mozambique: Who Calls the Shots?*, London, James Currey Ltd., 1991, p. 1.

4. Ibid. p. 1.

5. Ibid. p. 1.

6. Jeremy Harding, "Mozambique", in his *Small Wars, Small Mercies: Journeys in Africa's Disputed Nations*, London, Penguin, 1993, p. 243.

7. See E.N. Maganya, "The Nkomati Agreement and the Future of the Second Phase of the National Liberation Struggles in Southern Africa", in S.I.R. Msabaha and Timothy M. Shaw (editors), *Confrontation and Liberation in Southern Africa*, London, Gower, 1987.

8. Kenneth Macksey, *The Guinness History of Land Warfare*, London, Guinness Superlatives Limited, 1973, p. i.

9. For example, Samora Machel was renowned for making instantaneous public rallies, praising soldiers, whenever the government forces had made a major (successful) offensive against the rebels. Exhibiting a similar glorification of heroism, one Frelimo party official got so excited at hearing that I was studying war during one of my interviews with him. Calling himself *'mambo wehondo'* (literally king of war, but here meaning a very

brave soldier), and illustrating his points by taking various firing positions, he went on to narrate in detail his engagements with 'Matsanga' (local name by which the rebels are known, named after the movement's first leader, Adrea Matada Matsangaissa) and how he had heroically emerged as victor in all these engagements.

10. See among others, Joseph Hanlon, *Mozambique: The Revolution Under Fire*, London, Zed Books Limited, 1980, Diana Cammack, "The 'Human Face' of Destabilization: The War in Mozambique", in the *Review of African Political Economy*, Number 40, 1988, pp 65-74, and Alex Vines, *Renamo: Terrorism in Mozambique*, London, James Curry, 1991.

11. See among others, Marc Wuyts, "Money, Planning and Rural Transformation in Mozambique", in the *Journal of Development Studies*, Volume, 22, Number 1, and his, "Economic Management and Adjustment Policies in Mozambique", paper prepared for UNRISD conference 'Economic Crisis and Third World Countries: Impact and Response', Institute of Social and Economic Research, University of the West Indies, Kingston, Jamaica, April 1989, and Maureen Mackintosh and Marc Wuyts, "Accumulation, Social Services and Socialist Transformation in the Third World: Reflections on Decentralised Planning Based on Mozambique", the *Review of African Political Economy*, Number 24, May-August, 1982.

12. See Helena Dolny, "The Challenge of Agriculture", in John Saul (editor), *A Difficult Road: The Transition to Socialism in Mozambique*, New York, Monthly Review Press, 1985 and Vincent Tinker, "Structural Adjustment and Agricultural Pricing in Mozambique", in the *Review of African Political Economy*, Number 53, 1992, pp 25-42.

13. See Otto Roesch, "Economic Reform in Mozambique: Notes on Stabilisation", paper presented at Trent University, Ontario, 1988 and James H. Mittlemen, "Marginalization and the International Division of Labour: Mozambique's Strategy of Opening the Market", in the *African Studies Review*, Volume 34, Number 3, December 1991, pp. 89-106.

14. See for example, Tom Young, "The MNR/RENAMO: External and Internal Dynamics", *African Affairs*, December 1991, and Otto Roesch, "Renamo and the Peasantry in Southern Mozambique: A View from Gaza Province", in *the Canadian Journal of african Studies*, Volume 26, Number 3, 1992.

15. For journalistic writings on the conflict, see among others, Miles Bredin, *Blood on the Tracks: a Railway Journey from Angola to Mozambique*,

London, Piador, 1994; W. Finnegan, A *Complicated War: the Harrowing of Mozambique*, California, University of California Press, 1992; Nick Middleton, *Kalashnikovs and Zombie Cucumbers: Travels in Mozambique*, London, Sinclair-Stevenson, 1994. For official/authoritative works, see Robert Gersony, *Summary of Mozambican Refugee Accounts of Principally Conflict-related in Mozambique*, Washington, Bureau of Refugee Programs, Department of State, 1988; Prakash Ratilal, *Mozambique: Using Aid to End Emergency*, UNDP, Maputo, 1989; and, Reginald H. Green, "Four Horsemen Ride Together: Scorched Fields of War in Southern Africa", paper presented at a Refugee Studies Programme seminar on Forced Migration, Queen Elizabeth House, Oxford University, November 1992.

16. See David Hoile, *Mozambique: A Nation in Crisis*, London, Claeridge, 1989.

17. Africa Watch, *Conspicuous Destruction: War, Famine and The Reform Process in Mozambique*, London, Human Rights Watch, 1992.

18. David Hoile, review of "*Conspicuous Destruction: War Famine and the Reform Process in Mozambique*, The 1992 Africa Watch Report on Mozambique: Disappointing, Stereotyped and Fragmentary", London, Mozambique Institute Occasional Paper No. 2, 1992.

19. Alice Dinerman, "In Search of Mozambique: the imaginings of Christian Geffray in La Cause Des Armes au Mozambique", draft review paper, 1993.

20. See among many, Anders Nilson, *Unmasking the Bandits: The Face of the MNR*, London, Ecasaama, 1980, and Joseph Hanlon, *Mozambique: The Revolution Under Fire*, London, Zed, 1984, *Apartheid's Second Front*, London, Penguin, 1986.

21. Aquino de Braganca and Jacques Depelchin, "From the Idealization of Frelimo to the Understanding of the Recent History of Mozambique", revised version of paper presented at the United Nations (UN) University Conference on Peace and Development in Africa, Harare, August 25-28, 1986, p. 2.

22. Joseph Hanlon, op. cit.; James Mittleman, *Out From Underdevelopment*, New York, Macmillan, 1988, and John Saul (editor), *A Difficult Road: The Transition to Socialism in Mozambique*, New York, Monthly Review Press, 1985.

23. Horace Campbell, "War, Reconstruction and Dependence in Mozambique", *Third World Quarterly*, Volume 6, Number 840, 1984.

24. Vojin Dokovic, *Anticapital*, Harare, Sapes Books, 1994, p. 153.

25. Bjorn Beckman, "The Liberation of Civil Society: Neo-Liberal Ideology and Political Theory", in *Review of African Political Economy*, 1993, Number 58, p. 20.

26. See, among others, Mahmood Mamdani, "State and Civil Society in Contemporary Africa: Reconceptualising the Birth of State Nationalism and the Defeat of Popular Movements", *Africa Development*, Volume XV, Number 3/4, 1990.

27. For a detailed theorisation of the state see, Runaldo Munck, *Politics and Dependence in the Third World: The Case of Latin America*, London, Zed books, 1985.

28. See, among others, Paul G. Lewis (editor), *Democracy and Civil Society in Eastern Europe*, London, Macmillan Press, 1992 and Keith Tester, *Civil Society*, London, Routledge, 1992.

29. Keith Tester, ibid. p. 8.

30. There was a massive exodus of entrepreneurs, skilled personnel as well as deliberate sabotage of plant machinery by departing settlers at independence. The economic cost of this violent decolonization process is estimated to have been around 21 per cent of the 1975 GDP. See Roberto J. Tibana, "Mozambique Commodity and Policy Shocks: Terms of Trade Changes, The Socialist 'Big-Push', and the Response of the Economy (1975-1986)", Oxford University, Centre for the Study of African Economies Working Paper Series (WPS) Number 18, 1994.

31. Stalin proclaimed the State Plan to be the sole economic law in the socialist economy, and Machel was a faithful disciple of this creed.

32. Lenin, taking into account the economic backwardness of the largely agrarian Soviet economy, stressed the need for flexibility, in particular the importance of giving some free rein to market forces, in the popular euphemism; 'two steps backwards and one step forward' under the New Economic Policy (NEP) of 1918-1920. The NEP allowed the peasant to sell his surplus agricultural products freely in the market, permitted private commerce and the setting up of small private manufacturing enterprises, and gave a certain amount of freedom to private initiative and private capital. See, V. I. Lenin, *The State and Revolution,* Moscow, Progress Publishers, 1950.

33 See Jocelyn Alexander, "Political change in Manica Province, Mozambique: Implications for the Decentralization of Power", Oxford University, draft research paper, 1995.

34. See Irae Baptista Lundin, "Survival Strategies in Maputo City: An Anthropological Investigation, Working Paper Number 2, Department of Archaeology and Anthropology, University of Eduardo Mondlane, July 1986, Jovito Nunes and K.B. Wilson, "Repatriation to Mozambique: Current Processes and Future Dilemmas", paper presented to the Symposium on 'Social Change and Economic Aspects Of Mass Voluntary Return Movements of Refugees from one African Country to Another', United Nations Research Institute for Social Development, Harare, March 1991, and Jovito Nunes, "Peasants and Survival: The Social Consequences of Displacement: Mocuba, Zambezia", draft paper, April 1992.

35. Jack Goody, *Technology, Tradition and the State in Africa* London, Hutchinson University Library for Africa, 1971.

36. Ibid. p. 73.

37. Anthony Giddens, *Profiles and Critiques in Social Theory,* Berkeley and Los Angels, University of California Press, 1982.

38. Ibid.

39. Carl Von Clausenwitz, *On War*, London, Penguin, 1971.

40. Martin Carnoy, *The State and Political Theory*, New Jersey, Princeton University Press, 1984, p 78.

41. These estimates were provided by the Department of Planning (PlANO). Accurate figures were not possible to get as there was constant movement of people.

42. See among others, Ken Flower, *Serving Secretly: Rhodesia into Zimbabwe, 1964-1981*, London, John Murray, 1987, and Africa Watch, op. cit.

43. See Jeremy Harding, op. cit.

2 The local dynamics of the war: From banditry to civil war

Introduction

This chapter attempts to analyze the genesis and subsequent expansion of the Mozambican war. It seeks to understand how external and internal, political and economic forces interacted in fuelling the conflict. This is a complex undertaking. The complexity derives partly from the political distortion of Mozambican history, equating it to Frelimo's own history, and recounted in a triumphalist fashion; the acknowledged and large-scale involvement of external forces, which, by some, have been blamed for all the ills inflicted upon Mozambique, in instigating and fuelling the conflict; the multiplicity of interacting variables shaping the dynamic of the war; and finally, the varied pattern, both in time and space, of the war. This complexity is reflected in the contested characterization of the war by scholars and politicians alike: while some have dismissed the conflict as mere 'banditry', 'external destabilization', 'surrogate/proxy army', others have depicted it as a 'civil war' and the MNR as 'freedom fighters'.

These labels, whether ideologically motivated or not, depict dimensions of a much more complex phenomenon. Unfortunately debate has been falsely polarised over the propriety of these labels as well as who is to blame; this has obscured understanding of the nature of the crisis. According to the destabilizationist paradigm, the conflict represents the continuation of a long-standing pattern of aggression: at first from the efforts of Portuguese settlers to subdue and dominate the natives; second, the efforts of Portuguese colonial authorities to block the attainment of national independence; then from the Rhodesian racialist regime in its defence of minority rule; from the South African destabilisation (with tacit Western approval) of the new nations of Southern Africa "to force them into subordination to its economic and political hegemony"[1] ;and finally from the Kenyan and Malawian kleptocratic elites who probably had narrower private and commercial interests for getting involved in the conflict. In short, Mozambique like other weak states in the periphery of the global political system, is depicted as vulnerable to external pressure, and political objectives of extra-territorial forces tend to play an important role in shaping internal politics.

Notwithstanding the implicit attempt to abandon 'economic reductionism' or structural determinism, their analytical conclusions still very much under-emphasize other important non-economic factors, such as religion, neo-traditionalism and ideological struggles. These factors have played a significant role in sustaining the anti-state insurgency, and in shaping the contingent outcomes of the war. Noting that "commitment can sometimes blind one to the realities and only make one see the idealized version of that reality" de Braganca and Depelchin, emphasise that:

> [it is] necessary to reanalyze Frelimo's and Mozambique's own history, as a base for more correct analyses of the contradictions that are appearing today.[2]

Criticising Hanlon's and Saul's books[3], they point out that "it is possible to analyze the current contradictions of Frelimo, going over its own history, within the framework of the history of Mozambican society".[4]

More important, the voices of the dispossessed have been energetically suppressed in these dominant approaches (including non-Marxisant ones). For example, in the authoritative account of the impact of war on society by Green[5], the ordinary people are simply invisible. This is the case with many other publications produced by both local and international officialdom. Geffray's anthropological work in Nampula Province has gone a long way in correcting this imbalance.[6] By basing his evidence on the 'voices of the voiceless', Geffray projects the hitherto obscure men and women onto the political scene, and thus breaks new ground in Mozambican historiography. For Geffray:

> All of the local interpretations over the origin and meaning of the current war refer to [the importance of the political authority of lineage notables and the disastrous effects of their marginalization and humiliation]... and all of the accounts, without a single exception, referred to the question of the villages in explaining the motivations for entering into the war on Renamo's side.[7]

Unlike the 'external conspiracy' or 'destabilizationist' theorists who emphasize the global structures and political economy, Geffray focuses on the local and offers a sophisticated account and explanation of the conflict's indigenization. In short, Geffray's work made a vital contribution to the understanding of the historical specificity and irreducibility of culture.

It is quite misleading, however, to see rural people as merely interested in restoring their traditions and/or as the ideological and political pawns of powerful political elites. Such an interpretation would share the credence of somewhat antiquated views which depict rural populations as passive cultural dopes subject to the ideological hegemony and manipulation of political elites adept at evoking primordial sentiments of ethnicity, locality or kinship.[8] As the Manica experience suggests, rural populations resorted to traditional ideology not only to resist Frelimo, but also as a way of controlling Renamo brutality. They also took recourse to neo-traditional religions in order to explain their changing situation and bring order and harmony. Partly reflecting the power of the Church and the success of the Frelimo government's education programme, the dispossessed have also challenged traditional sources of authority and the religions that buttress their power.

Thus, although suppression of tradition really mattered, there was a multiplicity of other intervening variables determining how and why people positioned themselves in the ways they did: human desires have been frequently contradictory and their consciousness has shifted and moved elusively. By abstracting the internal from external class forces, and the political from the economic Geffray ends up reducing a far more complex conflict into a simple question of how to reconcile traditional authority with the modern state system. Undoubtedly, "the struggle between the world of the peasantry and the world of the cities"[9] is a vital element of the conflict, but there is more to it. The Mozambican conflict, as Finnegan aptly captures it in the title of his journalistic book was *A Complicated Conflict*[10] with many dimensions.

The problem with studying the past is it keeps on changing. This is partly because, as Benjamin once argued, "[e]very historical state of affairs presented dialectically, polarizes and becomes a force field in which the conflict between fore- and after-history plays itself out."[11] If the contested representation of the 'past' and 'present' of the war in Mozambique can be construed as such a field of conflictual ideologies, any wholesale embrace of either is as problematic as is the dramatization and celebration of the war. The point is, the causes of the war are not 'there' to be discovered, nor are they 'here' to be invented. Rather, the challenge is to shatter the reified continuity of history, as it has been presented in these dominant paradigms. In fact, as the Manica experience shows, the war was also fought at various levels of society by different individuals, with many different means, and for many different purposes.

Thus, whatever the merits of the destabilizationist and bona fide civil war theses, it is important to shift the terms of the debate about the conflict in a

27

new direction, which would lead out of the aporias of a totalitarian imposition of reason on a recalcitrant world. Whereas these perspectives remained locked in an ideological battle of blame and counter-blame, with their conceptual representations never fully adequate to their objects, this analysis focuses instead on the relations among subjects, people, and the basis of conflict between them. Conflicts, as Habermas paraphrasing Hegel and Marx points out, are:

> only the form of appearance, the empirical side of a fundamentally logical contradiction. Conflicts can be comprehended only with reference to the operatively effective rules according to which incompatible claims or intentions are produced within an action system.[12]

This places contradiction firmly with the intellectual's 'logic'. As Habermas further argues, class societies have fundamental contradictions, only because 'their organizational principle' necessitates that individuals and groups repeatedly confront one another with claims and intentions that are, in the long run, incompatible. In the *Legitimation Crisis*[13] he explains how such fundamental class contradictions can be displaced from the economic to other levels of social interaction, such as religious and quasi-nationalism in the case of Mozambique (see Chapters Four and Five).

Diachronically, this chapter traces the genesis evolution of the conflict, paying particular attention to the many intersecting variables such as the complex relationship between the state, rural communities and war. It tries to answer the questions of 'how' and 'why' a handful of malcontents managed to spark off a war that spread throughout the whole country like wild fire, forcing Frelimo to backtrack on a number of important policy issues. More specifically, what is the social content of the mass following of the rebel movement? What function did this mass (including the rebel forces themselves, who are mainly former peasants) have in the balance of forces, which is itself in a process of transformation? To what extent do the means conform to the proposed ends? And finally, what is the political and social significance of those demands presented by the movement's leaders which find general assent?

These questions revolve around the role and functioning of ideology in drawing masses of people into such situations of crisis and counter-revolutionary armed violence. It will be argued that the 'crisis of hegemony' of the state and the MNR's mobilizational strategy and it's evolving relationship with the peasants, combined in shaping the peasants' response to the war. In turn, the ways in which the peasants have positioned themselves in accordance with their changing circumstances and political consciousness, has provided the central dynamic to the war. These internal processes have been influenced by external factors to which we shall turn first.

The geo-political and historical context

At one level, Renamo owes its existence to the contradictions of the Southern African regional political economy. The requirements of capital accumulation and the struggle between states of the region to establish alternative social and political systems were decisive. Historically the penetration of international capital in Southern Africa led to the formation of a regional sub-system in which the principal poles of capital accumulation were located in South Africa. As with other states of the region, Mozambique became subordinated to serve the needs of capital accumulation in South Africa in various ways, mainly as a labour reserve for South Africa's mining industry and as a market for South African produced commodities.[14]

One long-standing objective of South Africa's regional policy had thus been to maintain this status quo, to entrench its interests and hegemony of capital in the region. The collapse of Portuguese colonialism in Mozambique in 1975 threatened this status quo. (Lacking its own capital, Portugal had granted concessions to multinational companies as well as entered into a labour export agreement with South Africa in exchange for foreign currency remittance to the colonial state). In the regional class and race war Rhodesia, which had unilaterally declared independence (UDI) in 1965, thus became the last bastion of white supremacist racialist ideology north of the Limpopo River.[15] Both Rhodesia and South Africa feared that the success of an alternative socio-economic system in Mozambique might inspire their own peoples to fight for the same system, generally independence and socialism. As a counter measure the Rhodesians and South Africans found it essential to undermine Mozambique's capacity to do so by destroying its economy.

The Rhodesian war and the MNR

Just after independence Mozambique closed its border with Rhodesia as part of the international sanctions against the illegal Smith regime. It also provided rear bases to Zimbabwean guerrillas. Both these moves probably had more disastrous consequences on the former than on the latter country. In response Rhodesia entered into war with Mozambique.[16] From 1976 till the end of the Zimbabwean independence war in 1979, Rhodesian air-raids and commando attacks on vital installations in Mozambique became the major feature of the strained relations between the two countries. The impact of this undeclared war was negative, and this led to further restlessness in the Manica Province.

In order to achieve maximum effect, the Rhodesians sought to enlist the services of disgruntled elements of the Mozambican society: exiled Portuguese settlers; former members of elite units in the colonial army; the embittered losers of political battles within Frelimo; and disgraced members of Frelimo's guerrilla army.[17] These were the people who, at the initiative of the Rhodesians, formed the nucleus of the rebel movement which they christened 'MNR' on 1 May 1977 in Harare.[18]

Thus the MNR was created as a 'fifth column' to the Rhodesian forces in their 'hot pursuit' of Zimbabwean guerrillas who had their rear bases in Mozambique.[19] It was a proxy force intended to further and protect interests of external forces. This view is increasingly being contested. The exact chronology of events leading to the formation of Renamo, and in particular those surrounding the defection from Frelimo to Renamo by Andrea Matada Matsangaisa (first leader of Renamo) and Dhlakama (the current leader), are still a grey area.

The Frelimo official version is that Matsangaisa and Dhlakama escaped from re-education centres to join Renamo after they had been arrested for theft. This is being dismissed as cheap political propaganda by some Mozambicans who have their own different versions. For instance, a senior Ndau government official with sympathies for Renamo contends that Matsangaisa was arrested not because of 'theft' but because of his perceived insubordination to his seniors. According to him, Matsangaisa, who was a commander based at Dondo (near Beira city), was arrested for refusing to obey orders to send troops under his command to repel a Rhodesian invasion.[20] Naturally, this was considered an act of high treason, and despite his 'reasonable argument' that his forces were ill-equipped to face the heavily armed Rhodesians and that he needed more equipment before he could engage them, he was sent to prison. He later escaped and joined Renamo. According to the same official, Dhlakama, whom he claims to know intimately, was arrested for giving favours (good food, cigarettes and other small basics not usually available in a military prison) to his colleagues who had been imprisoned for getting drunk and showing off with women in Chimoio city.

Another different account was offered by a former officer in the army, an insightful young man. According to him Matsangaisa was arrested allegedly for secretly hoarding arms in preparation for an uprising. Matsangaisa, the young man pointed out, was over-ambitious and was not satisfied with his post as Provincial military commander. It was this disillusionment and a perceived marginalisation of peoples of central and northern regions by the Southerners that motivated him into hoarding arms. Even during the independence war some members of the Popular Front for the Liberation of Mozambique (FPLM, Frelimo's military wing) had cached arms and turned bandit (about 2, 000 according to Samora Machel) either on their own account or working for the Portuguese secret police.[21]

Whether or not these accounts are true, one thing is certain: some elements of the Mozambican society, and within Frelimo itself, were disaffected by Frelimo policies and their latent opposition was galvanised and organised into effective counterrevolutionary opposition by external forces. Thus there was a historical coincidence of interests between internal and external forces, and this should not be surprising since, from a purely strategic/tactical point of view, 'the enemy of your enemy is your friend'.

South Africa and the MNR

With Zimbabwe's Independence in 1980, South Africa took over control of Renamo. By 1981 a full-scale war had begun.[22] Whilst the Rhodesians had used the MNR as a clandestine movement with a low profile, Pretoria, until the signing of the Nkomati Accord in 1984[23] had assumed a much more public profile. It pursued a double pronged strategy combining political and military initiatives to boost the MNR. Through this support Renamo graduated from being a mere 'Matsanga outfit' or bunch of bandits into being a formidable force to reckon with.

At the propaganda ideological level, Pretoria boosted the image of Renamo by setting up a radio broadcasting station, 'Voz da Africa Livre' (Free Africa), in Transvaal and by producing highly effective colour posters in French, Portuguese and English.[24] Pretoria also provided the MNR with mobile bases along the 500km L-shaped frontier between the two states, from Pfafuri in the north to Kosi Bay in the south.[25] As a pay result of these concerted initiatives, and the press-ganging recruitment methods of the MNR, the movement's force strength increased dramatically from less than 2, 000 in 1980 to 20, 000 armed men by the 1990.[26] Then this was two thirds the government's 30, 000 men of whom only 5, 000 were well fed and equipped.[27] These developments marked an important watershed in the historical metamorphosis of Renamo.

The objectives of Pretoria's destabilizationist foreign policy towards Mozambique were of a political/ideological nature. As Geldenhuys pointed out, Pretoria wanted Frelimo to abandon its active support for the ANC; loosen, if not cut its close ties - particularly in the military field - with communist powers; and tone down its revolutionary fervour and moderate its condemnation of South Africa.[28] An underlying economic objective was to maintain the Southern African states' dependence on itself. This meant making Mozambican land routes and port facilities unusable. The reasoning, which to some extent worked, was that with no alternative to using South African routes and ports (which were much more expensive than Mozambican ones) for import and export, the Frontline States (FLS) would water down their condemnation of South Africa and their call for mandatory sanctions. These geo-political considerations were tied to the ideological and military rivalries between Eastern and Western blocs.

The Super-power 'Cold War' rivalry

In the 'Cold War' of the 1980s Angola and Mozambique were viewed by Pretoria and the West as Soviet satellites or as "falling in the communist sphere of influence".[29] Indeed the former Soviet Union had been the ally of Angola and Mozambique supplying them with military hardware and equipment. The Reagan administration's over-arching commitment was to out-manoeuvre the former Soviet Union and under-cut the growth of communism in the 'Third World'. To that end, the West developed a strategic alliance with South Africa, which was dubbed 'Constructive Engagement'.[30]

Outlining the west's stance with respect to Southern Africa in 1982, the then Assistant Secretary of State for African Affairs, Chester Crocker stated categorically:

> In [South Africa] ... important Western economic, strategic, moral and political interests are at stake. [South Africa] is an integral and important element of the global economic system and it plays a significant economic role in its own region.[31]

Consequently, US political, ideological and economic ties with South Africa increased and South Africa was to serve as a "regional police force in the global imperial system managed by the US".[32]

For the frontline states and liberation movements struggling against apartheid, the United States' policy of 'Constructive Engagement' (with South Africa) was 'destructive engagement'.[33] According to Mittlemen, Section 512 of the Foreign Assistance and Related Programmes Appropriation Act specifically banned development assistance to Mozambique during the early 1980s.[34] In 1982-3 there was talk in the US Congress to supersede Section 512 by Section 513 of the Act, the so-called 'hit list'.[35] The hit list then comprised countries proscribed from development assistance under any conditions: then Libya, Iraq, South Yemen, Angola, Cambodia, Cuba, Laos, Vietnam and Syria.

Clearly Frelimo's experiment, whatever its shortcomings, was never given a chance. The struggle for development was superseded by that of survival. Even in areas which were promising fruitful results, such as health and education and women's liberation, there have been reversals. Thus to down-play the difficulties of charting an independent development path on the periphery of a regional system dominated by an aggressive and militaristic power like (former apartheid) South Africa would do but scant justice to Frelimo's achievements. External forces have, for various reasons, played an important role in stirring up havoc and chaos in Mozambique. Rhodesia created Renamo, and South Africa (with the West's connivance) as well as other private Western organizations and individuals have sustained it. It is important, however, to state firmly that there is more to the war than simply external aggression and conspiracy. The mono-causal analytical focus on outside forces characteristic of the 'destabilizationist' or conspiracy theories constitutes a major weaknesses in these studies' methodological approaches, and are not satisfactory.

Limits of the 'destabilizationist' and 'conspiracy' theses

Dependency theory inspired analyses, by emphasizing the importance of external influence/domination, lose sight of the internal economic and political dynamics of the war. The role of internal ideological, class, religious, gender and even generational struggles in fuelling the conflict is underplayed. Mozambicans are depicted as passive victims of external machinations incapable of making their *own* history. On the contrary, in their mutual reciprocal destruction and in their relentless struggle to survive, the Mozambicans have actively shaped the course of the war and their history, though not as they willed it nor in conditions of their own choosing. Moreover, the whole idea of 'destabilization', which necessarily assumes prior stability, is fundamentally flawed. Instability, conflict and contradiction have been the major defining elements of Mozambican history, even in the pre-colonial era. External factors thus only provided the broad parameters within which the internal conflicts and struggles were fought out.

The local dynamics of the war: Internal contradictions and struggles

From one point of view, the genesis of the civil war could be traced back to the unresolved questions of the independence struggle. Some of the issues over which the recently ended war has been fought, are strikingly similar to those that almost tore Frelimo apart within a few years of its inception. Frelimo was formed in June 1962 through the merger of three exiled nationalist groups, the Makonde African National Union (MANU), the Mozambique National Democratic Union (UDENAMO) and the Mozambique National Independence Union (UNAMI). As a result of its growth and the opening of 'liberated zones'[36] the Front experienced ideological divisions as opposing views on the organisation of post-independence society confronted each other. The disputes culminated in the assassination of its first President and founder, Eduardo Mondlane in 1968.[37]

As in the recently ended war, the most contentious issues were the role of traditional chiefs; the position of women; the involvement of whites in the struggle; the role of the educated cadres; the tactics for prosecuting the struggle; and the nature of the post-independence political and economic system. On all these issues, the revolutionaries radically differed with conservative nationalists, represented by Uria Simango (then the vice-president to Mondlane) and Lazarus Nkavandame among others.

For the revolutionaries, represented by Samora Machel and Marcelino Dos Santos, the chiefs were both collaborative stooges of the colonialists and an anachronism of the repressive and exploitative feudal society. Therefore their power had to be undermined. With regard to the position of women, they strongly argued for the total emancipation of women. The revolution would not only be incomplete, it would also not succeed without the liberation of women.

Through a combination of mobilization, agitation and under-hand tactics the conservative nationalists were defeated, and at the 1968 FRELIMO Second Congress the line of the revolutionaries was approved. The defeat of the moderate/conservative nationalists marked the transformation of Mozambique's independence struggle from being a mere nationalist struggle into being a 'socialist revolution'. This ideological and power struggle, like that within the Zimbabwe African National Union (ZANU)[38], was an intra-elite struggle and the triumph of the 'radicals' clarified a series of central tenets that have characterized Frelimo since then. In theory people were supposed to govern themselves, in practice the party governed them. Nonetheless, these proclamations and the limited transformations of the ideological superstructures, as shall be shown below, formed the focus of counter-revolution.

The state, peasant communities and war

Fanon, in discussing the weaknesses of political parties in Africa in particular and the Third World in general, identifies two major factors. The first weakness is, he argues, "the mechanical application of an organization (the party) which was created to carry on the struggle of the working class inside a highly industrialized, capitalist society".[39] This instrument of modern political warfare, he continues, "is thrown down just as it is, without the slightest modification, upon real life with all its infinite variations and lack of balance, where slavery, serfdom, barter, a skilled working class, and high finance exist side by side".[40] The second, and interrelated, weakness is:

the inherent defect in the majority of political parties in underdeveloped
regions has been, following traditional lines, to approach in the first
place those elements which are the most politically conscious: the
working class in the towns, the skilled workers, and the civil servants -
that is to say, a tiny proportion of the population ...[41]

Mozambique seems to have had more than its fair share of the "fetish of
organization" and the concomitant contempt for 'obscurantist' rural traditions,
defects which Fanon considers major obstacles to realizing the new energies
of the masses.

After gaining absolute power in 1975 Frelimo banned all opposition.[42] It
then imposed a one-party authoritarian regime which ruled the country until
the introduction of political liberalism and multi-partyism towards the end of
the 1980s. The relationship of the state to rural communities has been
characterized by suspicion and tension; in the former, modern ideas reigned,
while in the latter, tradition. The major schisms between the urban based
elites and the rural population emanated from the effects of the agrarian
reform programme (it interrupted peasant social organisation and their rural
economies); suppression of peasant religious and neo-traditionalist ideologies;
the futile attempt to build the nation by 'killing the tribe'; and the general
attempt to control society and change. The attempt to resolve and/or suppress
these tensions through the ideological mechanism for control and subjection
lies at the core of the local dynamics of the war in rural Mozambique.

In Manica Province these factors were compounded by the effects of the
Rhodesian war and sanctions. The failure of the new system to deliver the
goods, and the coercive imposition of anti-peasant ideologies caused much
discontent. In Manica Province collectivization and 'proletarianization'
through work in state farms affected different groups of the peasantry
differently. For instance, whilst for poor peasants collective villages might
have provided an opportunity to a better life, for some rich peasants it meant
loss of land and wealth. A combination of these factors have shaped the local
dynamics of the war in Manica Province.

The peasantry, agrarian reform and it's impact on the rural economy

Defining a peasant and drawing up typologies can be a barren exercise,
because it "blinds us to the process of change and imposes a static
picture".[43] Current conceptions of the peasantry have emphasised either
peasant 'culture', or its economic and political relationships with the wider
society. Emphasizing the first aspect, Kroeber defines the peasants thus:

Peasants are definitely rural - yet live in relation to market towns; they usually form a class segment of a larger population which usually contains urban centres, sometimes metropolitan capitals. They constitute part societies with part cultures.[44]

While accepting the 'part society/culture' notion, Saul and Woods stressed the partial integration of the peasantry into the wider economic system. For them:

[P]easants are those whose ultimate security and subsistence lies in their having rights in land and in the labour of family members on the land, but who are involved, through rights and obligations, in a wider economic system which includes participation of non-peasants.[45]

As is clear in these complementary schools, peasant societies are, in Godelier's words:

class societies within which the peasantry constitutes an exploited class, dominated economically, politically and culturally by a class which no longer participates directly in production.[46]

In Mozambique, as in peasant societies elsewhere, the social organisation of the peasantry was built, first around the relations of production as they grew from the economic constraints of agricultural activities, and next, around the necessity of reproduction of the productive unit.[47] For the peasantry, security consists more in the maintenance of social links with kinsfolk able to help in times of need than in the amassing of capital. However, as shown below, like the colonial state Frelimo also undermined the peasant's security by pursuing agrarian policies that reduced the peasantry to poverty and increased their social marginalisation. Through their participation in the dialectic of control, the peasants resisted these agrarian policies and their legitimating ideologies. When Renamo appeared on the stage a significant proportion of the rural population of Manica province switched their allegiance to it from Frelimo.

The ideological rationale and content of the agrarian reform

Frelimo's agrarian transformation programme was guided by Marxian anti-peasant ideologies. These ideologies depicted the peasantry as an inexorably disintegrating residue of the past feudal society.[48] To realise the 'socialization of the countryside' it was thus necessary to transcend the archaic social and economic organisation of the peasantry. The thrust was on increasing peasant productivity through introduction of large-scale and high-technology state and collective farms. This reflected an elemental belief in the superiority of large-scale production.

In Manica province about 8 per cent of the rural population was affected by collectivization campaign. Some were made labourers in state owned farms[49]. The overall effect was the marginalisation of the family farming sector. For example, 90 per cent of agricultural investment in 1977-1983 went to the state sector, 2 per cent to cooperatives, and virtually none to the small family sector.[50] The assumption was that although agrarian transformation disrupted the peasant economy, peasant needs could be satisfied more generously only by large-scale production in the long run.

Agricultural pricing policy was established within a conception of a planned economy, with a planning system responsible for the distribution of consumer and investment goods. The rigid pricing policies threw the rural market into disarray and removed incentives for increased market production. The combined effects of neglect of both the family and cooperative sectors and the deficiencies of centralised state planning led to a fall in production levels. The Frelimo view that the peasant does not regard the family as a household[51] resulted precisely in the destruction of peasant communities. Similarly, because the cooperative sector was starved of capital, the socialization of the countryside did not materialise. Moreover, due to bureaucratic red tape state farms and collectives never fulfilled their production targets. The plans, designed by the National Commission for Planning and passed on to the Provincial and District cadres, were too rigid and unrealistic. Also, low wages in the state farms also meant that the workers had little money to spend on consumption and investment. As a result, they reverted to family subsistence production for survival. Both peasant and workers' needs and aspirations were therefore not satisfied. This was the genesis of the crisis of hegemony of the state.

The discontent with the increasing price absurdities and consequent shortages of basic foodstuffs, in both rural and urban areas, led to the emergence of *candonga* (informal or 'blackmarket' economy). *Candonga* was ruthlessly punished, mainly through public flogging. But with the deepening of the economic crisis and collapse of the formal economy, it has become the major source of goods for many. Belated attempts to increase producer prices and to invest in the family sector had little effect. First enunciated at Frelimo's Fourth Congress in 1983, when the war had made rural production almost impossible, they were half-backed solutions. Another element of government agrarian policy which backfired, was the 'back to the land' policy.

'Operation Production', implemented in 1983, involved forcible removal of unemployed people from the cities and sending them to work in state farms far in the north. The move seems to have been based on a misconception of the problem: unemployment was not due to the unemployed's 'laziness' (as the officials contented), but rather to the failure of the economic system to create sufficient jobs. The urban unemployed's desire to follow 'decadent' urban lifestyles was a reflection of the broader changes that society was undergoing.

The policy was in some ways a form of victimising the victims by way of internal deportation. It was rushed and haphazardly effected. As a result many family members were arbitrary separated and dislocated. According to some Mozambicans not only did this cause promiscuity in the farms (as well as in the cities) as thousands of male and female youths, separated from their spouses and loved ones, were forced to live together: most of the 'deportees' also ended up joining the ranks of Renamo.

To sum up, for Frelimo the peasant system was incompatible with progress, and the development of society was overcoming it. In its quest to 'organize society to conquer underdevelopment' (through a series of 'Indicative Plans'), Frelimo set itself the task of demolishing the semi-feudal conditions on the land. In theory, this would set in motion a complete social restructuring for the benefit of the peasants. In practice, however, this meant the replacement of peasant culture and ideologies with official order. 'Accumulation on the back of the peasantry', in which surplus created in the agricultural sector was supposed to be invested in the industrial sector, had the opposite effect of disrupting peasant production and organisation. This constituted what might be called the 'undoing' of the peasantry, and the basis for strained relations between the state elites and the peasants.

The crisis of hegemony and the struggle between peasant and anti-peasant ideologies

Overall, the legitimating ideology of the agrarian transformation programme flouted the traditional ways and claims of the peasantry. As Machel put it:

> transposition of peasant ways to the city ... meant the city being changed to the rural way of living (with) the assimilated man replacing polygamy with promiscuity, eventually marrying one, the most polished, but not giving up the others. Traditional superstition will be supplemented by cinematic myths from karate films and models of the foreign bourgeoisie.[52]

The task of the revolution was therefore, as Machel declared:

to break with this (peasant) outlook, to bring man into culture, to relate to the mode of production and to economic development. The scientific knowledge instilled there plus the ideology and class sentiment provide the irresistible force that will sweep away the old world and implant a new world. Our schools are a mirror to society and to the contradictions, including those of culture, that we are facing.[53]

But 'sweeping away the old world' was not in tune with peasant aspirations. As one peasant put it:

Caetano [Portuguese leader in colonial times - here used to refer to the local Portuguese farmer they worked for] was better. He used to give us maize meal, dried fish and clothes [as payment in kind for farm labour]. Samora Machel gave me this large piece of land. What without capital, tools and other necessary inputs does he think I can do with it?[54]

Clearly the revolutionary elites and the peasants had different agendas: it seems while the former had waged the war in order to create a 'new society', the peasants had supported them (in only a handful of the northern provinces where the guerrilla war was fought - nothing happened in Manica) in the hope of gaining their land alienated by the Portuguese. They wanted to live their lives as they had done before colonialism.

There was a fundamental misunderstanding on what should constitute 'Independence' and a 'new society' between the various social groups in Mozambique. Consequently, and in order to impose their ideological hegemony, the urban-based elites deployed the full force of the party and state repressive apparatus against the dissenters. This forced many to ask, 'when will Independence end?'.[55] Traditional chiefs, who before the revolution were at the centre of peasant communities were arbitrarily stripped of their power. By performing ancestral appeasement and supplication as well as rain-making rituals, they had symbolized the ensemble of peasant ideologies.

As a former colonial policeman, *sapiao*, pointed out with respect to localities in Gondola district, where he had played a crucial role in the traditional succession ceremonies:

In their place party cadres were appointed, and chiefs who tried to resist this were sent to re-education centres (a euphemism for detention centres), where some of them never returned from. Traditional rituals and superstitious beliefs, viewed as it were as 'obscuntarist', were ruthlessly repressed.

39

Religious worship was also condemned as an 'opium of the people' and religious leaders were persecuted. In a quest to emancipate women from male domination, polygamists as well as parents who arranged marriages for their daughters were severely punished.

Echoing Marx's contempt for the 'idiocy of rural' life, Machel attacked the peasantry:

> Peasant societies essentially are underdeveloped because they are fatalist. Mozambican society, even in the urban sector, carries the dead weight of the fatalist, resigned, passive legacy of the peasant society.[56]

Underdevelopment and poverty was "not generally due to a lack of material resources", but instead reflected "man's ignorance in using existing resources and man's passive acceptance of his situation of wretchedness".[57]

Although in some specific circumstances peasant production may be based on routine, wisdom acquired through experience and risk aversion, this, as their ingenious and innovative survival strategies amply demonstrate (see next Chapter), is not always the case. Similarly, while their communities are based on patriarchy and genealogy with ritual (ancestral supplication especially) providing the corner-stone of the social fabric that holds together these societies, these are not rigid and static structures (see Chapters Five and Six). The point is, as Fanon notes:

> the young nationalist class ... is going to compete with these feudal lords in many various fields. There are marabouts and medicine men who bar the way to sick people who otherwise could consult a doctor, oracles which pass judgement and thus render lawyers useless, caids who make use of their political and administrative powers to set up in trade or to start a transport service, customary chiefs who oppose, in the name of religion and tradition, the setting up of businesses and the introduction of new goods.[58]

The people, who are exposed to competing traditional and modern forms of authority, organization, medicine etc, "therefore become a market to be contended for".[59] In Manica, the consequent wholesale attack on the bedrock of peasant society and ideology only led to rising discontent. In a vicious circle, deepening economic crisis led to increasing restlessness, which in turn led to rising state authoritarianism in order to contain the discontent.

In response to the discontent its policies caused, the government embarked on a combination of ruthless repression and a more vigorous implementation of its agrarian policy.[60] Peasants who resented having to leave their traditional homes for collectives were coerced. Sometimes their huts were burnt by the government soldiers who ferried them to their new state-designated homes. Black marketeers were flogged or arrested. One religious leader pointed out that many of his colleagues taken to re-education centres have never returned. Gloating at the weakening of Frelimo, he aptly summed up the situation in a traditional idiom thus:

> *Nyaya dzinotongwa nedzimwe nyaya. Kushata kwezvimwe ndookunakaka kwezvimwe* (Problems are resolved by other problems. In every cloud there is a silver lining).

In other words for him, seen dialectically, some problems created by Frelimo have been solved by the problems created by the war.

Thus, contrary to anticipated results, increased state repression had the opposite effect. In addition to terror, antagonism and confusion, it also created resistance among the disaffected. Little did Frelimo realize that in a way it was digging its own political grave. For instance, religious persecution was actually seen as fulfilment of prophecy, and hence an inspiration by religious organizations such as the Jehovah's Witness. The contest between Frelimo and the peasantry (as well as economic elites such as black marketeers), though reduced to merely a technical problem by Frelimo, was an ideological conflict. It was a manifestation of a deep-rooted contradictions in the modes of production and the development process.

By imposing the agrarian transformation programme and its legitimating ideology, the revolutionaries were unwittingly playing a decisive role in shaping the peasants' political outlook. The intended transformations were not attuned to the desires and aspirations of its supposed beneficiaries, the peasantry. They instead generated discontent, unrestlessness and resistance. This in turn formed the internal dynamics for the escalation of the military conflict: when the Renamo rebels came promising a return to the old ways of doing things, the most disaffected and disinherited peasants welcomed them as their liberators.

The MNR's ideological mobilizational strategy and its relationship with the peasantry

When Renamo first arrived in Gorongossa district on one night towards the middle of 1977 they looted a cooperative shop. After that they gave the shopkeeper a poster, which he was ordered to pass on to the authorities, caricaturing Samora Machel as a monkey sitting on a throne.[61] War pictures and cartoons of this kind play a crucial role in raising people's awareness as well as an effective propaganda instrument. The ideological message was that

Mozambique was being ruled by ignorant pseudo-revolutionaries who had seized and maintained power through 'monkey tricks'. The intended effect was to incite people to revolt against that rule, and the main task, to convince their potential constituency that an alternative to the status quo was realizable.

Typically, Renamo's ideological mobilization strategy developed haphazardly and synecretically. In particular, it was based on a combination of outright coercion, vague anti-communism, quasi-nationalism and an articulation (or appropriation) of peasant ideologies. It's success depended largely upon its capacity to tap and harness the existential dimensions of human subjectivity. In other words, whether or not its major propositions were in tune with what made sense to ordinary people's conception of the world was what mattered.

The task was made much easier by the acute legitimacy crisis in which the matrix of affirmations and sanctions underpinning the Frelimo regime and its ruling ideology were breaking up.[62] Exploiting and manipulating localised peasant grievances against Frelimo, Renamo managed to carve up a constituency for itself. Where Frelimo repressed peasant ideologies, Renamo articulated and presented them as its cause. For instance, Renamo has consistently argued that its war is 'a war of spirits' and that it seeks to give back to the ancestors, traditional chiefs and the elders their powers and proper position in the community. This made sense to the peasantry, whose world outlook had been condemned by Frelimo as anachronistic. Not surprisingly some supported the rebels.

The expansion of the war and the Renamo-peasant initial rapport

By 1979 the rebels had established a major base in the dense forests of Gorongossa mountain. Proceeding from there, and in a more or less coordinated campaign, the rebels spread into Manica Province destroying collective villages and *aldeia*s. They forced their inhabitants to return to their original homes. In some cases, as in some other northern provinces, the peasants willingly abandoned their state-designated collective villages in favour of their traditional homes. The latter then formed a kind of 'human fort and communication network' and buffer zone for the rebels.

For example, according to some displaced peasants from Doroe localidade (Gondola District) Renamo largely owe its early military success in the area to peasant cooperation. In an ingenious tactic, the 'liberated peasants' - liberated from state tentacles - would alert the rebels (and everyone else) of the approach of government forces through a coded whistling. The code was picked up by the next neighbour, who in turn would pass the message by another whistling. By the time government soldiers arrived the peasants and guerillas would have vanished into the bush. Such codes, which sometimes covered distances of more than 12km, provided essential intelligence information to the rebels. It enabled them to retreat when their enemy advanced, harass him when he halted, attack him when he evaded action and pursuing him when he retreated.[63] Reminiscent of Mao Tsetung's dictum that a guerilla should be like 'a fish in water among the peasantry'[64], the tactic served the rebels well.

Many displaced peasants pointed out that during the period up to about the beginning of 1982 incidents of brutal harassment and murder by the rebels were limited to ruling party officials and to those associated with the government in one way or another (quite a wide net). According to a Ndau witness, for example, when the rebels first attacked a collective farm in Buzi they only murdered the chairman of the collective and mutilated his wife. He narrated the incident with mixed feelings thus:

> My mother, with other women, laboured so hard at the *shamba de pove* (collective farm), but never got anything out of it. They were always told that the money was being saved to buy new equipment. Meanwhile the *chefe* (party boss) of the collective's belly was growing bigger and bigger.... But it (this injustice) was righted when the 'boys' arrived. They killed him and hacked off his wife's ears and nose.

His only anger was that the rebels were also after him, and other members of his family, because of their supposed connection to Frelimo through his uncle. As a general rule, many displaced peasants pointed out, before looting and burning a collective farm or an *aldeia* (resettlement camp), the rebels would ask the inhabitants to leave. According to inhabitants of Chacacaule resettlement camp, about 12km northwest of Chimoio city, in all the three attacks on the camp, the rebels first fired warning shots in the air to allow the people to flee, before looting and burning it down.[65]

Also, during this period, and reminiscent of the Robin Hood heroic bandit', who "takes from the rich to give to the poor",[66] the rebels distributed some of their booty to the peasants. Naturally, this helped them escape the clumsy traps of soldiers and policemen. For as long as no peasant gave them away and as long as many were willing to tell them about the movement of government soldiers, the rebels remained immune to hostile weapons and as invisible to hostile eyes as the myths and legends about 'Matsanga' invariably claim.[67] According to a Zimbabwean military intelligence officer (then based in Chimoio), by the early 1980s the rebels had consolidated their position and had gained a far greater upper hand in the battle-field:

When we arrived (in 1982), the Frelimo state was on the verge of collapse and it would not have been surprising to hear that Chimoio City had fallen into rebel hands. The rebels used to roam freely during day-light all over the place.

The peasants' sympathy, active and passive, was the rebels' major asset in their early successes. Without necessarily actively supporting the rebels, some of those who had been disaffected by the state's interruption of their traditional way of living felt relieved by the appearance of the MNR on the stage. These are the people who constituted the internal constituency of Renamo.

The social content of Renamo's followers

Witch-doctors and traditional healers who had been banished by Frelimo were among the first to join the rebel movement. They were re-empowered. Performing traditional rituals for the guerrillas, they played a vital role in expanding the social constituency of Renamo. In territory that Renamo controlled, chiefs who had been marginalized by Frelimo were also given back their lost powers. There were, in fact, cases whereby peasants followed their chiefs, as well as reputable witch-doctors joining the rebels *en masse*. In extreme cases, some peasants, as an excuse to go back to their original homes, even burnt down their collective villages and claimed that it was the work of rebels.

Men, like the rebel soldiers themselves, were allowed to marry as many wives as they pleased. The latter (to which we shall return to in Chapter Six) was resented by women as it is clearly a reversal of the gains they had made under Frelimo's limited emancipation campaign. It is a manifest example of the retrogressive nature of Renamo's political line. Another social group that readily welcomed Renamo, and in fact played a crucial role, was the rural 'lumpen proletariat', the unemployed youth.

Marx and Engels had dismissed the 'lumpen proletariat' as the most reactionary class which can easily betray revolutionary cause for immediate material gain, and indeed advised that any revolutionary who wished to succeed should first eliminate this 'absolutely brazen' social category.[68] In contrast, Fanon viewed the lumpen proletariat -"the wretched of the earth" - as the potentially most revolutionary social group as it had nothing to lose, and had not been contaminated by capitalist materialist values[69]; having been hardened by tough life, they provide ready-made soldiers. As Mozambique's experience suggests, there are a multiplicity of factors that determine whether or not a specific social class becomes revolutionary; in Uganda, it was the lumpen proletariat, many of whom street children, who provided the backbone of Museveni's resistance movement that toppled the dictatorial and corrupt post-independence regime.

The point is, as Girard forcefully stresses in his book *Violence and the Sacred*, violence, whether revolutionary or counterrevolutionary and as it appears in myth and ritual, "belongs to all men and to no one in particular".[70] The world-wide rise in violence, in all its manifestations and at various levels of society - from child abuse and wife battering within families, youth violence and police brutality in many capitals of the world, bush wars in Africa, Asia and Latin America, state terrorism in many countries to scientific atrocities against both nature (nuclear testing for example) and peoples of the world (for example the mass murder of Iraqis during the Gulf War and of the Kurds by Saddam Hussein) etc - suggest that the physiology of violence varies little from one individual to another, even from one culture to another. Indeed, as Girard, following Storr, point out:

> nothing resembles an angry cat or man so much as another angry cat or man. [Violence seems] to be a factor which is to an extent independent of those cultural variables that often unknown to us, or only dimly known, or perhaps less familiar than we like to think.[71]

As he further argues, "[w]hen unappeased violence seeks and always finds a surrogate victim ... chosen only because it is vulnerable and close at hand".[72] The genesis of *all* myth, for example about the sanctity of the nation-state, property, tradition, and religion etc, as the experience of the afflicted communities of Southern Africa show, is also the genesis of such violence and tragedy. Struggle against such hegemonic myths, therefore becomes, as Cabral aptly put it, "a normal condition".[73] For him, in such circumstances it is important, as he stresses in his revolutionary theory and practice - praxis - to analyse the forces that influence the revolutionary or counterrevolutionary potential of specific classes, and on the basis of that analysis develop strategies for raising revolutionary consciousness of the masses.

In the Mozambican civil war, however, as we shall see in Chapter Five, such a revolutionary consciousness was at best haphazard and fragmented, and at worst non-existent. For instance, for some unemployed youth violence has offered an escape from poverty, whilst for others it destroyed their opportunity of finding a stable job. As in the conquest wars, in which some of the rural poor found sustenance from the civil and military labour markets of the conquest[74], many unemployed rural youth found theirs in an auxiliary role on Renamo's investment in force. Thus war provided an outlet from 'rural idiocy' and poverty for the social marginals, if often at the expense of their fellows. For some violence was an empowering, and even cleansing process, yet for others, it was disempowering and degrading. More serious, in terms of its implications for post-war reconstruction, is the fact stressed by Storr that once the urge to violence has been aroused, it is difficult to quell it; "it is more difficult to quell an impulse toward violence than to rouse it, especially within the normal the normal framework of social behaviour".[75] Violence triggers certain physical changes that prepare men's bodies for battle and confrontation, and this tendency should not be regarded as a simple reflex that ceases with the removal of the initial stimulus; it instead lingers on, and especially in socially stratified societies in which the access to scarce resources is highly inequitable.

As the rest of Southern Africa, Mozambican society, rural and urban, is stratified and differentiated. Consequently, people's response to the violence war, and their relationship with Renamo, has tended to vary in accordance with their socio-economic status, as well as whether they were directly or indirectly affected by the war. In other words, people occupying different positions in the social hierarchy have been affected differently by the war. Those whose privileges had been threatened, chiefs and the rural 'kulaks' whose aspirations had been doomed welcomed the rebels and some willingly joined their ranks.[76] For example, one rebel junior commander said the war was the only way of achieving justice and fairness. He explained his reasons for joining Renamo thus:

> When collective villages were introduced in our area, the party ordered me to use my truck - which I had bought through hard-earned savings - to transport the produce to city markets at no pay. But when the truck broke down, neither the party nor the collective would help me have it repaired. I was the ultimate loser in this evil system, so this is why I decided to fight it.[77]

In contrast, and ironically, some entrepreneurs especially found security in Frelimo's 'socialism' rather than in Renamo's capitalism. Similarly, elements of the poor who had gained from Frelimo's egalitarian policies did not welcome Renamo's arrival and were among the first to flee. Another form of ideological mobilization quietly used by Renamo has been that of quasi-nationalism centring on the alleged domination of the state and party structures by Southerners.

Ethnicity, quasi-nationalism and the war

The perceived ethnic domination of official politics by the Southerners is perhaps the single most important one in Manica Province. The issue, which

46

is a prominent source of conflict within Frelimo itself, is a recurring theme in ordinary discourses among various social strata. The Southerners are accused by the Ndaus and by some Northerners (people from the central regions commonly refer to themselves as 'Northerners') of a superiority complex and of having dominated politics, with nepotism being the high road to power. The extent of this (perceived) ethnic domination is difficult to judge.

Claims of the affected, though biased, might offer us some insights. One typical example of perceived Southern ethnic hostility towards the Northerners, is the case of four senior government officials (two from Manica Province, one from Nampula and the other from Tete) who vehemently asserted that they would never want to work in Maputo.[78] They would not because, they pointed out, the Southerners, including those at lower status levels than them (the officials), would look down upon them.

They further claimed that the most important posts in their departments, such as personnel, are held by 'them'. 'Them' are the Southerners, portrayed as a devious caste apart which has maintained its hegemony through a network of personalistic and kinship-based clientelism. One of them, in support of his argument, cited the skewed ethnic composition of both the first and present cabinet; out of the eighteen ministers of the 1975 cabinet, there was only one from the central and northern provinces, and in the present one the only important cabinet posts held by non-Southerners are Defence, and Education.[79]

Another related issue, according to some Northerners, is the fact that opportunities to study at the local University or overseas are restricted to Southerners only. Of the many youths who complained that opportunities to study at the Eduardo Mondlane University and abroad were only available to Southerners, one was a young man from Gorongossa district (Sofala Province). He described how his ambitions to study at the local University were frustrated in 1982 thus:

> When everything was okay, (ie admission) we (the eight of them, from Manica, Sofala and Nampula) went to Beira where we were supposed to get a flight to Maputo. In Beira the Department of Education, which was supposed to provide us with air-tickets to Maputo, delayed us for about a week saying the tickets had not yet arrived from Maputo. When we finally arrived at the University, we were told that our places had been filled and advised to wait for the next intake the following year.

He was convinced that there had been some ethnically inspired politicking behind the scenes to stop them from studying at the University. For instance,

47

he could not understand why the Ministry of Education which was responsible for both their admission and their late arrival, could have done such a thing.

A similar incident of perceived tribal discrimination was the story of a senior Ndau government official who complained that his brother, an officer in the army, was killed (when coming from the frontline near Maputo) by his own 'comrades' for being a high ranking northern officer.[80] Incidents of this nature abound in the diverse life histories of many a Mozambican from Manica Province. One senior government official (Provincial level) summed it up in the following cynical or joking fashion:

> In the national division of labour in Mozambique the Southerners enjoy the wealth of the country, those from the central region labour for the country and the Northerners defend (or fight for) the country.

While these stories might be viewed as frustrated mumblings of elites who feel marginalised from the power centre, such ideas have noticeable resonance among the general populace. It should also be noted, however, that all these stories were offered by those who stayed with Frelimo. Their accounts could be different from those who are part of Renamo. Unfortunately, and for security reasons, it was not possible to interview the latter. Judging from what they say and do these officials could even be said to be working under-cover to help Renamo. For example, they engaged in practices that discredit Frelimo such as super-exploitation and harsh treatment of their servants and abuse of young women. Whatever the details of this, it is clear that the ethnic factor is a key variable in Mozambican politics in general and it has provided a dynamic for the war. The Senas, who come from around Beira and right up to the Zambezi, are the most despised ethnic group. This is evidenced by the Ndau and Manyika usage to scold an ill-behaved child thus; "Don't be like a Sena".

Ethnicity is therefore an important variable in the Mozambican conflict, and an element in politics in general. But unfortunately, the only political party, the Federal Party of Mozambique-Democratic Federalist (PAFEMO-DF), which recognises the ethnic diversity of Mozambique and, hence, the need for a federal system to accommodate these diversities has not been registered. Its application for registration was turned down by the Justice Ministry in September 1993, on the grounds that its statute violated Articles 32 and 69 of the 1990 constitution,[81] by advocating 'division' of the country.

Ethnicity in a historical and theoretical context

As in the rest of sub-Saharan Africa, Mozambique's ethnic pluralism is characterised by a vast cultural, linguistic and geographical base. This variety has multiplied the manner in which ethnic identity has been invoked in social conflict or collaboration. Mozambican ethnicity, like African ethnicity in general, is also marked by a weakness of secondary bases of identity, such as class, profession, vocation that arise with industrialisation and the spread of secular values. This fact has given ethnicity a prominent role in politics. The African ethnic diversity and the weakness of their secondary bases of identity have complicated national political management of civil society by materially poor and weak countries such as Mozambique.

Mozambique, like other African countries continued to resist ethnic pluralism on the ground that 'tribal' loyalties will sunder its fragile new state. Central to nation-building was therefore the need to transcend and/or negate the tribe, to 'kill the tribe to build the nation' in the then popular slogan. The attempt to resist ethnic pluralism was based on the assumption that tribal affinity in African politics is the premier scourge of good government.[82] But the negative connotations of the word 'tribe' is itself one enduring legacy of the divide *et emperium* era of colonialism; in Chege's words, the word tribe is "an invidious term of colonial vintage that denigrates African ethnic groups".[83] In a similar vein, and with specific reference to Southern Africa, Vail has argued that tribalism was a creation of the colonialist rule as part of their 'divide and rule' tactics.[84] But, given the ubiquity of warfare between rival chiefdoms for influence and resources (notably slaves) in the pre-colonial era, it appears the colonialists did not create tribalism. Rather they manipulated and exacerbated pre-existent tribal animosities for their advantage.

In the particular case of Mozambique it has been argued that the domination of politics by Southerners is one of the most enduring legacies of colonialism, in particular the concentration of development in the south. More specifically, the weakness of the Portuguese in the south allowed others, Protestant Missionaries especially, to build schools and a University there. Consequently, the educated Southerners had to lead the liberation struggle and the country after independence. Refuting this argument, some Northerners have cited Southern leaders, including Machel himself, who are or were less educated than some non-Southerners.

More important, the attempt to 'build the nation' by 'killing the tribe', rather than strengthen the tribe in order to build the nation, as PAFEMO-DF argues, has cost Frelimo much in terms of its popularity. The MNR has successfully exploited this to its advantage. Mozambique, like the rest of Africa, must learn to live with its fissiparous subnationalism and ethnic diversity, but the political and constitutional institutions conducive to pluralism are unlikely to be found in strong authoritarian state, as Frelimo's was. Building the nation and integrating diverse ethnic groups into statehood should not necessarily entail destroying the elements of the 'social whole'.

Rather, as PAFEMO-DF contends, federalism, which allows ethnic organisation, may ironically strengthen national loyalty. In Chege's words:

> By diffusing autocratic power and providing cultural autonomy and control over local resources, it may satisfy varied and sometimes highly idiosyncratic provincial demands. Strengthening the parts could then provide solidarity for the whole.[85]

In itself, identification with one's ethnic group is not a retrogressive phenomenon; only when ethnicity is 'politicized' in the struggle for scarce resources does it become a divisive and dangerous force. Both Frelimo and Renamo, in their different ways, are guilty of the latter.

Finally Mozambican ethnicity, like ethnic consciousness elsewhere, has used a number of primary identities, such as area of origin, religion, culture and language, to build a group's internal cohesion in the face of competition for power and resources from other groups. Such forms of identity, though prior to class, have become the basis for class membership in both Frelimo and Renamo hierarchy, and an issue of contention. Renamo has exploited these identities, as well as other peasant legitimate grievance against Frelimo to carve a social constituency for itself.

The constituency, however, disintegrated as the true colours of Renamo started to emerge. Coercion put an end to initial peasant rapport with Renamo. After that, the balance of force in the battle-field started changing; by the time of the signing of the cease-fire agreement in October 1992 neither side was in a position of militarily winning the conflict. More important, peasant response to Renamo violence, as well as drought, shifted the balance of force against Renamo.

Coercive mobilisation and the demise of the Renamo-peasant honey-moon

Kriger, with reference to the Zimbabwean independence war, has convincingly concluded that popular support is an irrelevant issue in the success or otherwise of a revolutionary movement.[86] She argues that although peasants' participation in organisations set up to provide logistical support for the guerrillas was unpopular, "this did not prevent the revolutionary movement from coming to power".[87] As with the Zimbabwean guerrillas, Renamo rebels' military success was not based on popular support. On the contrary, peasants had to invent strategies to avoid Renamo control or positions within its civilian administrative structure. The strategies ranged from flight, negotiation of a precarious existence and invocation of peasant ideologies to tame Renamo terror.

50

Coercive mobilisation became central to Renamo's strategy primarily for two main reasons, namely, the intensification of the war and the collapse of the rural economy as a result of both drought and Renamo's predatory treatment of the peasantry. During 1983-1984 the war intensified dramatically. Dirty war tactics based on "the construction of a culture of terror ... intended to subdue the civilian community into social and political acquiescence"[88] were elevated to a common strategy by the belligerent forces. The rebels, in their war of manoeuvre, engaged in frontal attack of the enemy. They burnt a goods train near Dondo (a few kilometres west of Beira), and assaulted nearby government forces, and pursued the survivors up to near the border with Malawi.[89]

The government responded by launching a ruthless campaign to 'drain the water from a rebellious fish'. Code-named, 'Operation *Tira-camisa*' (sheath/dirt-remover), the operation involved massive mechanized counter-offensives, as well as large-scale military conscription of all able bodied males of 16 years and above. The military call-up was so thorough that, in folklore, Marcelimo Dos Santos is reported as having said that he would give his daughter to anyone who was so skilful as to be able to escape it; quite a few, however, did manage to escape the military call-up.[90] The civilian population emerged not only as the principal victims, but also as the major spoils of the war.

In response to the government forces' offensives, coercive mobilization increasingly became the central element of the rebels' strategy. In order to boost their numbers and expand the territory under their control, press-ganging recruitment methods and grotesque violence - mainly mutilations and the public display of victims - became the norm. This was intended to instil terror, and hence obedience, among the civilian population as well as to demonstrate the myth of the invincibility of the government forces. At that time the latter were rapidly losing the capacity to protect the population.

Coercion became particularly necessary when the MNR became increasingly discredited among its rather reluctant supporters. This was due to its continued predatory relationship with the peasantry, and hence destruction of the rural economy, as well as its failure to defeat the government. Unlike the Shining Path (Sendero Luminoso) of Peru, whose violence matches or even surpasses that of Renamo, the latter has been unable to sustain itself economically. Although game meat provided a vital diet for rebel soldiers, they had to rely on peasants for maize and other food stuffs. But as their stocks of chicken, goats, grain etc started to dwindle, especially during the drought, peasants increasingly became reluctant to feed the rebels. Such refusal was almost invariably met with heavy punishment, usually beatings but sometimes even murder.

The devastating drought of the late 1980s to early 1990s played a crucial role in altering the balance of forces in favour of the government. From a purely military point of view, as the rapid swings in the military balance of force in Angola's civil war in accordance with the seasons amply demonstrates[91], climatic and topographic conditions are vitally important for the survival of rural-based guerrilla army. Green vegetation provides much needed cover, while rain both provides food in the form of agricultural produce, wild-life meat and wild fruits, and also hampers enemy aerial bombardments.

When the drought set in, Renamo lost all these advantages. It should therefore not be surprising that, at least in Manica Province, it was during the drought that many of the peasants started flocking from Renamo controlled territory to government ones in search of food. The food is largely provided by donor agencies. Not only did Renamo lose its peasant 'captives', on whom it had parasitically survived: it also lost a significant proportion of its soldiers as many opted to surrender under the government's amnesty rather than face death by starvation.

For example, almost all the displaced peasants as well as amnestied Renamo guerrillas interviewed in August 1992 at Matsinye resettlement camp (about 20km north-west of Chimoio) mentioned drought and hunger as the main reasons for fleeing from Renamo controlled territory.[92] Every day streams of people were flocking to the camp. One man who had just arrived at the camp with his family of three terribly undernourished children and his wife explained the reasons for his escape thus:

> We could not take it (hunger and Matsanga brutality) anymore. Before, when the rebels asked for food we would give them, and there was no problem. But later [due to drought and the predatory relationship of Renamo to the peasantry], when we told them (the rebels) that we had no food and we were also starving, they refused to listen. They said we were lying, and would search our granaries. If they found something, even just a little bit, that was your end. They would mercilessly beat you up, even when you told them it was for the kids... It was after so many beatings that I decided it was worth taking the risk to escape (escape was usually punished by death) to where others were going [the resettlement camp].[93]

Emphasizing hunger and suffering, a guerrilla interviewed on the day of his surrender - he arrived while we were at the camp - explained the reasons for his defection thus:

For me, like other guerrilla cadres, life was so difficult in the bush. For instance, whenever I was assigned a mission, sometimes to a place up to 100km from the main base (at Gorongossa), to assault and loot, no-one took care of my family - a wife, two children and an aging mother. In one such mission I got wounded, and my comrades left me with a *n'anga* (traditional healer), and I had to find my way to the base after about five months.

It was so hard living with the *n'anga* with none of your comrades to cheer you up. I was most disgusted when I finally made it to the base, only to see my family virtually starving. Another disappointing thing was that most of the loot we brought in was distributed among commanders. It was only when I concluded that I was suffering for nothing that I escaped, taking with me my gun to protect my family along the way.[94]

Judging from the surprising 'hero's welcome' he received from the displaced peasants on arrival at the refugee camp[95], he seemed to have been a popular guerrilla with the people.

One development led to another in a chain reaction fashion: drought forced the peasants to stop feeding the rebels, but this only resulted in brutal reprisals by the rebels, which in turn had the unintended effect of forcing the peasants to flee to government controlled territory, and finally, left with no one to feed them, the rebels soldiers themselves followed. It was precisely at the peak of this drought, and when this process was beginning to gather momentum that Renamo finally agreed, after foot-dragging for years, to sign the October 1992 Peace Agreement. Drought, by necessitating increased coercion, contributed to the weakening of Renamo by discrediting it in the eyes of the peasantry and by forcing its soldiers to defect.

Clearly, those defined as powerless were not mere victims. In reality they constituted the main actors in the conflict. Even by simply trying to escape, they actually fuelled the war, as attempts to escape resulted in 'hot-pursuit operations', and increased murders. In their attempt to negotiate for their free survival from both state tentacles and Renamo domination, the displaced actively shaped the course of the war itself.

Peasant resistance to Renamo terror: 'Cults of violence and counter violence'

One way in which peasants' responses to the violence actually fuelled the war, was their recourse to what Wilson has called "cults of violence and counter violence".[96] Wilson has documented the rising incidents of 'cults of violence and counter violence' in Zambezia Province.[97] Another typical example of peasants confronting Renamo violence with violence was the case of the Naprama religious warriors, led by Antonio Naprama who claimed to have arisen from the dead. Arguing that the people of Mozambique were tired of the war, and claiming that God had ordered him to 'bring peace', he organized a peasant army armed only with drums and sticks as well as spears to fight the rebels. Vaccinating his soldiers, who at one point numbered more than 500, he managed to 'liberate' many peasants from Renamo terror before his death.[98]

Similarly, in a *localidade* in Gaza province, a group of peasants have also resorted to 'violence to counter violence' by arming themselves to protect their families and property against both Renamo and government forces.[99] In Manica Province these 'cults of violence' have manifested themselves in many ways. Armed piracy against hunters or smugglers (see next chapter) and every day casual brutality have been the commonest forms of 'cults of violence'. These have been complemented by or competed with other forms of passive ideological resistance.

Passive ideological resistance

In challenging Frelimo's ideological hegemony by articulating peasant ideologies, Renamo was also equipping the peasants to turn against itself at an ideological level. In many areas around Manica Province, and in interesting paradox, the peasants also evoked these ideologies to resist Renamo abuse and brutality. One typical example is the case of a village in Doroe (a *localidade* of Gondola district) a few kilometres north-east of Chimoio city. According to an eye witness, during the late 1980s when Renamo brutality had become the norm rather than an exception, the village elders of the locality managed to negotiate for the re-instatement of human dignity and to 'tame' the rebels by turning Renamo belief in superstition against itself.[100]

They explained natural disasters, such as the devastating drought, as the ancestors' expression of anger at Renamo's abuse of young girls and married women and its prohibition of the living to bury their dead (murdered by the rebels for being sell-outs and therefore left to decay in open public places as a lesson to would-be sell-outs). After consultation with the local rebel commanders, a ceremony was organised, to which the 'boys' (rebels) contributed and attended, and after that the more grotesque Renamo brutalities ceased.

In some areas in the Province, peasant ideological resistance to Renamo has taken a variety of other forms, the most common and effective of which have been spirit possession by a *chikwambo,* and the threat of *mufukwa* or

54

ngozi.[101] Both *chikwambo* and *ngozi* are avenging spirits of the 'unjustly' murdered, which persecute the murderer or his family. According to Roesch, "virtually all Renamo fighters ...are persecuted by the muf[u]kwa spirits of the people they have killed and/or despoiled".[102] The threat of persecution has curtailed Renamo violence, though it is evident that "such forms of spirit possession have not always kept Renamo fighters from killing peasants and/or despoiling them of their possessions".[103] In short, and reflecting the importance of the dialectic of control in social relationships, the peasants have managed to alter the balance of force and carve out a social space for themselves, though within narrow constraints.

If ideology is conceived of as "the human condition under which human beings live their lives as conscious actors in a world that makes sense to them in varying degrees"[104], the claim that Renamo has no ideology has no basis. By resuscitating and defending peasant outlooks of the world, which had been suppressed by Frelimo, Renamo was articulating peasant ideologies. This largely explains its success in the countryside. To some Mozambican peasants, who had emerged from one form of social servitude only to fall into another, it appears the central conflict was between tradition and modernity: the 'peasant war' was fought to restore tradition, with Frelimo confronting it while Renamo defended it. As we shall see in the next chapters, the rising disorganization of the state's legitimacy in the eyes of the ruled led Frelimo to abandon one-party statism and to introduce wide ranging political and economic reforms. These reforms facilitated the emergence of a political society characterized by the burgeoning of civil organizations and movements that might best be conceived of embryonic elements of a civil society.

The initial rapport which Renamo enjoyed with the rural population was not only due to a desire for a return to the old ways of doing things; it also reflected a quest for more change and freedom to control one's life. It was a result of the need to resist the regimentation of society by an over-arching state bureaucracy. Such a quest, however, was not compatible with the narrow Renamo political ideology. The mobilizational methods of Renamo, lacking a coherent ideology as it were, flouted the basic dignities and freedoms of the peasantry. In the process Renamo destroyed its social constituency and its initial rapport with the peasants ruptured.

Summary: Theoretical and practical implications of the war

The foregoing discussion has attempted to demonstrate that the Mozambican war had many dimensions to it. External/internal, political/economic factors reciprocally fed on each other in shaping the course of, and giving a dynamic to the war. The operation of the Southern African regional political economies, as well as in the global political economy, gave an impetus to the rise of counter-revolution in Mozambique and, undermined the Mozambican state's capacity to contain it. The internal latent contradictions divided civil society between supporting Frelimo or Renamo, and gave the rebel movement a momentum of its own. Noteworthy, these contradictions are strikingly similar to those that almost tore Frelimo apart in the early 1960s.[105]

One of the central contradictions that confront African planners, especially with respect to agrarian transformation, is between the need to accelerate capital accumulation to create an industrial investible surplus, and the need to retain legitimacy among the rural population. Given the fact that these societies are primarily agrarian, with rural populations often comprising over 70 per cent of the total population, any meaningful capital accumulation has to be based on rural transformation. In Mozambique, the loss of 'transit' income and migrant labour remittances, and the exodus of Portuguese skilled personnel led to the collapse of government revenue. In turn this made the need to exploit peasant labour urgent. But the very quest for rapid rural transformation, involving as it were, changes in political and economic configurations, generated tensions and conflicts that undermined the whole process.

Agrarian reform based on 'accumulation on the back of the peasantry' stifled peasant production and threw the rural market into disarray. The consequent shortage of basic food stuffs in both rural and urban areas resulted in mounting discontent. In turn, this led to authoritarianism as the state tried to contain this restlessness. But increased authoritarianism and mounting discontent only served to provide fertile recruiting ground for the opposition. The extreme violence of oppositional politics has further exacerbated the crisis; the war and the economic crisis have been reciprocally fuelling each other.

Exploiting the crisis, the MNR ideological mobilization has been based on the fusion and condensation of several ideological discourses. Religious, neo-traditional and/or quasi-nationalist ideologies have been fused into a single threat taking a conjunctural form. They have all been appropriated in the legitimation of the anti-state insurgency. This partly explains why the movement has been characterised as 'Janus faced': its mobilization strategy, and relationship with the peasantry, varied with the localized or specific grievances and priorities of the peasants.

With Renamo providing counter-ideologies and backing them up by force, the ruling class' ideological domination and hegemony were torn asunder. Frelimo has had to accommodate the peasants and their ideologies. Some have argued that this amounts to a re-feudalization of society.[106] It is, however, not clear whether peasants are a revolutionary or reactionary force in social change. They have effects which are neither so coherent nor so morally straight forward. Their resistance and resilience also highlights the impossibility of changing society by decree.

The use of violence and terror, which became a central strategy of Renamo in the mid-1980s compromised its relationship with the rural populations. By resorting to violence and terror tactics, both Renamo and government forces have discredited themselves in the eyes of the mass of the peasants. The pathetic situation that has emerged is that neither seems to be able to meet the peasants' aspirations, to provide them with security or to allow them to realise their potential.

The notion of 'socialism with a Mozambican face' itself seems to have been deficient in a number of respects, and the viability of the 'transition to socialism' itself - popularised by Saul - should have been seen to be improbable given the context within which the independence struggle had occurred. First, as with other Lusophone African regimes (Angola, Cape Verde, Guinea and Sao Tome and Principe), the drive to establish a 'socialist' state took place against the background of an Africa "where the first wave of 'socialist' experiments was recognised to have failed"[107], and when the crisis of state socialism in Eastern Europe had already begun.

As Chabal argues, "there were no historical, structural or socio-economic reasons to expect in black Africa (except perhaps 'feudal' Ethiopia) revolutions in the mould of the 'classical' revolutions (France, Russia, China or even Vietnam)."[108] In other words, Frelimo set itself a task the material conditions for whose resolution were non-existent viz, a powerful economic base that will allow the socialisation of plenty rather than the socialisation of misery; and a large educated industrial working class that can become a conscious actor in this process and itself - instead of bureaucratic elites - administer the economic and political system.[109]

Due to these objective historical reasons, the elite, instead of the yet to be born working class conscious of its historic role in the revolutionary transformation of society, spearheaded the independence struggle, and subsequently took over state power. Influenced by their East European allies, which were already experiencing the crisis of Stalinist counterrevolution, Frelimo attempted to control, re-direct (or even forestall) change from below. In so far as this attempt inevitably stifled popular grass-roots initiatives, Frelimo was effectively, but unwittingly and unintentionally, becoming its opposite, a counterrevolutionary force. The statist and anti-peasant policies which it pursued with ruthless determination during the first decade of independence constituted a negation of the people's revolutionary potential.

The process began with the shift in emphasis from political debate to the prosecution of the military struggle after Machel's accession to power in the late 1960s, the banning of opposition in 1975, and the transformation of the front into Marxist-Leninist vanguard party at the Third Congress in 1977. In the post-independence era, these counterrevolutionary tendencies[110] manifested themselves in the suppression of the organized power of the subordinate social groups, parties, and other forms of association, physical curtailment of human rights; the physical suppression of opposition leaders, agitators, 'subversives' and 'enemies' of the state; and political orientation of the state in authoritarian directions. Not surprisingly, this alienated a substantial proportion of the people, in whose name the policies were being pursued. This in turn, provided a fertile ground for Renamo recruitment.

As with Frelimo, Renamo's resistance to change and its alliance with white racist regimes constitutes another counterrevolution. In particular, this counterrevolution consists in its attempt to restore the power, prosperity and privileges of traditional authorities, capitalists and other segments of the dominant social groups who were threatened with dispossession by the Frelimo regime. Thus, at the risk of over-simplification, what we have before us is a negation of one (Frelimo) counterrevolution by another (Renamo) counterrevolution, with the former having given rise to the latter. This counterrevolution, conceptualised at a politico-military level as Renamo anti-state insurgency, and at the socio-economic level as the transformation of the Mozambican state in rightist authoritarian directions, is partly a manifestation of the class struggle at the national and international level.

But paradoxically, and as a contingent outcome, the negation of a Frelimo ('Stalinist') counterrevolution by a Renamo (neo-traditional/quasi-nationalist and anti-communist) counterrevolution, has given rise to a potential revolutionary situation. Some of the social changes which Frelimo unsuccessfully sought to effect by decree, as shall be clear in the next chapters, are occurring spontaneously as contingent outcomes of the war, but with a different trajectory.

Conclusion

The main import of this critical exploration into the history of rule, obedience and resistance in post-independence Mozambique is the urgency it attaches to the need for a fundamental re-conceptualization of the state, traditional authorities and civil society relationships. As the experience of Mozambique suggests, the state in Southern Africa, given the present level of development, can only *absolutely* marginalise traditional sources of authority and the civil society at its peril. The ideological and political war against what Frelimo called 'obscuntarist' feudal ideas threw some peasants into conservatism and subsequently supporting the MNR. This raises important questions that bear on what kind of social organization or state formation is needed/appropriate for a peasant country?

Both modernization and Marxist theories of development alike assume as a rule that peasant farming is doomed. The peasant is dying from a number of ills at one and the same time: he is losing the much-needed supplementary income which he derived from his domestic handicraft which can no longer compete with industrially manufactured goods; land alienation, through displacement by war in the case of Mozambique, has deprived him of his cheap means of growing food and keeping animals; and finally, his life as an autonomous producer is being gradually squeezed out between the fore-finger of the state tax-collector and the thumb of the market (either regulated by the state or dominated by the larger capitalist producer). The expansion of capitalism into the countryside has done and is daily doing away with the peasantry.

The technocratic planners in Mozambique sought to accelerate the death of the peasantry[111] by converting it into a rural working class, labouring in state farms and collectives.[112] But, with remarkable resilience, the peasant astoundingly refused to die.[113] Dispossessed of their land by the war, they have survived as bear-foot entrepreneurs, wage workers, dealers etc in the war-torn city of Chimoio. Through participation in the dialectic of control, the peasants have developed counter-hegemonic ideologies based on neo-traditionalism, Christianity, as well as radical ideas. These dialectical contradictions are not transitory aberrations, but are instead central elements of the historical process of change and development.

Notes

1. Anderson Nilson, *Unmasking the Bandits: The Face of the MNR*, London, Ecasaama, 1980, p. 1.

2. Aquino de Braganca and Jacques Depelchin, "From the Idealization of Frelimo to the Understanding of the Recent History of Mozambique", paper presented at the United Nations (UN) University Conference on Peace and Development in Africa, Harare, August 25-28, 1986, p. 2.

3. Joseph Hanlon, *Mozambique: Revolution Under Fire*, London, Zed, 1984, and John Saul (editor), *A Difficult Road: The Transition to Socialism in Mozambique,* New York, Monthly Review Press, 1985.

4. Aquino de Braganca and Jacques Depelchin, op. cit, p. 2.

5. Reginald Green, "Four Horsemen Ride Together: Scorched Fields of War in Southern Africa", pare presented at a seminar on 'Forced Migration',

Refugee Studies Programme, Queen Elizabeth House, Oxford University, November 1992.

6. Christian Geffray, *La Cause des Armes au Mozambique: anthropologie d'une guerre civile*, Paris, Karthala, 1990. As Geffray's book has only been published in French, and recently in Portuguese, the interpretation presented here is based on reviews by, and discussions with, specialists in the field who speak French, and as such is only tentative.

7. Ibid.; Alice Dinerman, "In Search of Mozambique: the imaginings of Christian Geffray in *La Cause Des Armes au Mozambique*, draft paper, January 1993, p. 23.

8. For a discussion of this see Allen Hoben and Robert Hefner, "The Integrative Revolution Revisited", *World Development*, Volume 19, Number 1, 1991, pp. 17-30.

9. See Bridget O'Laughlin, "Interpretations Matter: Evaluating the War in Mozambique", *Southern Africa Report*, Volume 7, Number 3, January, 1992.

10. W. Finnegan, *A Complicated War: The Harrowing of Mozambique*, California, California University Press, 1992.

11. Walter Benjamin, "The Theory of Knowledge, Theory of Practice, in Gary Smith (editor), *Benjamin: Philosophy, History, Aesthetics*, Chicago, p. 60.

12. Jurgen Habermas, *Legitimation Crisis*, (translated by Thomas McCarthy), Boston, Boston University Press, 1973, pp. 26-7.

13. Ibid.

14. See among others, Ruth First, *Black Gold: The Mozambican Miner, Proletariat and Peasant, Brighton, Harvester, 1983*, and Carol B. thompson, *Challenge to Imperialism: The Frontline States in the Liberation of Zimbabwe*, Harare, Zimbabwe Publishing House, 1985.

15. The Portuguese colonial authorities had supported Rhodesia in its sanctions busting after UDI.

16. See among others, Tom Wigglesworth, *Perhaps Tomorrow*, Bulawayo, Mardon Printers, 1983 and H. Ellert, *The Rhodesian Front*

War: Counter-Insurgency and Guerrilla War, 1962-1980, Gweru, Mambo Press, 1989.

17. See, Paul Fauvet, "Roots of Counter-Revolution: The Mozambique National Resistance", in *The Review of African Political Economy*, Number 29, 1984.

18. Ibid., p. 118.

19. See Ken Flower, *Serving Secretly: An Intelligence Chief on Record, Rhodesia into Zimbabwe, 1964-1981*, London, John Murray, 1987.

20. The invasion in question appears to be the one in which Rhodesian commandos, led by a former Zimbabwean guerrilla, Nyathi, who had switched allegiance to Rhodesians, massacred more than 600 exiles at Nyadzonia camp on 7 August 1976. The commandos entered and exited Mozambique without encountering any resistance, and blew up bridges behind them in order to avoid follow-up operations. It is alleged that Nyathi had deceived border guards as well as soldiers manning the many check-points along the road leading to the camp, by telling them that the Rhodesians were captured prisoners of war. But this was inconsistent with the fact, emphasised by many of the survivors of the massacre, that the white soldiers wore black paint in their faces. While it is difficult to ascertain exactly what happened, it appears there was some conspiracy between elements within Frelimo defence forces and the Rhodesian commandos.

21. Paul Fauvet, op. cit., p. 118.

22. For example, in the period between 1981 and 1983 the MNR destroyed 1 00 shops, hundreds of vehicles, 40 locomotives, 20 sawmills, 840 schools - resulting in a 60 per cent decline in primary enrolment - 200 health posts, cotton gins and tea factories. See Joseph Hanlon, *Mozambique: Revolution Under Fire*, London, Zed Books Ltd, 1984, pp. 219-232.

23. The Accord was a non-aggression pact and obliged Mozambique to stop supporting African Nation Congress (ANC) guerrillas in return for South Africa's cessation of support of Renamo. South Africa did not honour the accord and, as the Renamo documents captured at Gorongossa when the base was overran in 1985 show.

24. To present Renamo as freedom fighters, guerilla motifs pioneered by FRELIMO were hijacked and made to serve thoroughly reactionary ends. For instance, Renamo deliberately portrayed itself as "the inheritor of the good

nationalist aspects of FRELIMO tradition", waging a "second war of liberation", and as "a shadow cabinet or government in exile". See Paul Fauvet, op. cit., p. 119.

25. The major mobile training bases along the border included the following: Skietog in Phalaborwa; Lake Sibaya base, south of Kosi Bay; Ndumu Game Reserve, which straddles the border with Mozambique; and one in the northern reaches of Kruger National Park in Pfafuri. See *Weekly Mail*, Johannesburg, Volume 6, Number 9, March 1990, p. 1.

26. British Broadcasting Corporation (BBC), *World Service: Focus on Africa*, 20 May 1990.

27. *Africa Confidential*, Volume 31, Number 7, April 1990, p. 1.

28. Cited by Robert Davies and David. O'Meara, "Total Strategy in Southern Africa: An Analysis of South African Regional Policy Since 1978", in S.I.R. Msabaha and Timothy M. Shaw (editors), *Confrontation and Liberation in Southern Africa*, London, gower, 1987, p. 263.

29. Ibid, p. 264.

30. See Mark W. Cheatham, "Constructive Engagement in Mozambique, 1980-1984: The Accord of Nkomati", Masters thesis submitted to the University of Oregon, Michigan, UMI Dissertation Information Service, 1985.

31. Cited by James Petras et. al, *Capitalist and Socialist Crisis in the Late Twentieth Century*, New York, Rowman and Allanheld Publishers, 1987, p. 19.

32. Both the US and Britain have considerable investments in SA - about 300 Transnational Corporations in the case of the US - and this largely account for their reluctance to impose mandatory sanctions on SA as this would have had serious negative repercussions on the British economy (and in turn the US) whose iron and steel industry is very much dependent on SA.

33. See Phyllis Johnson and David Martin, *Destructive Engagement: Southern Africa at War*, Harare, Zimbabwe Publishing House, 1986.

34. See James Mittlemen, *Out From Underdevelopment*, New York, Macmillan, 1988.

35. Ibid., p. 154.

36. See Paul Fauvet, op cit. Recently the very much celebrated idea of 'liberated zones', with new socio-politico arrangements has been challenged and dismissed as a myth detached from reality: new power relations, based on guerrilla coercion, simply replaced old forms of repression. Discussion with Jean-Claude Legrand, UN field representative and researcher on Mozambique, Chimoio, 1992.

37. Some observers are sceptical of the Frelimo official version of the story, that Eduardo Mondlane was assassinated by agents of the Portuguese secret police, with the assistance of 'insiders' (or internal enemies). As one such observer put it: "How could Machel, until then a junior military commander, have risen to power so rapidly to power after Mondlane's death? ... He eliminated all the moderates (including Mondlane) who he thought would delay the revolution as well as frustrate his vaulting ambition for power".These new versions of the story, which appear to be just a tip of the iceberg, and which are surfacing due to the relaxation of the political atmosphere, justify a re-writing of Mozambican history.

38. Paradoxically, the Frelimo 'revolutionaries' who had won the ideological battles within their movement, later supported moderate ZANU nationalists against the radicals in the ideological disputes of the mid-1970s within the latter (see below).

39. Frantz Fanon, *The Wretched of the Earth: The Handbook for the Black Revolution that is Changing the Shape of the World*, New York, Grove Press, 1968, p. 108.

40. Ibid., p. 108.

41. Ibid., p. 108.

42. There were a dozen of political parties at Independence, some of which products of splits within Frelimo and others created and financed by the Portuguese as part of their divide and rule tactics. Most of the leaders of these parties, including Uria Simango who had been a founder member of FRELIMO, were sent to re-eduction centres (a euphemism for detention camps), where most never returned from. It is alleged that Samora, fearing that Renamo which was advancing towards the detention camp might overrun and free the inmates of the prison, ordered the execution (murder) of Uria Simango in April 1986, six months before his own death in a plane crash; other sources put the dates as early as the mid-1970s, early 1980s, See, David Hoile, (review of) *Conspicuous Destruction: War, Famine and the Reform Process in Mozambique, The 1992 Africa Watch Report on Mozambique:*

Disappointing, Stereotyped and Fragmentary, Mozambique Institute Occasional Paper Number 2, 1992.

43. Martin A. Klein, *Peasants in Africa: Historical and Contemporary Perspectives*, London, Sage Publications, 1980, p. 9.

44. Cited in Alfred Kroeber, *Anthropology*, New York, Harcourt, Brace Joanovich, 1948, p. 284, by Martin A. Klein (ibid), p. 10.

45. Saul and R. Woods, "African Peasantries", in T. Shanin (editor), *Peasant and Peasant Societies*, Harmondsworth, Penguin, 1971, p. 105.

46. Cited in M. Godelier, *Perspectives in Marxist Anthropology* (R. Brain, translation), Cambridge, Cambridge University Press, 1977, by Martin Klein, op cit. p. 11.

47. See C. Meillassoux, "The Social Organisation of the Peasantry: The Economic Basis of Kinship", *Journal of Peasant Studies*, Volume 1, 1973.

48. For Marx, the peasants' conservatism is a drawback on the workers' revolution, see Karl Marx and Frederick Engels, *Selected Works*, Moscow, Progress Publishers, 1984, and for a critique of Marx's position on the peasants see David Mitrany, *Marx Against the Peasant*, Chapel Hill, North Carolina Press, 1951.

49. Most of these farms are being re-claimed by their Portuguese owners, 'bought' by state elites or foreigners or have simply collapsed.

50. Cited in Samora Machel, "Facamos de Decada da Victoria Subdesenvoivimento Coleccao Palavras de Ordem", Maputo, 1979 by Maureen Mackintosh and Marc Wuyts, "Accumulation, Social Services and Socialist Transformation in the Third World: Reflections on Decentralised Planning Based on Mozambique", Development Policy Working Paper, Number 9, January 1988, p. 4.

51. Cited in Samora Moises Machel "Organizing Society to Conquer Underdevelopment", a speech given at the start of the school year in Maputo, 13, February 1982, by Barry Munslow, (editor), *Samora Machel: An African Revolutionary*, Harare, Zimbabwe Publishing House, 1987, p. 130.

52. Ibid., p. 131.

53. Ibid. p. 130.

54. This remark, which became a popular joke among Zimbabwean exiles (at Doroe camp Base Five in particular), was quite common among the peasants of Manica Province during the period between 1976-79.

55. This is quite a common remark, especially among the resigned elderly women and men.

56. Samora Moises Machel, op. cit., p. 130.

57. Ibid, p. 130.

58. Frantz Fanon, op. cit., p. 110.

59. Ibid., p. 110.

60. For a detailed account of human rights abuse by the government, as well as Renamo, see African Watch, *Conspicuous Destruction: War, Famine and The Reform Process in Mozambique*, London, Human Rights Watch, 1992 and David Hoile, op. cit.

61. Eyewitness whose uncle worked at the said co-operative shop, and whose grandfather was the chief in the area.

62. As noted above, this breach developed when interests of the rulers and the ruled started diverging, and was manifested in a rise in apathy or a 'retreat into tradition' and subsistence economy, and the emergence of the black market.

63. As Sun Tzu pointed out, spies are a most important element in war because upon them depends an army's ability to move. Cited by James Clavell, *The Art of War: Sun Tzu*, London, Hodder and Stoughton, 1991.

64. Mao Tse-tung, "On Protracted War", *Selected Works of Mao Tse-Tung*, Volume 2, New York, 1954.

65. The resettlement was visited and inhabitants interviewed in September 1992.

66. See E.J. Hobsbawn, *Revolutionaries: Contemporary Essays*, London, Quartet Books, 1982, p. 164.

67. For more on the 'Matsanga' myth, see Alex Vines, *Renamo Terrorism in Mozambique*, London, James Currey, 1991.

68. Karl Marx and Fredrick Engels, *Basic Writings on Politics and Philosophy*, (edited by Lewis S. Feuer), Washington, Anchor Books, 1959.

69. Frantz Fanon, op. cit.

70. Rene Girard, *Violence and the Sacred,* (translated by Patrick Gregory), London, The John Hopkins University Press, 1989.

71. Ibid., p. 2.

72. Ibid., p. 2.

73. Amilcar Cabral, *Unity and Struggle: Speeches and Writings*, London, Heinemann, 1980.

74. See Bruce Berman and John Lonsdale, *Unhappy Valley: Conflict in Kenya and Africa*, London, James and Curry, 1992.

75. Rene Girard, op. cit., p. 2.

76. It is interesting to note here that, while all amnestied rebels interviewed claimed they had been captured or coerced into joining Renamo, they also said they knew some guerrillas who joined willingly. Their allegation of having been gang-pressed might be interpreted as a carefully calculated response intended for official ears, but the fact that they defected might lent credence to it.

77. Interview with Roy Perkins, who had talked to the guerrilla during her captivity in 1987, Gondola city September 1992.

78. The first interview was held in Maputo with the said government official who was a delegate at a Ministry of Education meeting. As he had said, he left Maputo as soon as the meeting was over because he felt uncomfortable there. The other three interviews were held, separately, in Chimoio city.

79. This was probably an exaggeration because, in addition to these two ministries, the Minister of State Administration, Mazula, is from Niassa, and that of Youth and Culture, Katupha, who is important in the Polity Bureau, is not from the south.

80. The lawyer who was pursuing the case was also murdered in Maputo. Interview in Chimoio.

81. Iain Christie, "Mozambique's Unarmed Opposition", in *Mozambique Peace Process Bulletin*, Special Supplement, October 1993, p. 1. Articles 32 and 69 allow for the outlawing of political parties if they are perceived by Frelimo as regional or as threatening to undermine national unity. See David Hoile, op. cit., p. 9.

82. Michael Chege, "Remembering Africa", in *Foreign Affairs*, Volume 71, Number 1, 1992, p. 150.

83. Ibid. p 150.

84. See, Leroy Vail (editor), *The Creation of Tribalism in Southern Africa*, London, James Curry, 1989.

85. Michael Chege, op cit., p. 151.

86. Norma Kriger, *Zimbabwe's Guerrilla War: Peasant Voices*, Cambridge, Cambridge University Press, 1992.

87. Ibid., p. 7.

88. Carolyn Nordstrom, "The Dirty War : Culture of Violence in Mozambique and Sri Lanka", in K. Rupesinghe (editor), *Internal Conflicts and Governance*, Macmillan Press, 1992

89. Interview with a survivor of the attacks, a former government soldier.

90. There were many tactics used by the youth to avoid military call-up. These ranged from understating or overstating one's age, faking illness, physical or mental disability (madness), bribing the officials in charge, keeping on the run, hiding or being 'invisible', escaping to neighbouring countries or even joining the rebels.

91. The pattern of war in Angola is fairly predictable: the government forces, with their heavy Soviet-made artillery, have usually been able to launch major successful offensives against Unita rebels, but with the rains in the summer providing vegetation cover, making many roads unusable and aerial visibility difficult, the rebels have usually been able to gain an upper-hand.

92. This resettlement camp, which was then ever growing, was visited on a number of times between July and September 1992.

93. Interview at Matsinye, September 1992.

94. Interview at Matsinye Resettlement camp.

95. Within minutes after his arrival, a crowd had gathered around him. They hand-shook him, enquired about life in general and the whereabouts of some of their relatives or neighbours.

96. See Ken Wilson, "Cults of Violence and Counter Violence in Mozambique", in *Journal of Southern African Studies*, Volume 18, Number 3, 1992.

97. See Ibid.

98. The movement invaded Renamo bases by beating their drums so loudly as to scare the rebels, who believed their bullets would not be effective against these vaccinated religious warriors, into fleeing. However, after the rebels consulted a witch-doctor and got vaccinated as well, they stood their ground in one attack and it was a blood birth when the defenceless warriors were subjected to hail of machine gun fire. The movement is now in disarray.

99. Interview with Joao Gravinho (May 1993), Phd student working on Mozambique, and based at Oxford University..

100. It is worthy noting the parallel with the Zimbabwean war here. While at the official level, Frelimo and ZANLA were allies claiming to be fighting for similar objectives, at the politico-religious level ZANLA's approach was much closer to that of Renamo than Frelimo. Both relied extensively on spirit mediums and ancestors, while Frelimo condemned these as obscuntarist. On the role of neo-traditional religion in Zimbabwe, see David Lan, *Guns and Rain: Guerrillas and Spirit Mediums in Zimbabwe*, London, James Curry, 1985, and Terence O. Ranger, *Peasant Consciousness and Guerrilla War in Zimbabwe*, London, James Currey, 1985. On Renamo's use tradition see, Otto Roesch, "Peasants, war and 'Tradition' in Central Mozambique", paper prepared for the symposium "Symbols of Change: Transregional Culture and Local Practice in Southern Africa", free University of Berlin, Berlin, Germany, January 7-10, 1993. On Matsangaisa's mythical legend and superstition within Renamo, see Alex Vines, op. cit.

101. The difference between *chikwambo* and *ngozi* is that, the former possesses its victim (the wrong-doer or a relative) through whom it makes its demands, and one can become a *chikwambo* after death only after taking some medication (from a traditional healer) while still alive, or when the relatives go through the rituals of medication posthumously. Unlike a *chikwambo*, *ngozi* does not possess its victim and one does not need to take some medication to become a *ngozi* after death. The demands of, and modes of

compensation for, a *ngozi* can only be known by consulting a spirit medium, and if this is not done a whole family may get misfortune or even perish. The treatment of *chikwambo* and *mufukwa (ngozi)* as the same, as Roesch does in the above cited article, is therefore inaccurate.

102. Otto Roesch, op cit.. p. 17.

103. Ibid. p. 16.

104. Goran Therborn, *The Ideology of Power and the Power of Ideology*, London, Verso, 1980, p. 2.

105. See Alex Vines, op. cit., p. 6.

106. Currently the Ford Foundation is sponsoring research on how to incorporate traditional chiefs into state administrative structures.

107. Patrick Chabal, "Some Reflections on the Post-colonial State in Portuguese-speaking Africa", in *Africa Insight*, Volume 23, Number 3, 1993, p. 130. On the first wave of 'socialism', see also C. Rosberg and T Callaghy (editors), *Socialism in sub-Saharan Africa*, Berkely, Institute of International Studies, University of California, 1979.

108. Ibid. p.131.

109. See Ronaldo Munck, *Politics and Dependency in the Third World: The Case of Latin America*, London Zed Books Ltd, 1985, p. 216. For a more detailed analysis of the material/objective conditions for a successful socialist revolution, see also Karl Marx and Frederick Engels, "A Critique of Political Economy", in *Selected Works*, Moscow, Progress Publishers, 1985. They argue that no social system will ever perish before all the forces of production (and contradictions) in it have matured to their fullest.

110. On what constitutes counterrevolution in the African context, see among others, P. Anyang-Nyongo, (editor), *Popular Struggle for Democracy in Africa*, London, Zed Books, 1982, and Nzongola-Ntalaja, *Revolution and Counter-Revolution in Africa: Essays in Contemporary Politics*, London, Zed Books Ltd, 1987. ,

111. With respect to the Russian peasantry, Bebel had consistently argued that, as the small farmers were the most backward they should be the first to be expropriated. Cited in David Mitrany, *Marx Against the Peasant*, Carolina, University of Carolina Press, 1951, p. 16.

112. Proudhon, who was dismissed as utopian by Marx, suspecting the constricting effects of large economic units had, for economic and philosophic reasons, argued for the peasant to be owner of his farm. See ibid, p. 5.

113. John Stuart Mill, in contrast had wished to see the industrial worker converted into the peasantry. Cited in Ibid, p. 15. In fact these ideas were attempted in Zambia, under the 'back to the land policy' following the collapse of the copper-based economy during the mid 1970s. In Mozambique, a slightly different version of the policy was implemented under the inauspicious 'Operation Production' of 1983 which forcibly sought to remove all unemployed people from the cities and send them to work in remote state farms in the north. But for reasons discussed above the programme did not work, It appears that, since peasant subsistence agriculture has proved itself able to survive and resist forced rapid change, as Bernstein and David argued, a more viable system would have been co-operative socialism assisted by pro-peasant policy. See Ibid, pp. 15-20. But the most desirable policy, at least from the point of view of the peasant himself, would be simply to give the peasant his farm, and possibly support him with the necessary inputs, credit facilities and effect an equitable marketing and trading system.

3 War, economic crisis and the emergence of the grass-roots war economy

Introduction

Officially, and primarily due to the war, the economy of Mozambique is in a state of disaster. By the end of the war the country had become one of the five poorest countries in the world, while by 1990 seventy six per cent of its budget came from foreign aid (of which 40 per cent was spent on defence) and food aid accounted for 90 per cent of the marketed grain supply.[1] Like many other African countries of which Zaire is a typical case[2], exports could not keep up with imports, production lagged, industry barely functioned, scarcities were rife, the infrastructure had deteriorated drastically, wages were at starvation levels and nothing worked as it should have. But the reality on the ground was this: despite the severe economic crisis, the war weary Mozambicans found the means to survive, and actually some were and are thriving and becoming wealthy.

Against formidable odds and refusing to die passively (of hunger and starvation), the dispossessed have taken the initiative to provide for themselves what the weakened state could not. On the ruins of the war, they have erected alternative, and even more dynamic, economies and social relations. As more and more former rural dwellers, pushed by economic necessity, become petty traders there has been a spontaneous emergence of markets virtually everywhere in the peri-urban slums. These developments challenge both the collapsing dominant structures, conventional wisdom of peasant adaptability, innovativeness and endurance as well current conceptions about the 'informal economy' .

This chapter explores the complex process of accumulation, social differentiation and class formation in a grass-root war economy. It seeks to identify the possible range of relationships between the economic changes occasioned by the war and social organisation. More precisely, it examines a wide variety of individual survival strategies, and their transformative potential. It also assesses the magnitude of the grassroots war economy, in particular its capacity to offer a solution to Mozambique's pressing economic problems. Focusing specifically on wartime micro-level economic activity, it shows how the operation of the grass-roots war economy has transformed pre-capitalist relations of production of kin, clientage and lineage ties into capitalist relations. In turn, this has resulted in the positive liberation of subordinated social groups, such as youths from elders and females from males (see Chapter Six).

The analysis emphasizes the resilience and resourcefulness of the dispossessed in dealing with the problem of scarcity in a war situation, as well as the dialectical relationship between war and historical economic processes. Such resilience and innovativeness lead to one major conclusion that, while it is possible to look at the interaction between war and economics in terms of its negative impact on societies and economies negative effect, it is also necessary to view it as a historical process capable of multiple consequences; among other things, it released hitherto latent entrepreneurial potentials which catalysed economic change, especially at the 'grass-roots level'.

Given the virtual collapse of the official economy, the centrality of this economy in the livelihood of many displaced persons who sought refugee in the relative safety of the peri-urban slums of Chimoio city and in other towns of Manica Province need not be over-emphasized; were it not for the grass-roots, and its unacknowledged, and often harassed, heroes and heroines, many more would have starved to death. This chapter explores the extent to which the 'grass-roots war economy', based on a wide variety of individual and collective survival strategies as it were, could offer a solution to Mozambique's pressing post-war economic problems. The thrust of the analysis is on highlighting the scope of the impact of war on the economy, as well as its transformative potential.

The analysis is divided into three broad sections. The first section briefly looks at the structure and recent economic history of the country. Starting from the premise that the outcomes of war are often conditioned by the economy's pre-war productive and revenue raising capacity, it examines how the politico-military conjuncture surrounding the country's independence determined the nature of the economic system set up by Frelimo, and its subsequent performance. The next section examines how the 'grass-roots war economy' emerged, its dynamics and impact on household income distribution and general livelihood. It starts by raising problems of conceptualization and measurement, and attempts to develop a framework for understanding the dialectical relationship between war and economic change. The final section assess the implications of this development for post-war reconstruction. It also discusses options for economic intervention to alleviate the damage, and raises theoretical questions about war and economic processes.

Structure and history of the economy

The Mozambican economy is largely agrarian and dependent on export of raw materials for import of essential manufactured goods - mainly military hardware during the war. The major agricultural products include cashew nuts, cotton, citrus products and copra. In times of peace 80-90 per cent of the working population would be employed in rural agriculture, and before the conflict about 80 per cent of exports were agricultural products; not surprisingly the government's options were severely limited when raw material production (cotton farming, etc) virtually ground to a halt due to the war. Maize and cassava are the main staple food for the rural population, and in times of peace the country could potentially feed itself using the 3,000 plantations left by the Portuguese. Prawns/shrimps and fish are the main marine export products; as this was the only sector relatively safe from the direct effects of war, there was a tendency to over-exploit it to a point that threatened the long-term viability of the industry.

The country also has considerable mineral resources. The most significant minerals are pegamite in Zambezia province, which are mined for colombo tantalite, beryl, mica, bismuth and semi-precious stones and gold in Manica Province. The Manica reserves are officially estimated to be over 50m tonnes, and in 1986 Lonrho[3] negotiated an agreement to mine in the province. Potentially, tantalite exploitation is the country's most important mineral export, but mining of this had to be abandoned in the mid-1980s due to war. Similarly, by 1984 exploitation of the country's principle mineral potential deposits of 100 million tonnes of iron ore in Tete province had ceased altogether.

In addition, in times of peace, the country has a great tourist potential with a ready market in South Africa. One estimate calculates that Mozambique could potentially earn in excess of US$80 million from tourism in three years, equivalent to about 50 per cent of the country's total merchandise export value.[4] Vital to this tourist industry, Mozambique has the potential to earn large sums of foreign exchange from its rail and port infrastructure. The country has three excellent ports, Maputo, Nacala and Beira, each providing access to world markets for neighbouring landlocked countries. Zimbabwe, for instance, had to commit up to 10,000 troops to protect the route to the outside world, the Beira Corridor, and this was costing the country Z$1 million a day.[5]

Finally, the historical penetration of international capital in Southern Africa led to the formation of a regional political economy in which Mozambique, like other countries of the region, became subordinated to serve the needs of capital accumulation in South Africa in various ways. With the principal poles of capital accumulation located in South Africa, Mozambique became a labour reserve for South Africa's mining industry as well as a market for South African produced commodities. In Manica Province, the majority of migrant workers went to Zimbabwe. The remittances of these migrant workers were a valuable source of capital accumulation and expansion of the economy. In colonial times, however, revenue from port and rail services to neighbouring countries and from the export of primary goods was not channelled into industrializing and developing Mozambique. It was instead drained away on the import of practically all consumer durable and other consumer goods, such as farming tools, domestic utensils, textiles, clothing, footwear and wine, mainly from Portugal.[6] Only from the beginning of the 1970s were appreciable quantities of investment goods imported into the colony, resulting in the emergence of an infant manufacturing industry. In Manica Province, such infant industries were the clothing factory Textafrika in Chimoio city, the Timber Factory at Ifloma plantation (between Chimoio and Manica town along the Beira road), and a wine and beer brewery in Manica town. The first two were the major employers in the Province, but due to the direct and indirect effects of the war, by 1992 both of them were facing serious financial difficulties. In a nutshell, as a legacy of 500 years of Portuguese colonial domination Mozambique became independent as one of the poorest countries in the world, with an annual per capita income of US$ 117 at current prices[7], and with a structurally dependent and extremely vulnerable economy.

Frelimo's economic and politico-military revolution, 1975-1985

Implicit from the foregoing, the economic system set up by Frelimo was conditioned by the needs of managing, initially, a 'crisis economy' and later a 'war-economy'. The independence war and the decolonisation process entailed massive economic ruin, disruption of economic activity and losses in output. With the exodus of skilled personnel (human capital), capital flight, illegal exportation of plant equipment and deliberate sabotage by the departing Portuguese, GDP fell by around 21.3 per cent from 1973 to 1975.[8] The undeclared war with Rhodesia (mainly in Manica and Sofala provinces), which started when Mozambique closed its borders with Rhodesia in compliance with United Nations sanctions against the former's unilateral declaration of independence, had cost the country about US$550 million by the time Rhodesia became independent Zimbabwe in 1980.[9]

Faced with desertion, sabotage or bad management of many farms, factories and shops in the early days of independence, the new government was obliged to intervene in order to avoid a complete collapse of these units. At its Third Congress in 1977, with the aim of tackling the economic distortions and the social inequality inherited from colonialism, Frelimo adopted a strategy of development based on the model of a centrally planned economy. In this model almost all policies and decisions in the economic sphere were made in the context of a central state plan, which set production targets and allocated financial and material resources. Monetary and pricing policies played a limited role in the distribution of goods and services. The role of the state in the economy was consolidated by the development of state farms and cooperativization of agriculture and the promotion of heavy industry.

The overall consequence was that an inefficient bureaucratic structure, albeit without sufficiently qualified personnel, was set up to run the economy. As Pitcher notes, 'poorly managed, state-run enterprises in agriculture, industry and commerce were unable to produce a profit and went into debt'.[10] This statist approach not only created discontent and hence a social constituency for Renamo, but also by their very nature such state enterprises became easy economic targets for Renamo. As shown below, their subsequent collapse heralded the demise of the official economy and the ascendence of the grassroots war economy.

Further, with the revolution threatened from within and without (by the disaffected Mozambicans and their Rhodesian, and later South African allies), production was seen as the best defence.[11] The defence of the revolution was ultimately completely dependent on the strength of the Mozambican army, which in turn was dependent on the productive capacity of the economy; 'an army moves on its stomach'. Without an army capable of resisting internal uprising or external aggression, the final conquest of freedom and independence would never take place. But a strong army was viable only at the cost of huge expenditure, since arms and other necessary supplies had to be procured from abroad. These economic and politico-military considerations were coupled by a desire to meet the rising revolutionary expectations, and the result was an ambitious development strategy dubbed 'the socialist' big push.

According to Tibana, although the populist policies of the 'socialist big push' were conspicuous for their investment drive, they were financed through foreign income and hence increased indebtedness.[12]In addition, this public sector investment boom also generated resource requirements far in excess of domestic capacity or propensities to save.[13] To the extent that it involved massive government intervention in the economy in ways that became irresponsive to changing circumstances, 'the socialist 'big push'

75

amounted to a shock of its own, with powerful implications for the behaviour of both private and public economic agents'; it introduced absurdities in the consumption, savings and investment patterns of economic agents.[14] By the late 1970s and early 1980s, however, the investment boom had led to fiscal and current account imbalances, and the net accumulation of public assets was very low relative to resources manipulated through government revenues and spending policies.[15] These distortions were amplified by the effects of fluctuations in world market prices, or terms of trade shocks, especially the steep rises in the price of oil, high interest rates and variations in exchange rates during the early 1980s.

However, whatever the weakness of Frelimo's development strategy, the point remains that it was never given a chance to experiment with its radical ideas. Indeed, between 1977 and 1981, before the escalation of the conflict after South Africa's takeover of Renamo, there was some positive growth. This growth reached a peak of 2 per cent in 1980 before falling by 8 per cent the following year. The interpretation of this growth is contested; on the optimistic side, UNICEF[16] calculated that without the destruction of the war and assuming the achievements of up to 1981, Mozambique's economy could have grown at a rate of 4.5 per cent per year, and on the pessimistic side others, for example Tibana, contend that the growth reflects 'an investment blip'.[17] Whatever the case, it seems more useful to stress (rather than engage in speculation) that, apart from improvements in education and health, most of the benefits of this growth were concentrated in elite hands.

Juxtaposing this past with the present, it seems history is repeating itself, but this time as farce; although war has engendered the development of new economic and social forms of organization, the benefits of such re-organization seem largely to be concentrated in elite hands too. This very lack of difference, the reproduction of old divisions and hierarchies, with different actors though, testifies to the centrality of class struggle to historical movement; in fact, at another level the civil war itself was an intra-elite struggle for power and hegemony, with disgruntled Frelimo leaders defecting and forming a rebel army. The war intensified this class conflict and historical movement, and indeed it was the final blow to the faltering official economy.

Forging a war economy

The cost of fighting the war has been enormous. Although the war represents only one set of 'shock events' that affected the economy, and hence operation of the 'grass-roots war economy', it was the most devastating. Throughout the

1980s defence expenditure averaged a staggering 38 per cent of total government expenditure, one of the highest rates in the world.[18] About 70 per cent of this expenditure was on imports, which reduced the capacity to import non-war related products and diverted scarce resources from national investment programmes. By 1992, aid accounted for 50 per cent of the government budget, paid for over 75 per cent of imports and accounted for more than 70 per cent of the country's GDP.[19] A year later the country had become the most-aid dependent nation in the world with a GDP per capita of less than US$100.[20]

The war has been described as 'one of the most brutal holocausts against the human condition since World War II'.[21] Estimates of the costs of the conflict to the official economy vary enormously. According to Saferworld's report, Aranda da Silva, the Minister of Commerce and National Authorizing Officer estimated that by 1989 the country had lost some US$4.4-6 billion, whilst a 1989 UNICEF report put the losses in the region of US15 billion. The latter figure is equivalent to four times the 1988 GDP.[22] Whichever is the case, the point is the war destroyed the country's productive capacity, and amplified the problem of scarcity. The problem of scarcity was at the core of economic behaviour of the actors within the grass-roots war economy of Manica, and the ways they dealt with it had fundamental implications for the structure of economic organization, then and in the future.

Compounding this was the colonial loss in human capital, which is probably the most valuable resource as it much more difficult to replace than machinery, (for example a doctor, engineer or teacher etc). By 1986 100, 000 people had been killed, 95 per cent of whom were civilian casualties. Nearly one million people were forced to flee the country and become refugees in Malawi, Zambia and Zimbabwe, while another six million were internally displaced as Frelimo development projects, schools and clinics in the rural areas became a prime target of Renamo. For example, by 1989 Renamo had destroyed 44 major economic units, including three sugar factories, various tea factories, and a number of cashew nut factories, as well as highly productive agricultural complexes, such as the 120, 000 hectare scheme in Manica Province.[23] In addition more than 1, 120 rural shops and 1, 300 vehicles were destroyed, and the effect was to strangle the rural commercial network.

The combined effect of all these factors was a general deterioration in the official economy's productive and capital formation capacity. For instance, by 1984 capital formation had fallen by 5 per-cent from its 1982 level of 20 per-cent of the GDP, while production also fell by about 23.4 per cent in the period 1981-83. Similarly, gross agricultural production fell by 22.8 per cent in that period, while industrial and transport likewise fell by 30.9 per cent and 26.6 per cent respectively. By 1986 real GDP was just below 60 per cent of its level in 1980[24], the year it had fallen to 80 per cent of its 1975 level. Inevitably, and compounded by drought, there was a major food shortage throughout the country in the 1980s. The collapse of the economy was so rapid for a number of related reasons viz, lack of management skills, lack of price incentives for producers, and the easy with which Renamo could destroy collectives and state farms, among others.

The state sector, which was based on abandoned/destroyed farms was not in a position to respond in terms of output, notwithstanding Frelimo's Fifth Congress declaration in 1989 to 'increase rapidly food production'.[25] Neither was the private sector able to make a significant contribution, for hitherto it had been starved of capital, and often disdained. The belated introduction of food-rationing only fuelled the economic crisis as increased speculation and hoarding by both consumers and merchants led to further shortages and consequent price rises and inflation. By the end of the war the official economy of Mozambique was in a state of disaster; in response to this nationwide economic crisis, the dispossessed of Manica province invented the grass-roots war economy.

The grass-roots war economy: An anchor in detail

Economic activities taking place outside the official system, known variously as informal, underground, parallel, unrecorded, second, hidden, shadow, endogenous, irregular, alternative, unofficial or black economy, exist alongside official ones in most countries in the world.[26] The analytical separation of these economic activities from the mainstream formal economy was first shown by Hart in 1971.[27] Based on his research in Accra, Ghana, Hart found that people solved the problem of inadequate wages by holding more than one job or by engaging in petty enterprises of all types: "Denied success by the formal opportunity structure, these members of the urban sub-proletariat seek informal means of increasing their incomes".[28] In Mozambique, the added dimension of war has given this economy distinctive features which are usually lacking or less amplified in other countries where alternative economies have evolved gradually over time and under relatively peaceful conditions. It is in recognition of this uniqueness that the term 'grass- roots war economy' is used in preference to the others currently in vogue.

As in Mozambique, in South Africa and Zimbabwe, for example, many millions of people work in the informal economy, and incomes secured in this sector have shaped the course of their working lives.[29] Similarly, in Uganda *magendo*, the black market economy, is estimated at two thirds of, or even to exceed the GDP while in the Central African Republic illicit trading

78

operations represent 75 per cent of the national budget.[30] In Morocco, the size of the black market economy is estimated to be about one third of reported GDP, while in Tanzania on average about 30 per cent of economic activity is not accounted for in the official statistics and takes place in the alternative economy.[31]

Whether its effects are considered to be good or bad varies with ideological inclination and social position. To the international agencies and researchers wrestling unsuccessfully to develop post-war reconstruction projects, the concept of the informal economy offers some hope. It offers the "the promise of new income-generating activities which would help the poor 'without any major threat' to the rich".[32] From this optimistic perspective, the informal sector is supposed to further development because it is less capital intensive and less dependent on foreign exchange and technology than the formal economy. Its supposed relative autonomy gives it a potential for expansion.[33]

From another perspective the informal economy is denigrated as exploitative and repressive. Portes and Walton have criticised the informal economy in general for subsidizing the big capitalists of the mainstream economy both directly and indirectly: as a source of cheap goods and services for their labour force it allows them to pay extremely low wages.[34] Other scholars advanced methodological and substantive objections: Why assume there were two (and only two) sectors? Is the dichotomy not a false one or might 'formal' and 'informal' not be better thought of as poles at either end of a continuum? Were the two sectors really independent of each other? How are the two sectors related to the state, culture and religion? Was the individual, the household, the locality, or the enterprise the unit of the informal economy? Were all informal workers really poor, and all in the formal sector labour aristocrats?[35] These are difficult questions which this empirical analysis will begin to explore as a prelude to detailed investigation.

The history of the Informal economy in Mozambique

The history of the informal economy in Mozambique dates back to the earliest phase of colonialism. As early as the sixteenth century alternative economies had started emerging as a response to the colonial administration's repressive policies. According to Beach, after taking Sofala from the Muslims in 1506, the Portuguese tried to impose a royal monopoly on trade. This proved unworkable, and "instead an unofficial private trade developed", which avoided taxation and "was difficult to detect".[36]

Similarly, as now, African traders of Manica Province defied colonial boundaries and engaged in transborder trade which linked people in trade networks over vast distances in both Mozambique and Zimbabwe (then Rhodesia). During the colonial era, following the collapse of the official marketing system, illegal trade, locally known as *candonga* (black market), flourished. In spite of the repression of the trade by the state, for instance, by public flogging, it continued to grow as the official rationing system faulted. With the collapse of the formal economy, this form of trade became an acceptable and principal survival strategy for many. Mozambique is not unique in the size of its alternative economy. The added dimension of war, however, gave the grass roots war-economy its distinctive character.

The grass-roots war economy: Concept and processes

The concept 'grass-roots war economy' is essentially vague. It relates to a set of social relationships, a number of different ideas and processes, many of which are often incapable of precise definition To start with, deciding which activities are 'grass-roots' or what economic behaviour is caused by war must involve a certain amount of arbitrary demarcation. Similarly, the multiplicity of interacting variables poses difficulties in ascertaining analytical primacy/weight to any of the variables in understanding the unfolding processes. Nevertheless, as will emerge later, it appears to be the best concept that captures the essence of the phenomenon under consideration; wartime economic activity at a micro level.

In this analysis the 'grass-roots war economy' will be defined loosely to mean that multitude of economic activities halfway between tradition and modernity that have sprung up unbidden among the dispossessed as they shifted their ground from rural subsistence production into spontaneous micro-entrepreneurship in peri-urban slums. It is a production and exchange system based on adaptation and flexibility, and operating in such a way that the war weary community could deal with various contingencies and make choices to reach certain goals, primarily survival and progress. The economy, run largely by self-trained barefoot entrepreneurs, arose through a process of voluntary and involuntary adaptation to new circumstances, uprootedness, created by the war. It is the sum total of the diverse survival strategies, '*manheira de ganhar*' or '*busy*' (as they call it - tactics for surviving or business), adopted by various individuals that constitutes elements and dynamic of this economy.

It is important to see the dispossessed's diverse survival strategies not simply as solutions to household survival or individual subsistence problems, but also as challenges to both the conventional wisdom on peasants' adaptability and the development model based on state economic authoritarianism, as well as a vehicle for social change. Their activities around production and consumption, the accumulation process, have been the major force shaping the emerging socio-political arrangements, in particular the strengthening of civil society vis-a-vis the state. In addition to shaping the course of the war itself, production and consumption processes, trade and exchange, also played a central role in linking the polity and the socio-economic system.

Main features of the grass-roots war economy

Forced physical and social dislocations of the rural population was the principal cause of the emergence of the alternative economy on a much large-scale than had been the case hitherto or was the case in relatively stable economies. As fields were ravaged, entire villages destroyed, and survivors often compelled to flee to inaccessible, unproductive locations to avoid rebels, the operation of the rural economy was undermined and its productive capacity impaired. Accelerating this process of rural underdevelopment was the loss of the most productive members of the rural communities, young people who constituted the major combatants in both belligerent armies. The collapse of the rural economy, as well as of the official economy, significantly shaped the character of the grass-roots war economy, especially via changes in the terms of trade between rural and urban areas (see below).

The break-up of state power and the rise in anarchy generated psychological insecurity and fear, and brought to the fore human-beings' basic survival instincts. This, coupled with the wide availability of arms received from European countries, made more efficient the process of predatory destruction. The adoption of extremely violent survival strategies, such as piracy around the border area and in the forests of Manica, were a manifestation of the extent to which the culture of violence had permeated civil society and the easy availability of guns. Similarly, the resurgence of aggressive and 'vicious market fundamentalism', based on crude exploitation of the destitute, reflects this presence of 'violence' in the atmosphere. In a nutshell, by virtue of its disruption of the existing social order, war gave the grass-roots war economy its violent and aggressive dimension; often victims of violence reacted to violence by adopting violent survival strategies, what Wilson aptly calls 'cults of violence and counter-violence'.[37]

Furthermore, whereas in other countries the informal economies emerged alongside relatively well established capitalist social relations, in Mozambique it arose within the context of a radical 'transition' from a command economy to free market one. Not surprisingly the emergent grass-roots war economy was based on 'economic hybridization' with market relations adulterated by non-market ones, such as socialist and traditional 'economy of affection' ethics. Also, the large scale involvement of international aid agencies in the 'emergence rescue operation' as well as foreign troops, influenced the character of the war-time economy in significant ways; foreign economic actors brought both material goods, which found their way to, and revitalised, the market, and new values, which were actively reappropriated by the

81

Mozambicans. Finally, the disruption of decolonisation, a series of severe natural disasters (such as the 1977-78 floods, and the 1981-83 and the 1991-1992 droughts), swings in international commodity prices of major exports and imports also influenced the nature of the grass-roots war economy.

A combination of these factors gave a kind of 'quantum leap effect' to the emergence of the grass-roots war economy, and as in the world of quantum physics[38], events in the grass-roots war economy are governed by probability. War and displacement accelerated the transformation of peasants into barefoot traders by *forcing* them to become innovative and flexible, or face death by starvation; the break-up of state power removed obstacles to capital accumulation; the adoption of structural adjustment programmes (PRE) in 1986/7 legitimated the acquisitive spirit, which hitherto had been condemned in the name of socialism, though dynamic elements of the latter were evident in the emergence of voluntary collectives/cooperatives; and the large-scale intervention by international aid regime not only injected money, goods and values into the system, but also led to the increasing integration of the Manica economy into the international economic system - both formal and informal. In a striking similarity with the effects of slavery, war and displacement engendered economic and social processes offering opportunities to some and drawbacks to others, with fundamental implications for the evolution of the Mozambican political economy.

Problems of measurement: 'Tracing statistical fingerprints'

An evaluation of the *interaction* between war and economic change, inevitably involves identifying mechanisms responsible for the uneven distribution of the costs/benefits of war; the changes in the exchange ratios between commodities (eg. between basics, luxuries and investment); changes in the proportions of total income received by different people with different skills (including comparative advantage in violence); assessing the magnitude of direct physical destruction of infrastructure; and evaluating the indirect longer term development costs. There were, of course, great difficulties in gathering accurate statistics on these matters.

This difficulty was not nearly so great in the war period as it was in the past, as the IMF and the World Bank and other international agencies have intervened in the economy to an unparalleled degree, making much more information available than before. However, such macro data, especially on inflation, price and income changes, reductions in consumption, GDP etc, even if they are good statistics, they are notoriously full of pitfalls. The macro-economic changes shown by cost of living indices in wartime may not give a true picture of what really happened for a number of reasons.

First, in many cases consumption patterns were changed out of all recognition, either by consuming less of normal foods, or other goods or dispensing with them altogether.[39] As such, any comparison of prices based on a pre-war system of weighting is not likely to be an accurate reflection of what happened to the cost of living. Second, and of central importance to this study, many commodities, even if obtainable, were only bought through barter exchange or at 'informal economy' prices whereas the majority of indices only reflect officially controlled prices. On the whole, and precisely because unrecorded economic activity and prices were much more common, it is probable that these official indices underestimate both the rise in the cost of living and the contribution of unrecorded economic transactions to the national GDP. Therefore, in order to get a truer picture of what was really happening to Mozambique's war-time economy, it is important to attempt a measurement of the magnitude of economic activity at the grassroots level and its contribution to national GDP.

Measuring the magnitude of grass-roots economic activity is an extremely complicated task. First, war itself ensured that there was a dearth of accurate quantified data as neither the government nor international agencies had access to all parts of the country during the war. As a result micro-statistics were non-existent or, if they were, they were notoriously unreliable, and could at best indicate only point estimates. Also lack of technical wherewithal compounded the problem. There were, however, more serious theoretical problems that one encounters in undertaking such an evaluation.

To start with, there were obvious difficulties of applying economic and statistical analysis to unrecorded economic activity, such as consumption, savings, capital accumulation and investment etc. Uncertainty and ambiguity among the economic actors about the ethical and long-term effects of their economic engagement and the processes they set in motion also meant many were not willing to divulge the sources and amount of their incomes. In any case, since these processes were governed by probability and the exigencies of the war, and not by the will of the actors, there were great sudden variations in prices, incomes and opportunities which mock the idea of averages; sudden changes in the military situation often altered demand and supply, and hence prices, of goods. In addition, prices were almost always negotiable (on the spot), and this flexibility, which is one crucial factor that distinguishes the grass-roots war economy from the official one, gave this economy an added advantage over the latter. As already alluded to, the merging of the 'formal' with the 'informal', with goods and economic agents continuously crossing the boundaries between the two sectors, also creates considerable difficulties in ascertaining the scale and magnitude of the grass-roots war economy's contribution to household income, national income and

GDP. Related to this, is the vexing question of identifying the appropriate unit of analysis.

The traditional focus on the family household (nuclear or extended) as the main unit of analysis in understanding economic and social change seems inadequate to capture the essence of the 'transitions within transformation' unfolding in Manica Province. As a direct and indirect consequence of the war, the traditional family household was rapidly disintegrating and being replaced by multiple forms of cohabitation among people who find themselves thrown in similar predicaments by the exigencies of the war. For example, some households consisted only of females, daughters, mothers, aunties and grandmothers, or young males separated from their families living together sharing food, income and engaged in some kind of division of labour.

In view of these difficulties, this broad survey will be largely qualitative. Discussion of the principal reactions and new economic relations of production will be mainly based on an estimated statistical picture of the general changes in prices, incomes, capital asserts, number of enterprises (in both the official and informal sectors) as well as proportions of population employed as soldiers, workers (in the two sectors), self-employed entrepreneurs. The analysis also combines direct techniques (from official and other secondary data) and indirect techniques of assessing informal sector activity. With regard to the latter, the underlying assumption is that macro-economic indicators leave behind them 'statistical fingerprints' which researchers can trace and interpret, and build a picture. Such indirect techniques include, for example, assessing changes in foreign currency demand, volume of transactions' within the grass-roots war-economy and the discrepancy between expenditure and official income. Using these techniques, which of course have their shortcomings, it would be shown that Mozambique's GDP during the period under consideration must have been far much higher, about 40-60 per cent higher as an officer at Machipanda border post estimated, than official figures indicate.

The units of analysis were both the individual and the enterprise. Focus on the individual is important because each individual's experience of war is unique, and also leads us full circle to the understanding of social relations within which these individuals stand. The point is, the individual economic actors are but the personifications of the *whole* economic and social relations that exist between them, and in order to understand the *whole* (which is of course more than the sum of its parts), it may be useful to understand the parts. As we shall see, the many individual survival strategies developed by the dispossessed involved new wage and social relations of production; the producer related to others either in production or via the market. Even 'self-employment', for instance, involved hiring some labour, whether family or wage-labour (and often both). Yet existentially, as the experience of orange traders at Sete de Abril (discussed below) demonstrates, many people were simultaneously labourers, working for a wage, and capitalists, employing wage labour. Thus, although where the focus will be on individual survival strategies, it is important to bear in mind the dangers of excessive individualization' of what were and are, in reality social relations of production. To avoid this danger, and depending on the point being made, the focus on the individuals (as embodiments of particular class-relations and class-interests), is complemented by a focus on the enterprise.

As with the definition of the grass-roots war economy, that of 'enterprise' is also quite problematic and contested. No consensus has yet been reached on a single definition, and the definition proposed here is not free from problems. Take for example the cases of a wealthy shop keeper who employs family labour and a mechanic who employs hired labour, but with very little turnover in countries like Mozambique. Whose undertaking qualifies as an enterprise? The tendency to recognize the former, and not the latter, as an enterprise runs the risk of condemning to invisibility a large proportion of economic actors whose contribution to the economy has yet to be acknowledged.

In order to give voice and pay homage to these resilient entrepreneurs who lived their lives outside official history, here the enterprise is defined broadly to mean an undertaking that involves wage labour relations and production for exchange, and not immediate personal consumption. The activities of emerging 'capitalists without capital', in so far as the chief part of their products was destined for market exchange, are encompassed within this definition. What is being stressed here is not the amount of capital, but rather the specific relational aspect embodied in the concept 'enterprise' as used here. The emergence of enterprises defined thus was accelerated by 'dispossession', a process whereby peasants were violently separated from their means of production. Divorced from their social means of subsistence, former agricultural producers were transformed into either wage labourers or barefoot entrepreneurs in the urban areas, where unlike in the rural economies, the producer and consumer were no longer united in the same person.

Finally, to some extent, the process of measurement itself will influence results, for as quantum mechanics says, 'nothing is real unless it is observed'.[40] Needless to mention that, due to the obvious constraints of doing research in a war situation (March-October 1992), it was not possible to follow strictly the standard procedures of random selection in selecting the case studies presented here. This, considered in relation to the twentieth century Chinese observation that it is 'it is too soon to say what to think of the French Revolution' it cautions a reluctance to be definitive about such a great social upheaval as that unfolding in Mozambique. Thus the data presented below only provides some indication of trends, rather than a definitive political economy of war in Manica Province; the most enduring evidence that the grass-roots war economy did make a significant 'invisible' contribution to the economy is the that Mozambicans still managed to thrive, and even become rich, in the face of national economic collapse.

The emergence of the grass-roots war economy: 'Hunger is more dangerous than war'[41]

Displacement and dispossession on a mass-scale in Manica province began in the early 1980s. It was during that period, following South Africa's take-over of Renamo from the Rhodesian Central Intelligence Organization (CIO) upon Zimbabwe's Independence in 1980, that haphazard banditry developed into a full-scale civil war. Forced to flee for their lives, many people became refugees in neighbouring countries, especially Zimbabwe, while others managed to negotiate a dangerous survival in the rural areas. An unknown number joined the rebel army, and yet many more fled to the relative security of Chimoio city, Gondola and Manica towns, and after the 1990 partial ceasefire, into the Beira Corridor.

More than 250, 000 out of an estimated total of 635, 000 people have been displaced in Manica Province. About 100, 000 have found relative security in the periphery of Chimoio city, which hitherto had accommodated only 50, 000 people. On arrival in Chimoio city, the first historical act that the dispossessed had to undertake was to find the means for providing for their basic needs. They had to produce and reproduce their material existence: eat, clothe and shelter. But this was 'another war', a war against hunger and certain death, fought differently at different levels by people with diverse social backgrounds. As one displaced man in Chimoio city put it: 'Hunger is more dangerous than war. You can run away from war, but not from hunger'.

Economic crisis, dispossession and 'Manheira de Ganhar'

In the relative security of the war-paralysed city of Chimoio multitudes each day succumbed to the despair of hunger, disease and homelessness. The majority of the displaced population lost a substantial proportion of their property on relocation. As the majority were peasant farmers, their means of sustenance, hoes, animals and land, as well as other valuables such as crops etc were left behind in the countryside as they fled for safety. Many families were split up, with some of their family members remaining with rebels or being murdered. In an attempt to check the over-crowding of already over-crowded towns the government and Non-governmental Organizations (NGOs) did not distribute free food and clothes in the city. Thus on arrival in the new accommodation centres the lucky ones made use of personal and kinship ties to piece together their lives in their new found homes. In addition, some brought previously acquired skills and proven cultural resources to bear, proven in defining trust, loyalty, authority and interdependence between kin and neighbours in the face of rapid change and uncertainty about the future. Nonetheless, this entire social group can accurately be characterized as a motley group of people with varying social backgrounds whose common denominator was *dispossession*, which in many ways was tantamount to a death warrant.

Given the collapse of a significant number of state owned enterprises as well as cooperatives in the province, the prospects for getting formal employment were extremely limited, if not nil. For instance, during the 1988-1992 period, and as a result of the closure of companies and/or failure to break even, 4, 377 people were retrenched bringing total registered unemployment to 8, 563 in the whole province.[42] In the same period, of the 5, 484 people who registered for employment only 3, 078 were employed, of whom only 141 were women.[43] Due to high inflation rates and the depreciation of the Meticais (Mt), the real purchasing power of incomes declined sharply during the same period.

The average wage of 40 000 Meticais (Mt) (about US$10) per month was far too little for procuring even the mere basics. In Chimoio, this average wage was sufficient to buy only either 20 cans of South African-made soft drinks, 20 loaves of Zimbabwean bread or 50kg of maize grain -which is not enough for an average family of seven for a month. In fact, an average family of six could only feed itself for four to six days on this wage. This partly explains, as shall be shown below, why for many, formal employment, which was often supplemented by other informal activities, had little to do with the actual earnings. It was instead valued for the opportunities it offered for making important contacts and for procuring bribes or tips. Formal employment was both difficult to get and insufficiently paying to guarantee one against being constantly haunted by hunger. In such a crisis situation, where the 'one man for himself, and God for us all' philosophy seems to be the operating principle, the new arrivals could survive in the city through flexibility, adaptability and ingenuity in finding new survival tactics and strategies *manheira de ganhar*.

Barefoot entrepreneurs making history: A general description

The war weary city of Chimoio was a hive of activity. The bustling markets in the peri-urban mud suburbs and the city centre hummed with economic activity. Vendors and petty-traders, selling all sorts of goods ranging from cigarettes, vegetables, bread, maize meal, toothpaste, soap, clothes, handicrafts etc spent stiflingly hot days walking around the city or sitting behind their market stalls waiting and hoping for customers. Everyday trucks/vans shuttled between Machipanda border town and Beira city, then the 'peace corridor', packed to the brim with traders and their various goods as well as ordinary commuters. The Beira Corridor had effectively become the economic life-line of the central region.

As more and more former rural dwellers, pushed by economic necessity, become petty traders there spontaneous emergence of markets virtually everywhere in the peri-urban slums.It was as if, as one of my research guides put it, "every household had suddenly become entrepreneurial, with too many people struggling to sell the same commodities to fewer and fewer customers". Thus, for instance, while in 1992 in neighbouring Zimbabwe women and young children in urban areas spent long hours every morning queuing for bread, their counter-parts in Chimoio had difficulty in selling their home-made bread because there is just too much of it.[44] Also rural urban trade continued as many Mozambicans risked their lives daily by moving between Renamo and government controlled territories, getting and selling many different items, and exploiting the price differentials. It is impossible here to detail all the survival strategies adopted by the disinherited new entrepreneurs. What follows is a selective analysis of the main aspects of the operation of a grass-roots economy, namely 'who was who' in the grass-roots war economy, how much were they making and re-investing, what were the sources of their goods and income, what were their motivations, and finally what are the implications of their economic behaviours and engagement?

The case of Sete de Abril market

Sete de Abril (7th April, the official International Women's Day, pushed forward to coincide with the anniversary of Samora Machel's first wife) is one typical market at which peasant-cum-capitalists struggle to shape their livelihood and economies, and which exhibits all the contradictions and ambiguities of the grass-roots war economy. The market was located about 2/3km south-east from the city centre near the 'Y' junction joining the Beira-Machipanda road and the minor road leading to Macate, a *localidade*

88

(locality) 48km southeast of Chimoio. The market, situated in the largest *bairro* (suburb), was probably one of the busiest and largest spontaneous markets in Chimoio. It was divided into three main sections, which roughly corresponded to types of tradable commodities, economic status of the entrepreneurs and income earned.

At the biggest and most active of the three sections of the market second-hand clothes (popularly known as *calamidades*, Portuguese for 'emergency aid') donated by Western aid agencies were the major commodity on sale. This section of the market had in fact become the major destination for Zimbabweans who bought cheap second-hand clothes for re-sale at profits of up to 500% in Zimbabwe. Zimbabwean dollars were not only accepted, but were in great demand at this market. Most of the entrepreneurs there were employed by commercial bureaucrats, who had easy access to donated clothes. Quite a significant proportion were entrepreneurs in their own right, though. By and large, and primarily due to the fact that clothes tended to fetch more money than most other basics, entrepreneurs in this business had a higher social status and were relatively better established than their counterparts involved in food vending, for example. Although women were represented in this category of entrepreneurs, it was generally the preserve of men.

The second section of the market, which had a more or less equal representation of males and females, spread around a pre-war dilapidated marketing hall. Manufactured consumer goods such as soap, tinned fish, salt, sugar, oil etc were the major commodities sold. With new entrepreneurs establishing market stalls around the old building the market was ever expanding. Owning a stall there indicated relative success. The third, smallest section of the market centre was comprised largely of new-comers to the city and concentrated on basic consumer goods, including wild fruits, sugar cane and cassava. The 'barefoot entrepreneurs' at this section of the market were among the most unprivileged. Unlike the traders at the second-hand clothes market, those at the 'basic survival goods' market were merely eking a living, and as such their struggle to graduate from being 'peasants' to 'capitalists' is of particular significance to this study.

Some socio-economic aspects of barefoot entrepreneurs: Age, gender and class

The majority of men and women present at the market were former peasants who had recently arrived in the city. As marginal entrepreneurs, they were also stratified and had different levels of prosperity or poverty. Gender, class and social status were interlinked. About 44 per cent of the 91 petty-traders present at the time of the survey (conducted in August 1992 at the smallest section of the market) were females of various age groups. The majority of

89

the women were in the 13-18 age group (17), followed by the 25-30 and 7-12 ages groups respectively. There were only 3 females within the 19-24 age group, the age which was also constituted the largest proportion of sex workers, one below 7 years and none within the 31-36 age group. Most of the women were selling maize flour, vegetables, firewood, home-made buns, bananas, sugar-cane, salt, dried fish and cooking oil.

White maize, which was more expensive, was bought from the rural areas, while the less desirable food aid yellow maize from either wholesales in town or from informal channels; the traders would buy the maize in larger quantities and then re-sell it in smaller units, the smallest of which was a kilogram, popularly known as *banamba*. Vegetables were either home-grown, usually in the so-called 'green zones' around the city, and quite often on a collective basis, bought from a few of still operating farms, or in the case of cabbage, imported (mainly via smuggling)from Zimbabwe. Firewood was bought from the rural areas, or fetched from the ever diminishing forests near the city, while bananas, and sugar-cane were mainly got from the rural areas. The basic manufactured goods were either bought from Beira or imported from Zimbabwe; at some stage Zimbabwean troops played a vital role as 'entrepreneurs in khaki' providing emergent entrepreneurs with a cheap source of goods and foreign currency. While most of the females were selling agricultural produce, the majority of men were selling manufactured commodities, which in relative terms tended to fetch more money.

All the small shops selling manufactured commodities like matches, tobacco, coca-cola etc from Beira or Zimbabwe were owned by men, most of whom were over 24 years. Young boys and girls, who were said to be less likely to be tempted to steal money or goods, manned these shack shops, while the owners concentrated on establishing networks of contacts to facilitate the procuring of goods. The goods were obtained through both legal and under-hand tactics that, more often than not, included smuggling. Younger men provided the conduit facilitating the movement of goods between rural areas controlled by Renamo and Government controlled ones. Starting humbly like this, and depending on the type of the enterprise, or the manner in which labour and capital were brought together, some made miraculous success while many others barely manage to survive. For example, some shopkeepers at Popular Feirra (Fepo), said they had started from savings they had made from such shack shops, which in turn they had set up by selling oranges. The case of orange traders is worth looking into in more detail as it highlights some of the contradictions and injustices of the grass-roots war economy at a very micro-level.

Most of the oranges sold at the market, as in many other markets scattered throughout the city, were either worked for or stolen from a nearby citrus plantation, about 6km away. At the plantation, people were allocated a number of trees around which they worked weeding grass, in return for oranges. Since there were always more people ready to work than was usually needed, there tended to be a huge disproportionality between the work these people did and the oranges they received in payment. Many people worked hard continuously for 6 hours from 8:00 am just for a sack of oranges. They would have woken up 4-5 hours earlier and travelled up to 10km from their homes to the plantation. On re-sale in the city one sack would earn them just about 1,500-2,000 Mt, which was insufficient for a decent meal in a city restaurant. But if this was done daily for a month, the earnings would exceed the minimum wage of 40,000 Mt, which as noted earlier, was sufficient to feed a family of six for about a week.

Some, unwilling to engage in a deal which was apparently very exploitative involving so much work for so little, simply availed themselves of the oranges without the consent of the legal owner. As one militia man who guarded the plantation divulged, dozens of women and children swamped into the plantation at midnight, filled their sacks and left. He said that when he asked them to stop most of the women would humbly reply: "Shoot if you want. I have children to feed. I can't let them die while I look on". He added that he himself, knowing how painful hunger could be, would not shoot at them, though this endangered his own job. But, as a 25 year old woman who laboured for oranges pointed out, "those who did not work sold their oranges cheaply, making it difficult for us to work and break even. Also those who get their oranges free of charge, through contacts at the citrus plantation, undermine us". Not only did this create tension among the marginal traders themselves, as a testimony to the 'violence' of the grass-roots war economy, but it also set in motion a process of social differentiation and stratification.

In the drought of 1992, for those who either had contacts or had the courage to steal the oranges at night, trade in oranges was obviously a relatively lucrative business. For instance, a sale of fifty bags would make enough savings to set up an average size mini-shop (It did not take much to set up one in the informal sector of Mozambique), which was often the first step towards more lucrative ventures such as foreign currency dealing or importing. As with other traders, a single individual could be simultaneously a labourer (working for the oranges), employer (employing children to sell the oranges), and trader (selling other manufactured goods purchased from savings made on selling oranges). The 'orange easy option' to accumulating initial capital outlay was not open to all, and the examples below, show the difficulties, fears and anxieties of these less fortunate economic actors.

Becoming a wartime entrepreneur: Problems and difficulties

The story of Rosina Zacarias, a 30-year old single mother of four, is typical of the hardships that forced people to be enterprising and the difficulties that becoming an entrepreneur entailed. She was waiting for bananas from Macate (then under Renamo control). According to her she earned most of her meagre income "little by little", by selling tomatoes and vegetables she grew in one of the many 'green zones', Dzembe. Her 9-year old son also helped her raise the income by selling firewood, before and after school, which he also collected from Dzembe.

Like many women in her situation, Rosina worked for far more than 8 hours a day, preparing food for her children, walking to and from the fields (usually carrying frighteningly huge bundles of firewood and vegetables on her head and back), working in the fields and selling her goods at the market. Daily she risked her own life merely by going outside the city perimeter: although Dzembe is just about 7km south east of Chimoio, the risk of being captured or murdered by Renamo could never be ruled out. In fact, before the partial cease-fire agreement of December 1990, MNR attacks within the city were quite frequent. Additionally her crops could be stolen, as many others' had been: there was an increase in the number of people who earned their living by 'reaping where they did not sow'.

Fetching wood[45], which was in greater demand as it was used for cooking, heating, fencing and building in the surrounding bushes/forests was also fraught with dangers such as amputation from anti-personnel mines or attack by wild animals. Since the further one went into the bush, the higher the risks of endangering of ones's life, many people resorted to cutting trees in the city perimeter, causing environmental degradation and deforestation. Most of the vegetables and other crops grown within the city or in 'green zones', are grown in river banks. This has caused so much soil erosion and consequent siltation that some of the small streams have completely dried up.[46]

Avoiding such unintended consequence of specific survival strategies will be a major challenge facing policy makers in the post-war reconstruction period; denied support to re-build their lives, the dispossessed, as they have done, will always do whatever they can in order to meet their immediate needs regardless of laws or knowledge of the effects on long-term developmental sustainability. Although it was impossible to ascertain what exactly was going on in the rural areas, it appears in the few safer areas natural resources were also exploited to an extent that undermined environmental sustainability. Below we glean some insights into this from the experience of rural-urban traders.

Rural-urban traders

Another category of people present at the market were rural folk who had come to sell their agricultural produce and to buy basics such as salt, clothes and soap for consumption as well as re-sale in the country-side. One such man was 21-year old Manuele Antonio, who had come from Macouya, a village further beyond Macate deep in Renamo controlled territory. Manuele was the oldest man at home.(Apparently believing that we were officials registering people for military call-up, Manuele initially lied to us that he was 17 years old). He was selling 100kgs of white maize, which he had bought from local farmers in Macouya. His mother and father were ill and his two elder brothers had died in the army, he said.

Like many such marginalized but resilient barefoot and rugged entrepreneurs, Manuel's profits were very small, if they existed at all. He would get 72, 000Mt (about US$18) after selling the maize in small units of 10, 12.5 and 18kg from the 100kg which he had bought for 66, 000Mt. Subtracting the cost of transport (the privately owned truck comes only three times a week), of 2,000 Mt for the sack and another 2,000 Mt for the person, his actual net profit was only 2, 000 Mt. This, as he puts it was, *"nao e muito dinheiro* (it is not much money)"*, especially taking into account the fact that the road he travelled through was extremely dangerous.[47] He added, *"Kutofamba nekushinga nekuti urombo hunenge hwanyanya* (It's suffering that gives us the courage to take risks)". Manuele was also selling locally produced cassava and bananas to supplement his income. From his income he would buy soap, salt and clothes for consumption as well as re-sale in the rural areas. Whether the re-sale was through barter or money, the extreme scarcity of manufactured goods in the rural areas, ensured a significant margin of profit.

Central to the success of Manuele's business, were the dilapidated and un-roadworthy trucks.[48] Most of these trucks were owned by urban based commercial elites who had businesses in the formal sector or who occupied positions in the state bureaucracy. Capitalizing on the crisis, these entrepreneurs did brisk business. More important, such ventures demonstrated the interconnection between formal and informal economies and how state elites could actually facilitate rather than constrain the informal sector.

Those who manned the trucks were vulnerable to losing their lives through ambushes or land-mines in their long and dangerous trips through no-man's land into rebel controlled territory and back again. Unconfirmed rumours had it that some of these drivers actually negotiated for their survival by making deals with the rebels in which they would bring them urban manufactured goods in return for their safety. Sometimes they even acted as rebels' informers. A more plausible explanation for why these men were prepared to take such risks, especially if one considers that they were very poorly paid, seems to be the unprecedented opportunities - which they exploited to the fullest - of 'making quick money' by exploiting price differentials between rural and urban areas.

By trading in chicken and clothes, for instance, such drivers could accumulate a far larger profit in a much shorter period than an average self-trained entrepreneur. For example, a chicken costing roughly between 200-600 Mt in the rural areas, would sell for 6,000-8,000 Mt in the city, while a piece of cloth costing 1,000-2,000 Mt in the later would sell for above 5,000 Mt in the former. Very closely related to this, was involvement in the 'big money' business of trafficking in ivory, rhino horns, precious stones and minerals as well as selling wildlife meat. Given the anarchy caused by the war, these goods (contraband of war) were easily available in the rural areas and easily tradable in the cities (see below).

Also, since there were no tickets for payment of fares, the drivers and their assistants could easily pocket some of the money without detection by the owner. This seems to partly explain why the trucks were always packed to the brim with people, sacks, animals, chicken, wood etc. In addition to this, by offering special privileges to some of their customers, these drivers not only obtained influence as well as respect, but also important business contacts. Rural-urban trading was thus very vital, rewarding but extremely risk.

Another group of entrepreneurs at the market who earned their living through rather unorthodox means was comprised of three youths aged 13, 14 and 18 years. These youths were playing a gambling game called *Rifa Mundil*. Their clients were other youths as well as women breast-feeding their children. The game involves spinning a stet/dice, with numbers, corresponding to those written on the table, written on all its six sides, in an empty coke cane. The clients bet, putting their money (100Mt, just enough to buy matches or a cigarette) on the number they think will come on top. The one who wins takes all the money, except 100Mt which must always go to the spinner. If no-one wins, the spinner gets all the money. Young kids spent the whole day hoping to win at the expense of others in this apparently non-productive game, which is becoming increasingly popular. The elite also played it in hotels and pubs. The only difference was that, with the former, it was small money that quickly changes hands in the marginalized's attempts to survive, whereas in the latter it was big money that changes hands in the elites' attempts to rapidly accumulate wealth.

To recapitulate, the hierarchies and divisions of the grass-roots war economy were also reproduced at a micro-level at Sete de Abril market. The second-hand clothes section represented, in relative terms, the upper tier grassroots war economy. Entrepreneurs participating in it were not only surviving, but were also getting rich. It was difficult to enter, but some of those who succeeded were said to have used the savings to open shops in town or purchase cars. Second, the fact that some of the most successful enterprises there were owned by officials (who had easy access to donated clothes), or traders (especially Asians) who had shops in town (who were given quarters or had influential contacts), reveals that the supposed dichotomy between the informal and formal sectors is indeed a fiction (see below). It seems more instructive to see them instead as integral elements of the same process whose complementarity is governed by the continuous variations in the labour market of an economy in crisis.

Related to the above, the grass-roots war economy was based on economic differentiation as evidenced by great disparities in income between traders in the affluent and poorest parts of the market. Traders at the latter were mainly recent arrivals to the city or were based in the rural areas, and a larger proportion of their income was spent on consumption. Exceptions were 'smart' orange traders and truck drivers, whose comparative advantage in their respective trades could easily be translated into a means for upward mobility within the anarchical war economy. Thus, no doubt, a preparedness to take calculated risks, such as being arrested while stealing oranges or being captured by rebels or blown up by anti-personnel mines, seemed a decisive factor in shaping the possibilities or constraints open to one; without having a 'go', the chances of success remained nil.

As we have seen, class, age and gender hierarchies and divisions were quite apparent, and were constantly being redefined, at this market. Gender determined the kind of 'acceptable' activity a person could engage in, and in turn the profitability of the activity determined one's class. Such unwritten economic rules and codes of behaviour resulted from the historically specific structure of social relationships between economic actors within the Mozambican political economy.They, however, were not unchanging. Under economic pressure, and this seems to vary with the period spent in the more fluid urban life, such rigid definitions of what was acceptable were being challenged by more and more women who were venturing into areas that had hitherto been the preserve of men. Not only did women's trade increasingly become a primary source of essential household income, but also gave them a greater degree of autonomy and independence, as well as provide an impetus to the on-going struggle to adjust the relative position of men and women. As shown below, the general description of the activities of entrepreneurs at Sete de Abril, one of the major markets which emerged spontaneously in Chimoio, roughly applies to many other such markets that emerged spontaneously in the city.

Similarities, variations and specializations in the markets

By and large, the newly emergent markets exhibited more similarities than differences. For instance, at Pedaco market in Bairro Pedaco, which was a more recent settlement, and hence much smaller than Sete de Abril, all the small shops were owned by men, while vegetables were sold mostly by women. Similarly, children (a significant proportion of whom did not go to school) helped their parents in various ways like selling goods, fetching firewood for own use and sale, and household work. There were, however, some variations and differences.

Due to a number of interrelated factors, such as the specifics of the local social and ecological environment, fluctuations in demand and supply, and above all, the exigencies of war itself, some activities and/or goods were more predominant in some locations than in others. In particular, the movement of goods and nature of markets was conditioned by the following: the natural resources available locally; geographical location; the factors governing supply and demand, both internal and external; political and economic conditions in neighbouring Zimbabwe; and local and national transportation conditions. For example, at the markets in the outskirts of the city, especially terminals of rural traffic or near forests such the ones at Nhadjecha (terminal of traffic from Sussundenga district, once considered the 'iron curtain' or 'granary' of the province), Agostino Neto (terminal of traffic from Matsinye locality, where many displaced people from Gorongossa had found refuge), and 7 de Abril, there was much more, and cheaper, firewood than in other centres in the city. This was because of their geographical proximity to the rural forests where firewood was fetched. Similarly, in other markets, notably in Bairro Cinco and Sete de Abril, because of their proximity to the citrus plantation in Dzembe, there were many and much cheaper oranges, than at Chimpfura or Villa Nova, both of which are near the city centre.

Also, the period of resettlement was a key factor determining the nature of activities and the markets. Markets in older 'new accommodation centres' were larger and relatively well built, and a larger variety of goods was sold. Newly settled 'new accommodation centres' had fewer commodities and more table stalls than properly built small shops than old ones. This was partly because most of the 'would-be' entrepreneurs were still busy building their homes and re-establishing themselves. Both the of experience of war and duration of re-settlement seemed to be key variables conditioning the effects of war at an individual and local level.

Diverse, complementary and contradictory survival strategies

Complementary to and in competition with the main established markets, many individual small shops and table stalls were flourishing throughout the peripheral slums, and along the Beira Corridor. Apart from that, many productive entrepreneurs, that is, those who engaged in real production, such as craftsmen, dress-makers/tailors, carpenters, mat-makers, etc conducted their activities in their homes. They produced their goods at home and sold them from there or sent their children to sell them at established markets or in city streets. Souvenirs, clothes, tables and chairs as well as building materials, sleeping mats, clay pots and pottery etc were among the most common items produced at homes. Services such as hair-dressing, divination, welding etc were also mostly performed at home. A few examples can illustrate these observations.

Naftal Matos, using a home-made blast-furnace made of an old truck axle and a bicycle tire rim and wood, was well established as a self-trained welder in his locality. He was serving almost the whole Bairro in which he lived. In the early 1970s, Naftal had worked in Zimbabwe (then Rhodesia) as an unskilled assistant motor mechanic. When he came back after Mozambican independence in 1975, he settled in his home area near Gorongossa mountain as a farmer. But when the rebels took control of this territory in the early 1980s, he was forced to work for them as a motor-bike mechanic.

In 1991, when he escaped from the rebel controlled territory he came with virtually nothing except for his family and a few household utensils. On arrival in Chimoio, he joined hands with another new arrival, gathered some discarded metal pieces and began the welding business. When their business started picking up they parted company with counter-accusations of laziness and misuse of funds - this appeared not to be a rare occurrence - and Naftal set up his own business at his home. He was helped by his 12-year old son (who he said was not going to school because the local school authorities wanted a huge sum of money as a bribe to give him a place) whom he had also trained.

Previous experience as well as committed determination were the crucial factors in the success of this man. He, unlike some few fortunate entrepreneurs, did not bring any material goods or valuables to start off with nor, as he pointed out, was he helped by kinsmen/relatives, but he managed to establish himself and gain respect and influence among his folk. There were many more examples of young men establishing themselves via technical innovations of this nature. One such self-trained radio technician was a young man who repaired, and even modified radios, using lemon juice as the cleaning liquid, fire-wood fire to melt the lead for welding together the radio wiring system, and sharpened wire as screw-drivers.

In marketing and trading, which are the dominant spheres of economic activity, cases of individuals starting from nothing and graduating into some localised prominence abound. Agostinho Capao, a 17 year small-shop owner had virtually nothing when he first arrived in Chimoio coming from Buzi was one such example. Luckily for him, his elder brother, who worked in Chimoio and owned a shop which was manned by their younger brother, offered him some accommodation. Agostinho had raised his initial capital by working as an shop assistant at a shop more or less similar to his. As a sign of success, he was planning to employ another person so that he could concentrate full-time on procuring the goods for the shop, and hopefully open another one.

As in the above example, the use of family bonds, kinship relations and ethnic connections for gaining access to goods or other resources, for practical help in facilitating these activities or reducing their costs, and for supporting mutual trust and co-operation, has been a common practice characterising activities in the grass-roots war economy. This transformation of kin relations into commercial ones is not unique to Mozambique. All over Africa, the poor have used the informal contracts kin and clan relations create as endogenous social security nets. As Jagganathan points out, such personal ties are "social assets that create earning opportunities for the poor."

In addition to the services mentioned above, cooked food - roasted nuts, cassava, bread - as well as sweet beer were mostly prepared at home and taken for sale at the market, main roads and in the city centre. Traditional opaque beer was also prepared and sold/consumed at home. It had become a major source of income for those who brew it as many people could not afford imported or locally manufactured beer. The alienated turn to it as a way to drink away their frustration and sadness - only to rediscover their frustration when they get sober. Fast-food shacks made of bamboo, sack and thatch, which sold hot tea, rice and chicken/meat, were also becoming increasingly fashionable. The food was roughly 40% cheaper than that found in concrete restaurants, although the hygienic standards were lower. This should not be surprising given that the vendors were mainly illiterate, starved of capital, and, to minimize costs, employed under age children who were paid far less than adults. In fact, the ubiquity of child labour made this phenomenon one of the most visible consequence of war. Given the fundamental implications for the future this has, it is important to look into phenomenon in some detail: Are the child labourers, denied formal education, a lost generation or are they, by virtue of their having to learn survival skills at an early age, pioneers of a new vision? A survey of the experiences of these children of tribulation may through some insights into this question.

In Manica Province, many children were war orphans, and many more were separated from their families by the war. The destruction of schools by the war meant that just about only 25 per cent of pupils eligible for primary school can get a place in Manica province.[49] Thus children as a whole, seem to be one of the social groups most marginalised by the war. In response to this crisis, and in their different ways, children engaged in economic activities and adopted various strategies that met their current needs and helped establish links among and/or with kin and business contacts.

In Chimoio city, Manica and Gondola towns and along the Beira Corridor children as young as seven years old were engaged in all sorts of economic activities ranging from begging, selling cigarettes as well as money (mainly local currency in exchange for foreign currency), working in small shops, smuggling etc. Some ingeniously made wooden wheel-barrows or beautiful kerosine lamps and/or bird-shaped ash trays with empty coke cans. Others worked hard and learnt new survival skills which included building their own huts, running their own small enterprises and providing a multiplicity of services etc. It is not clear, however, whether this kind of child labour did not retard their growth and, if at school, hampered their studies.

Consider, for example, the case of children who, without rank or money, miserable and in rags, spent their lives loitering at Machipanda border area, hoping that some good samaritan would recognise their suffering and respond to their humble pleas for help. On crossing the border from the Zimbabwean side, the first depressing signs of an abnormal situation were the hopeful faces of visibly hungry children standing by or leaning on the border fence, their gaze fixed on in coming travellers. These children swarmed around travellers crossing the border like chicken to a person feeding them, and literally pulled their bags shouting: "Please *tio* (uncle) let me carry it (the luggage) for you. Please tio do you have (Zimbabwean) dollars for exchange" or simply "Can you please help me with money". Small battles ensued, as they fought amongst themselves to carry the traveller's luggage or to get close enough so that any coins the travellers decide to part with fell into their hands. In some of these small fights, characterized by accusations and counter-accusations of lies, some even went on to say that only those whose parents were dead should be helped. Many of these children, most of whom were aged between 5 and 12 years, did not go to school and said they needed the money to buy food, give their parents or to go to Zimbabwe.

This army of destitute children, as well as other suspect people (that is those without the right papers) were frequently 'swept' away from the border area by officials, for allegedly pestering travellers. But this, like many other attempts by the weakened state to frustrate the dispossessed's attempts to survive, was not successful. In fact, some of the elder ones who managed to save a little money from carrying travellers' goods and selling money, ended up working in the Zimbabwean border city of Mutare as vendors selling eggs, cigarettes and vegetables. Although they did not get much from this kind of work, it was much preferable to languishing in Mozambique; the hard currency (Z$) earned offered the initial income to start up a more lucrative activity, such as dealing in money, when they returned. This explains why, in spite of constant arrests and deportations to Mozambique by the Zimbabwean authorities, they, like some of the recently repatriated refugees, still come back. In doing whatever they did, these children were either helping their parents/guardians or working for themselves.

In either case, as the following brief life histories show, the proportion of children's labour contribution to family survival (or own survival) roughly determined the extent of their relative autonomy from their parents or guardians. Jorge Kanimambo, then a 17-year old boy who lived with his sick mother in Chicacaule *aldeia* (resettlement camp)was one of the many young men who learnt survival skills at a very early age. As his two brothers were both in the army, his father dead and mother ill, he shouldered all the responsibilities of running a household. For instance, according to him, after each of the three rebel attacks which they endured he, with the help of his friend who he had a reciprocal work relationship, was the one who had to re-build their huts.

Another boy of the same age who had also to learn survival skills at an early age was Alberto. Alberto had just escaped from a Matsanga attack in Dombe, leaving all his family. Like Jorge, he was building his own hut with the help of a newly met younger friend who lived in the area with his parents. He was also selling thatch grass in order to get money for food. To some extent, these young men tended to enjoy a certain amount of freedom, but this new found or enforced autonomy tended to vary with age. Younger children, in spite of their labour contributions, remained more or less dependent on their parents or guardians. For example, all the young children who dug building stones/gravel with their bare hands for sale in Bairro Villa Nova, said they would give the money to their parents to buy *a banamba*.

To sup up, children's contribution in the production and reproduction of society, apart from keeping themselves and families alive and attaining some independence for themselves, contributed to the process of social differentiation and class formation. Notably, while the traditional patriarchal family was weakened, the relationship between mothers and children was strengthened precisely because of their productive relationship. Although children as a group occupy the lowest rung in the social hierarchy children from elite and peasant background live in totally different worlds; the former could easily cruise through life without having to learn to fend for themselves at an early age as their counterparts from poor backgrounds. Thus the study of the survival strategies of poor children, by virtue of their being at the bottom of the social pyramid, necessarily leads one full circle from an analysis of incidents of activity to a consideration of overall social organization and change, and in turn their bearing on the individual.

So far the focus has been largely on legal or semi-legal economic activities. But the most distinctive feature of the grass-roots war economy was semi-illegal, outright illegal and violent survival strategies of the scheming, greedy and cruel, those economic actors Keen identified as the beneficiaries of war.[50] It was precisely the collapse of state power, law and order, that ensured that, corruption, crude exploitation of the destitute, enslavement, robbery, murder, briefly force played a greater part in this group's primitive accumulation of capital.

Illegal and violent survival strategies and wealth accumulation

The International Labour Organization (ILO), the agency that has formalised the term 'informal economy', characterized the informal economy as 'a sector of the poor' in which 'the motive for entry into the sector is essentially survival rather than profit making'.[51] This statement, when considered in relation to the grass-root war economy of Manica Province, needs to be qualified. On the contrary, not all of those who participated in the grass-roots economy were poor nor were their motive for entry merely to survive. Corrupt bureaucrats and professionals used their office, influence or contacts to acquire via the grass-roots war economy, through for instance, smuggling, fraudulent export, barter, speculation, bribery, and embezzlement, and invest in building houses, hotels/restaurants or in transport.[52] Similarly corrupt commercial elites, religious leaders, international agency personnel, as well as international racketeers and their middle-men, smugglers, money dealers, pirates, and slavers and abductors, not to mention soldiers in the warring armies and foreign troops, were among those who yielded substantial benefits, and in many cases, became obscenely rich, by participating in the grass-roots war economy.

The collapse of state power and corresponding rise in anarchy offered the bureaucratic and commercial elite unprecedented opportunities of accumulating wealth via the grass-roots war-economy. First, the state's incapacity to enforce labour laws combined with the weakening of the labour movement allowed these two groups to base their accumulation of capital on the super-exploitation of labour. Most employed the poor desperate for cash in conditions that bordered on slavery. Others used their political positions to accumulate wealth, mainly through underhand tactics, mainly diverting public resources for personal gain and demanding bribes.

101

In Chimoio, some of the young elite, especially those who had been overseas, made huge profits by charging young children - most of whom worked hard to raise the money - to watch imported western videos. Western videos, just as the presence of Western international aid personnel, had a profound impact on culture and values, in particular the promotion of the entrepreneurial ethic. But the worsening living conditions, coupled with the visible widening gap between the increasingly consumptionist elite and mass degradation in the cities, increased the irresistible desire to get rich quick by any means, especially among young men. Consequently, many young men with low educational backgrounds turned to money dealing, smuggling, piracy, killing illegal hunters and miners and looting their belongings, highway robbery along the Beira-Machipanda road, and even slavery.

Money dealers and the circulation of financial capital

Central to the activities of all the economic actors (especially importers and travellers), the monetarization of the grass-roots economy, and the integration of the Manica grass-roots war-economy into the global informal economy were foreign currency dealers. This army of foreign currency peddlers, with their small bags full of Zimbabwean dollars (Z$), South African rands, American dollars (US$)and, as they put it, 'the debased and valueless Meticais'(Mt), slung on their shoulders, spent their time hanging around the main stations of Chimoio, Manica, and Machipanda waiting for clients.

Most of those interviewed in Chimoio said they had started as petty-traders with stalls at the main city market. Almost all of them still had these stalls but had employed young boys to man them, while they oiled the operation of the grass-roots war-economy by providing an essential service in a much more efficient way than the cumbersome bureaucratic 'red-tape' procedures of the state owned banks: if the foreign currency required was available, the transaction just took a matter of seconds. They also had the added advantage of always being ready to negotiate the exchange rate on the spot. In fact, the exchange rate was remarkably flexible in response to demand and supply, and this gave the dealers another added advantage over the fixed official exchange rate. For example, within a period of six months from March to October 1992 the informal exchange-rate had changed far more dramatically as compared to the official one which changed more gradually (see table below).

Table 3.1

**Changes in grass-roots war economy
exchange rates in Manica Province***

Currency	March 1992	June 1992	Oct. 1992	Feb. 1996
US$1	2,300Mt	2,500Mt	3,000Mt	11,000Mt
Z$1	300Mt	500Mt	650Mt	1000Mt
SA Rand	700 Mt	800Mt	1000Mt	2250Mt

* Since the grass-roots war economy exchange rate could always be negotiated at the sport, these figures are unavoidably spurious, but what they purport to depict was real enough.

The exchange rates varied with towns as well, with the Z$ for example completely valueless in Maputo, in significant demand in Beira, and in greatest demand in Chimoio city, Manica town, and the Machipanda border post where it fetched most.

Although this was a very lucrative economic activity, it was not only difficult to enter, as one had to have vital contacts in order to have a constant supply of hard currency (especially US dollars and South African Rands), but it was also very vulnerable to external fluctuations. For example, in 1992 the effects of the devaluation of the Z$ were felt overnight in Manica Province and reverberated through to Beira, and resulted in a simultaneous decline in the demand for US dollars and a supply of Zimbabwean dollars. What seemed to have happened was that the deterioration in the exchange rate between the Z$ and the US$ meant that more Z$ were needed to buy US$, and this caused a temporary decline in demand for US$ in Zimbabwe. This meant that Zimbabwean dealers who bought US$ in Mozambique (pumped into the economy by international agency personnel) for resale in Zimbabwe to Nigerian, South African, Zimbabwean etc smugglers, racketeers and travellers, lost their local market. In turn this affected their demand for US$ and, hence, supply of Z$ in Mozambique. In short, this reflects the extent to which the regional informal economies are increasingly getting integrated, with smugglers and money dealers playing a vital role in the supply of scarce goods and hard currencies across the region from Mozambique to Namibia, South Africa to Zambia. The circulation of money capital has thus been a vital element in shaping the changes and forms of the unfolding local and regional economic processes, and this in spite of the obstacles presented by the artificial colonial boundaries.

As already noted, most of the manufactured basic commodities that were being sold in the markets surveyed above were imported from Zimbabwe. For instance, nearly all the sugar and bread (these were goods mainly consumed by the elites - the poor made their own bread) were from Zimbabwe. But importing these goods was itself problematic. To start with, for entry into Zimbabwe one required a visa. The single entry visa fees, then 25,000Mt, was more than two weeks wage, and prohibitive for the unsalaried. (The fee for entry into Mozambique was Z$126.00 single entry for one month, and this was equivalent to about a week's wage). In addition, getting a visa involved extra costs, for instance, travelling to the embassies or consulate as well as bureaucratic hassles. Similarly, bribes were too costly and unaffordable by many unemployed people who needed to import and re-sale. In addition, not only was the import duty on certain goods too high, but on the Zimbabwean side there were severe restrictions on the quantity of certain goods that could be exported. For example, when the export of bread and sugar started creating shortages and price hikes in Zimbabwe, the maximum number of loaves of bread that one was allowed was limited to two. These costs meant that those who managed to import through the proper official channels only made marginal profits. Consequently, many turned to smuggling, came up with ingenious smuggling strategies to beat the system that served them well.

Smuggling involved a lot of risks, for not only was there a possibility of being arrested by the army and police patrols (and usually set free after relieved of the goods by the hungry soldiers/police), but there was the greater danger from pirates who survived entirely on raiding and robbing smugglers. To counter police patrols, the smugglers cooperated with emergency taxi drivers, who had the advantage of speed, and of whom they were major clients (as they charged each bundle of goods separately). Using coded messages and whistles, they developed an intelligence network that ensured they were always a step ahead of the police and that police moves were always known in advance. Similarly, the insecurity caused by pirates, who lay in cover in the border jungles waiting for unsuspecting smugglers, had an interesting unintended consequence; it resulted in the creation of employment for the local youth as border guides and couriers, escorting and protecting smugglers against pirates, transporting the goods, and keeping an eye on police movements.

Other traders/smugglers, not willing to risk being arrested for illegal entry, met and exchanged their goods between the border posts of the two countries and returned to their countries. Many such traders made more than one trip (to Zimbabwe) a day, dumping their goods at the border before going back to get more. Judging by the number of trips that these traders were willing to make in a day, such activities seemed quite lucrative. Quite interestingly, the customs officials at Machipanda border post turned a blind eye to hundreds of smugglers who daily illegally jumped the border, through bush paths far less than a kilometre from the post, during broad daylight.

No doubt, smugglers kept the grass-roots war economy moving. According to an officer at the Machipanda border post, more than 60 per cent of bread, beer, sugar imported from Zimbabwe were smuggled. Smugglers also made brisk business; even all the costs, especially transport, were taken into account, importing and selling yielded profits of over 200 per cent. It was the final consumer who bought, for example, beer and bread in Chimoio for far more than double the prices at the border, who footed the bill. Those involved in these kind of activities were certainly not just making ends meet, but were getting rich as well.

Many smuggled goods ended up not only in the informal markets, but also in the shelves of established concrete shops of Manica. In fact, some merchants in the formal economy entirely relied on smugglers and/or middlemen for certain scarce goods which were difficult to import because of high duties imposed by the Zimbabwean customs. Finally, as with other new entrepreneurs in the grass-roots war-economy, although there were cases of petty deception and cheating, what was very remarkable was the level of cooperation, trust and the observation of unwritten codes of business conduct among these traders. Closely related to smugglers, were hunters, pirates and traffickers who, by exchanging their commodities on the market, and using money to facilitate their transactions, provided an impetus to the growth of the grass-roots war economy.

Hunters, pirates and traffickers: The local and international informal economies

The increasing possibilities of making a fast buck by trafficking in items such as precious stones, minerals, rhino horns and elephant tusks resulted in the gradual growth of underground armies of hunters and pirates. Armed with guns or traditional weapons (bows and arrows) the hunters went hunting deep into the forests, sometimes for long periods of time ranging from weeks to months. In the jungle, their lives were endangered from all directions - government soldiers, MNR rebels, animals and 'hunters of hunters', pirates. On contact with government forces in the bush these innocent men trying to eke out a living were automatically arrested as suspect bandits or their informers (which some of them usually were as a price of not being harassed by the rebels) or shot at if they tried to flee. In contact with the rebels, they were either captured and coerced into the ranks of the force or murdered if they tried to flee. The animals they hunted, elephants and rhinos as well as buffalos (for meat), are particularly dangerous, especially when threatened. However, the more dangerous threat came from the army of professional 'hunters of hunters'.

This army, unlike the rebels and government forces who occasionally 'relieved' the hunters of the products of their labour, solely thrived on raiding and robbing the hunters. According to a police officer at the police station in Matsinye (literally meaning 'cruelty' in Shona) locality, which is about 12km northwest of Chimoio city, violent piracy was the most serious problem in the area. For example, within a period of two weeks in September 1992, the officer reported, three hunters had been killed by pirates, one of whom was later brought to trial. In other words, the war was not only being fought between government forces and the rebels: actual battles were also fought at various other levels, between the pirates and hunters on the one hand, and between these two groups and the former two groups as well as against nature (killing of animals and firing of forests). It was not these poor men who risked their lives and put that of other poor men at risk who really benefited from this business.

On the contrary, it was the 'big fish', the professional racketeers in their fancy suits and posh cars, not only from Mozambique but from other countries as far north as Zaire, Nigeria and Sierra Leone and Germany. Indeed, by 1992 Maputo had become a 'camp haven' for foreign dealers, who resided in the city's hotels, and who were busily creaming off the wealth of the country and setting up big 'legal' enterprises in their own home countries. One such example was a Sierra Leonean man, who boasted about having opened a number of supermarkets in his home country with money raised from dealing. When I met him, he was in a great hurry to go to Nampula (were precious stones and minerals were presumably cheap), and was desperately looking for a 'contact' to help him. Unsurprisingly, by its very nature, racketeering and trafficking was dangerous. For example, in typical gangster fashion, one day towards the end of September 1992 there was a dramatic incident at the Mozambique/Zimbabwe border, when a dealer was conned of gold worth about 2 million South African Rands by a South African, who on getting the gold, sped off at a terrific speed without paying for it. It was alleged that some members of police, army and foreign troops[53] were also involved in trafficking, one reason why the state could not clamp down on this specific practice and illegal activity in general. In short, trafficking involved a number of actors, interwoven in an extensive worldwide network linking local dealers to international barons, and with respect to Renamo, to arms peddlers in the international arms informal market.

Local rumours abound that some of the NGOs and international agency personnel were also involved in this racketeering.[54] In fact some government officials as well as ordinary citizens doubted the credibility of certain NGOs and other foreign agencies which they saw as mere 'fronts' for siphoning off their wealth to Western countries. As one former employee of one such agency, decried:

> These people (the agency's personnel) are intelligent crooks. They now know much more about this province than the Government. For example, they have taken a satellite picture of the whole province and they know where all our minerals are located. They don't show us all their plans, and the (local) Director is stupid. He just follows what they tell him to do. You never know what they take with them when they go home.

These concerns, shared by many patriotic Mozambicans, though difficult to prove, cannot be dismissed as unfounded. Suffice to mention that, as the Isaacmans note, the country's enormous mineral wealth, large natural gas deposits and the increasing likelihood of offshore oil, has attracted the attention of mineral and energy-starved countries such as Italy, France, Japan, and former East Germany[55], and lately the British firm Lonhro which was extensively involved in the peace process.

In this context, Mozambicans can be forgiven for seeing their well-intentioned 'good samaritans' as nothing more than tourists in a crisis, focused only on profiting from the situation. If the above allegation was correct, then the actual beneficiaries were the jewellery firms in the West which got raw materials cheaply. The only local group that benefited in a 'smart' way were the 'contacts' who go-between the actual labourers and the professional international racketeers. This group, like the local workers of NGOs and international agencies, was graduating from the sea of mass poverty into becoming the so called, 'new *assimilados*' (under colonialism, *assimilados* were those Africans, by virtue of their education and wealth, deemed 'civilised' and hence accorded equal status with the Europeans).[56] But such opportunities were not available to all: many had to adopt dehumanizing survival strategies, such as slavery.

Abductors, slavers and unscrupulous capitalists

Slavery in Mozambique is not a thing of the past. In 1992, it was reported that a South Africa based slave syndicate operating in the eastern Transvaal homeland of kaNgwane had abducted many young children from Maputo for sale in South Africa.[57] In the central region a clandestine group of abductors were also involved in similar activities. The slave traders entice the young children into crossing the border with them, by making false promises. In

107

Zimbabwe they then sell the children to white commercial farmers in the South-east of the country.

According to one such former slave - a 17-year old lad at the time of the interview, 1992 - who was abducted from Chimoio in 1986, the living and working conditions were appalling. They lived in barrack-like semi-circular asbestos buildings with no windows. Working from dawn to dusk for no pay, they were also not allowed to mix with the local population.[58] Zimbabwean rich peasant farmers, as well as urban petty-traders, also employed cheap Mozambican labour in poor conditions. This reflects the increasing integration of the regional informal economies, and shows that it was not only some Mozambicans who benefited (and lost) from the effects of war, but also other economic actors within the region.

To sum up, Mozambicans of Manica actively produced and reproduced their material existence, by seizing, creating or even missing opportunities for upward mobility. Different people responded differently to the war-induced economic crisis. Not all the dispossessed were able to adapt to their new circumstances. Inevitably, this process produced tensions and alienation as, in a 'zero-sum game', some social groups have substantially gained political and economic power while others have lost it. It appears, for many who have fallen by the wayside, that the main constraint, apart from helpless childhood, old-age or mere indolence, was the lack of initial capital outlay to start off with: many, because of the circumstances in which their uprootedness occurred, simply did not have the financial or the technological where-withal to get off the ground. Lack of technical managerial skills meant that most entrepreneurs only managed to operate at the level of a 'hand-to mouth economy' - 'partly living' - or worse still, their investments simply collapsed before take-off.[59]

Summary: The grass-roots war economy and development

Rimmer, commenting on the economic effects of war in Africa, begins his analysis by quoting Thucydides and Hobbes who argue that a 'state of war of each against all' and the absence of a "common power to hold the population in awe, with a number of rival powers disputing violently for supremacy, resulted in no commerce, and no safe communication [and] there [was] no place for industry; because the fruit thereof [was] uncertain". In Africa, he concludes, the situation is not remote from these imaginary states described by these classic theorists on violence and conflict. Later in the same analysis, he points out that in Western Europe, the devastation of the Second World War was "overshadowed by the effects on living standards of subsequent advances in science and technology, expansion in trade and accumulation in assets".[60] With respect to Africa he concludes:

> No such positive side effects of the African wars are apparent. The results appear wholly negative. Societies and states have not been strengthened by conflict. Only the killing arts have been refined. Fanon's idea of renovating violence, that solely through the fire could true liberation be won, can have few adherents nowadays. Violence in Africa has begotten violence - not freedom, not dignity, not socialism, not nationhood.[61]

However, in contrast to Rimmer's conclusion, the accumulation of outcomes of essentially random choices of possibilities in Southern Africa in general, and Mozambique in particular suggests that the results of violence are not unambiguous.

No doubt from a statistical and even a structural standpoint (the expansion of the grass-roots war economy, for example), the war did not produce miraculous development, such as a modern, urban, industrialized society which 'overshadowed' the effects of war as in the West. However, to deny the importance of new forms of livelihood, economic organization and social relations in altering the relationship between people and the state, the nation-state and capital, not only obscures the larger 'systematic' reasons why this is taking place, but is also to barter historical truth for ideology. In fact, with respect to Mozambique in particular, and Southern Africa in general, Rimmer's conclusions are so outrageously far from the truth that one can hardly imagine how any reader of 'his-story' could discover the dynamics of the invisible revolution unfolding in Southern Africa, let alone the elements of the solution in the problems.

First, his conclusions completely silence the voices of the participants. For instance, some of the entrepreneurs in the grass-roots war economy said they had voluntarily left their low paying jobs in the formal economy, such as teaching and shop work, to become entrepreneurs in their own right. One such young man vowed that he would never work for anyone, the government or private company, because it was, in his words "working for the *chefs* all the time". "I want to be my own *chef*", he confidently declared, and, he confided, it was because of his philosophy that he had avoided military call-up throughout the war. In other words, the grass-roots war economy - a by-product of violence - has offered the participants involved *relative* freedom from the suffocating grip of the state and from (direct) exploitation by big capital, as well as freedom of movement across national-boundaries in spite of the celebrated sanctity of the nation-state.

Second, if violence is so irrational, why should it persist? In Mozambique (in both wars for that matter), Namibia, South Africa and Zimbabwe, and notwithstanding the unfulfilled aspirations of freedom and justice, which are inevitable given the global economic power structure, violence did in fact bring respect, independence (and even socialism in Mozambique before the counterrevolution) for Black people. Third, and perhaps more important, the unintended consequences of violence have been to completely discredit economic nationalism and to demystify national boundaries, both of which are the bedrock of imperialism in Southern Africa, and core principles of Western civilization. As borders become more and more porus, through war, violence and economic crisis, the freedom of movement of peoples of the region has remarkably been enhanced. Nationalist leaders, well schooled in the sanctity of the nation-state, yet incredibly and irredeemably at odds with the demands of the new times, the desires and aspirations of the people they claim to represent, have relentlessly attempted to frustrate this new found freedom of movement; yet the more they try, the less is their labour rewarded, for it is to sail against the winds of world history.

In the particular case of Mozambique, what needs to be stressed, however, is that, the effects of the war on the economy have been conditioned by the nature of the war itself, the pre-war organization and performance of the economy, as well as by outside forces. The disarticulated and technologically dependent nature of the pre-war economy, the most enduring legacy of Portuguese colonialism, did not provide a strong basis for scientific and industrial innovation, but instead, without this foundation and building blocks, creative energies were directed towards trade and services. In the same way, the post-independence commandist organization of the economy hampered flexibility in response to the crisis. Similarly, the contraction of the global economy, unlike the post-1945 expansion which enabled Western Europe to recover rapidly, does not provide much prospect for externally driven recovery. Cause and effect tended to merge, as war and economic crisis fuelled each other.

While, as Thucydides, Hobbes and Rimmer speculated, war destroyed markets and commerce, it must be stressed that it also *created* others where non-existed before, and *more* rewards for those prepared to take the risk. For example, in theory and as Rimmer notes, 'political instability, insecurity or outright conflict increased risks - and hence costs - that transaction will not be completed profitably, or at all'. In reality, however, and in some specific trades it was precisely the presence of risks that was the basis for large profits for those prepared to take the risks. Related to this, his ideas on violence and development, in particular his dismissal of Fanonian romanticisation of violence, is contestable. As the evidence from Chimoio suggests, violence is

110

a social force which provides an accelerative process to change and development. As Clements put it:

> Any calibre of social change is rooted in the idea of two ideas colliding and the nature of this collision is dynamic. if we posit the status quo with statism, then incidents which change the status quo ontologically are dynamic which by its very nature are violent.[62]

Certainly in Manica, violence was an active disintegrative and integrative force, with association and competition, cooperation and conflict co-existing in dynamic tension.

It appears, while continued absolute war would have completely destroyed the economy, absolute peace would have been static and stagnant and without exciting creativity. Qualitatively, the emergent economic forms and relations documented above sharply contrast with the pre-war situation in many rural communities where products were destined for direct use by the community and did not take the form of a commodity, and where the social production and organization was based on the 'economy of affection'. For subordinate social groups such as women and children, the collapse of the economic basis of rural patriarchy and gerontocracy afforded them more freedom in terms of the economic activities they could engage in and the surpluses accruing therefrom. Similarly, the collapse of state power enabled social groups and movements within society to participate more effectively in the 'dialectic of control' and redefine the state-civil society relationship, and in particular, expand their political space. This transformation of the political economy, mainly via production and exchange, seems to have cleared the way for capitalist development, a transition to which Frelimo had violently attempted to forestall under the slogan; 'kill capitalism when it is young like a crocodile'.

Indeed, the state itself, since the adoption of the World Bank and IMF structural adjustment programmes in 1987, has been "reducing its intervention and privatizing those enterprises (mostly agricultural) that it took over following independence in 1975".[63] As Pitcher observes:

> Most of the new enterprises that have been created are in the form of joint ventures, with the state holding an equal or minority share in the new company alongside domestic or foreign capital. Many former Portuguese settlers who abandoned their farms at independence are now reclaiming their land and foreign investment from South Africa, Portugal and Great Britain is entering the country.[64]

Such an unholy alliance between the state and capital has been depicted by Marxists as a betrayal of the workers by the state, which now acts, as a weaker partner, on behalf of capital. In contrast neo-classical economists and public choice theorists, whose perspectives inform the World Bank and the IMF, applauded this retreat of the state as a necessary condition for prosperity and organizing the economy according to principles and priorities of the market. The point is, the state needs capital to shore up its legitimacy, through employment creation for example, while capital needs the state for the stability and security necessary for maximum accumulation of profit through super exploitation of cheap labour.

What is interesting to note, however, is the fact that as with Frelimo's 'big push', the structural adjustment programme and this new economic arrangement have been imposed from above, and their unintended consequences are certainly uncertain. More important, however, seen in global terms, this internationalization of capital, in so far as capital creates its own grave-diggers, is a necessary step towards international socialism. Thus war, in addition to bringing modernity to Africa as Bayart stresses, has accelerated the contradictions and crisis of capital, which in the long run, according to Marx, will inevitably lead to the victory of socialism, the withering away of the state. and the final emancipation of labour.

At the risk of imploding the concepts of development and violence, one may hazard a hypothesis thus: It seems there is a correlationship between violence and development, in which a certain amount of violence may be necessary to initiate change to the status quo, but at a certain stage diminishing returns set in as total violence starts undermining the capacity for innovation and enterprise. Duration and intensity of conflict appear to be key factors. Thus for instance, the central region (Manica and Sofala), owing to the longer experience of war it had, the partial ceasefire along the Beira Corridor in 1990, and the fact that it was Renamo's stronghold - which meant that the Province was spared the extremes gruelling brutalities of the war that it unleashed in Frelimo strongholds in the South of the country - is now one of the most urbanised part of the country. The length of the period involved meant that state and traditional structures which had obstructed change were undermined gradually[65], while both the partial ceasefire and Renamo's comparatively low profile brutality (at least against ordinary people during the early and last part of the war) allowed economic activity and innovation to continue. Thus without glorifying violence, with respect to Africa, it is necessary to modify Thucydidean and Hobbesian notions about 'the state of nature', 'the social contract', and 'the absolute sovereign'. The point is, as Kant rejecting both Hobbes' 'state of nature' and Rousseau's 'social contract' theses once put it; "we do not know what sort of opinion we should form of our species, which is so proud of its supposed superiority".[66]

112

Sadly, Rimmer's blind faith in these ideas led him to propose recommendations which amount to no more than re-baking the old beans, and naturally worsening the taste. More important, the recommendations reflect a deeply ingrained Eurocentricism that, following an American Huntington, celebrates building political institutions and the bankrupt notion of 'nationhood' as a panacea to Africa's problems:

> The prevention of conflict therefore requires the development of structures, and the fixing of norms of conduct, that make compromises more readily attainable, power contingent, and the holders of power removable by civil procedures. ... the rule of law, effective checks on the state executive, and disbarment of the military and police from politics appear to be requirements if Africa is to become peaceful. In addition, government must be competent in upholding the law and providing personal security; there must for each people be a common power to keep them all in awe.[67]

Essentially this amounts to call for the re-invention of Africa's future in Europe's image, and a denial of other possibilities that may have organic roots, such as the experiment in Uganda (which, though, is also nationalist).

More seriously, in Mozambique it was precisely because of the omnipresence of 'a common power to keep them all in awe' that, when the rebels appeared on the stage promising to relieve people of the 'awe' the common power induced, many welcomed them as their liberators. More control is not what the people of Mozambique in particular, and Africa in general, want, but economic justice, at a local, national, regional and international level. Distilled to its basics, as the interconnection between war and economic crisis testify, war in Mozambique is about bread and butter, or as Keen, modifying Clausewitz's dictum put it, war is indeed a continuation of economics by other means.[68]

Clear from the survey of Manica attempted above, the dispossessed were not mere passive victims of violence, but were instead active participants in the 'dialectic of control', shaping the outcomes of war and economic crisis. Mozambicans of different social backgrounds and positions reacted differently, adopting various individual and collective survival strategies (the list identified is not exhaustive), whose interaction constituted the dynamic of the grass-roots war economy. Their economic motivations were related to their class position; for peasants-cum-capitalists, it was primarily survival, while for the new economic elite, it was accumulation of wealth.

Owing partly to the diverse backgrounds of the these economic actors, and partly to the exigencies of the war itself, the grass-roots war economy was based on a hybridization of forms of economic organization and cooperation (and conflict), with the entrepreneurial ethic increasingly getting more and more entrenched; as one barefoot trader selling wildlife meat put it idiomatically, 'In times like these, *mupfuri anodyira pasi*' (the iron smith - who makes, among other things, plates - eats from the ground), when explaining how he and his family, in order to save some money for setting up a more viable business enterprise, ate their *sadza* (staple maize meal porridge) with vegetables. These barefoot entrepreneurs, like the classic entrepreneur, operated within an overall economy whose operation - influenced by the activities of these agents - provided both constraints and opportunities for these entrepreneurs to reproduce themselves and expand.

Although operating within these constraints, the grass-roots war economy was more predictable and rational in many respects than the official one. Illegal and unrecorded trade was not haphazard but institutionalised, operating according to a system of rules known to all participants. Examples included the standardized equivalences observed for barter transactions, the set rates for paying border guides, the arrangements set up for the terms of clientage, and the reciprocal obligations of other personal ties. The organisation of a grass-roots war economy depended to a great extent on these reciprocal obligations of personal ties. The trust and confidence inspired by personal relationships or common cultural background provided the reliability and predictability that were so conspicuously lacking in the official economy. To some extent, therefore, the grass-roots war economy generated alternative economic opportunities for people as well as an alternative society, with parallel religio-economic institutions alongside official ones. Although for the individual economic actors involved their new economic behaviours may have represented a pragmatic response to a crisis situation, overall their actions represented an institutional shift and a challenge to the development strategy that Frelimo had pursued since coming to power in 1975.

Inevitably, such fundamental changes in economic behaviour and attitudes wrought indirectly and directly by the war had a strong impact on the organization of society. In particular, they engendered shifts in the balance of power and political alliances at various levels of society as age old values and norms rapidly gave way to new ones dictated by the new economic reality. As these contested processes unfolded one could scarcely fail to notice a repugnant, sacrilegious injustice; the disparity between the vices of some and the virtues of others and between the expensive dress draping some and the rags draping others. Although it is difficult to separate cause from effect, there is indeed detectable a causal relationship between the shifts which occurred during the war in the general economic and productive balances and the position occupied by individuals in the economic hierarchy. What then are the implications, possibilities and constraints of these changes for post-war reconstruction and development?

Issues and options in post-war reconstruction

Mozambique's grass-roots war economy, as with the informal economy in general, is the subject of much controversy. Some observers feel it holds considerable developmental potential, as an untapped resource of entrepreneurship which offers a solution to post-conflict reconstruction. Indeed optimists consider it, following De Soto,[69] as an 'invisible revolution', or the 'other path' to development. Others view it in a negative light and see it as a mere haven for refuge at near-subsistence levels and ground for labour exploitation and class formation[70]. Yet others still, especially bureaucratic elites, have contemptuous disdain for the spontaneity of the informal economy as some of their remarks reveal: 'Have you ever seen anything like this in the West?' 'It is degrading and makes our cities dirty'.'All this will end after the war'. Significantly, the barefoot traders themselves indicated their wish to continue enterprising after the war, with some of them declaring that they would never work in bureaucracies or for anyone else. Such a diversity of views on this phenomenon bears testimony to the ambiguities and contradictions of the grass-roots war economy; the reality is that these contesting views only depict and emphasize an aspect of what is an extremely complex process. It also reflects the ideological inclinations and assumptions of the individuals and institutions concerned.

We have seen that the grass-roots war economy provided a livelihood to many people, some of whom even got richer, and generated growth in certain sectors of the economy. True, it is also based on crude exploitation and social differentiation; but as we have seen, in some cases collectivist and 'economy of affection' ethics provided an antidote to the extremes of unbridled capitalism. Finally, whether or not there are informal economies in the West, it can be noted that as unemployment continues to rise in the West more and more people, especially minorities, migrants and the underclasses in general, are turning to informal economic activity to supplement their unemployment benefits; certainly some aspects of the economy, like sex-work, piracy and slavery, were degrading, but not all activities in the grist-roots war economy were; and lastly, judging by the experience of other African countries and Mozambique's short post-war experience, the informal economy seems here to stay, and may even become the mainstay of the economy.

Given this contradictory reality, which is reflected in scholarship and policy, the task of intervention will unavoidably involve a deconstructive and constructive project; a deconstructive project of shattering myths about war and development, the state and common goals, peasants' adaptability, the supposed virtues of agrarian messianism, tradition, socialism and capitalism alike, and about the grass-roots war economy. It will also involve a constructive project of giving a positive form to the demonstrated *potential*

115

of the grass-roots war economy to act as an engine of growth and development in the post-war era. To put it differently, owing to the diversity of needs, priorities and conception of the problem, the post-peace reconstruction programme will be a contested process whose outcome will be decided by the balance of forces, viz the relationship between the state and civil society, and the forces within civil society itself. Thus, to explore the possible contribution of the grass-roots war economy to development out of the ruins of war, it is necessary to understand how the grass-roots war economy has affected the balance of these forces and the shifts in development ideologies.

Bayart asserts that:

> [I]n underdeveloped countries, the state is the creator, and not just the arbiter, of capitalist relations of production. Violence is required to establish such relations in a context where they would not otherwise occur. Thus violence and repression come before any attempt at legitimation.[71]

When considered in relation to Mozambique, this generalization needs to be qualified. As noted elsewhere in this analysis, and contrary to Bayart's assertions, in fundamental respects the Frelimo revolution was an attempt to violently forestall the development of capitalist relations of production. It was instead, anti-state violence and the grass-roots war economy that gave rise to these relations of production; later, and weakened by the war, the state had little choice but to give in to pressure from the IMF and the World Bank and become the new 'creator' and 'arbiter of capitalist relations of production'. Thus policies for post-peace reconstruction should consider the impact of the grass-roots war economy on state structures, and vice versa, and the role of the state in development.

To some extent the grass-roots war economy undermined state power by providing avenues for accumulation of wealth, which was translated into political power. In other words, the creation of an autonomous space of economic activity, outside state control, enabled the participants to breach and counteract the simultaneous totalisation unleashed by the weakened state, thereby altering the state-civil society relationships. Not surprisingly, there has been a hostile relationship between the state and the informal economy. Maliyamkono and Bagachwa conclude that the over-expansion of the grass-roots war economy, "in its new and excessive form...poses a challenge to state legitimacy in Africa.[72]

Although the Mozambican statist elite has expressed similar concerns, a closer look reveals the opposite; on the contrary, the grass-roots war economy in Mozambique, by providing what the state could not, hence reducing political restlessness, actually extended the lease of life for the state and allowed it to quietly retreat from its responsibilities. Otherwise the discontent could not have been contained, and state legitimacy would have been even more threatened. In any case, illegal economic activity thrived not only because of the state's incapacity to enforce regulations, but also because the state had opted out and simply ignored much of what was going on. Perhaps more important, the state could not clamp down on the grass-roots economic activities precisely because the wealthy and powerful consolidate their position through participation in its activities. Also, at a close look, the supposed distinction between the official and alternative economies is a myth; as we saw, economic actors operated in both economies just as goods moved from one economy to the other.

In spite of these obvious advantages of informal economic activity to the survival of the state, the state remains the major obstacle to the expansion of this sector, in particular through restrictive legislation and bureaucratic requirements which stifle initiative. Flustered by the enormity of the problem, and unable to see elements of its solution, the Provincial Planning Department, for example, produced an endless list of priorities within priorities which were not only more confusing than illuminating but also bore little relevance to what was happening on the ground. Thus a fuller realization of the potential of the grass-roots war economy presupposes a re-conceptualization of the role of the state in development; rather than be an anti-development machine, by stifling the developmental potential of the masses, the state should create conditions conducive for economic innovation and enterprise. Given the limited resources at the state's disposal, perhaps it makes sense for the state to streamline its responsibilities and concentrate on key areas such as provision of infrastructure, education, health and removal of bureaucratic rules that hamper economic activity. In other words, the state needs to redefine both its attitude towards informal economic activity and its role in the economy as well redirect its energies into critical areas, and allow the micro-entrepreneurs to chip in where they have a comparative advantage.

Closely related to this question, is the issue of development goals and priorities. The most perplexing aspect of the grass-roots war economy was its diversity, in terms of both the range of its activities and the wealth of the entrepreneurs; while some barely managed to survive, some became obscenely rich through the grass-roots war-economy. This diversity in needs and survival strategies, which partly derives from the different social backgrounds of the participants, poses a serious dilemma for policy makers in getting their priorities right. Basically, the problem involves choosing between or mixing *triage*[73] and morality; on the one hand, the need for rapid post-war recovery dictates that scarce resources be directed to where they can yield quick returns that could be ploughed back into investment, while on the other, morality dictates that those in greatest need should be given first priority.

The logic of the former, which is irresistible within the context of global capitalism, means supporting well established entrepreneurs, investing in areas where there is already a functioning infrastructure etc. This would result in widening social and regional disparities and, were it to happen, would be a recipe for another wave of violence. One need not overemphasize here that poverty, in particular the lack of jobs, fuelled the war as many youth escaped the idiocy of rural unemployment by joining the rebels. Similarly, the government's prioritization of securing productive resources for war created a shortage of basic essential commodities, and this fuelled the war as some of the disenchanted switched their political allegiance and joined the rebels. Thus, to avoid a replay of this scenario, it is imperative to address the needs of the poor.

But implementing this ethically informed development-reconstruction strategy is not an easy task. Apart from the obvious problems of resources and government administrative and technical capacity, the poor are not an homogenous social group. Their needs are also diverse. Some need basic essentials such as food, others, the majority, need farming implements, and yet others, especially young men need jobs and skills, while children need education. In this context it is important to note that about 50% of the young men interviewed in Chimoio said that they would prefer to remain in the city after the war:, and their reasons ranged from finding a job, becoming/remaining an entrepreneur, or fear of another war starting again. In the first category many had enthusiastic hopes for peace: one unemployed young man put it thus, "there will be many more jobs than people looking for jobs". A former Renamo soldier who had surrendered under the government amnesty declared "we are young and fit, and can use our hands... the government should get us jobs". And yet another former rich peasant asserted; "we don't want charity, it's humiliating. We want the war to end so that we can support ourselves as before". Among those who wanted to become/remain entrepreneurs, the main complaint (about 80 per cent of the respondents) was lack of sufficient financial and technical capital to run a viable enterprise. It is noteworthy here that there was a remarkable increase in output as well as improvement in quality of goods when an Italian non-governmental organization supported iron smiths and artisans at Matsinye resettlement with equipment.

The preference of a significant proportion of the displaced to remain in the city after the war, coupled with rapid urbanization (without industrialization) should caution us against celebrating rural resettlement as the optimal solution to the consequences of war and displacement; taken to its logical conclusion, this strategy effectively ends up condemning poor people to poverty, and poor countries to their traditional role as the ghetto of the world in the international division of labour. In the case of Mozambique, it is important to remember that forced ruralization, under the infamous 'Operation Production' of 1983, in which thousands of unemployed people in the cities were rounded up and sent to work in state farms in the north, actually fuelled the war, as most escaped and joined the rebels. Thus, to avert this scenario policies for reconstruction should be sensitive to the needs of various social groups, and should aim to integrate the economy, by for example simple technology industrialization geared towards supporting both the rising urbanisation and trade and rural agriculture. Given the fact that there are still an estimated 1-2 million anti-personnel mines that still have to be demined in the rural areas, and that there is inadequate technical capacity and personnel to undertake this task, such an industrial development of peri-urban slums becomes even more plausible. In a nutshell, the success or otherwise of any post-peace reconstruction programme will to a large extent be influenced by the operation of the grass-roots war economy. This economy was based on an uneven distribution of benefits and losses, offering unprecedented opportunities to some, while it ruining others. Although it was impossible to have accurate statistics about the magnitude of its contribution, it is clear for example that the increase in illegal cross-border trade flows from Zimbabwe to Manica Province and further to Beira provided a major stimulus to sustained economic expansion, social differentiation and shifts in power bases. It is also clear that, the collapse of state power removed some of the traditional obstacles to change, and gave rise to a new entrepreneurial class (of bureaucratic entrepreneurs, artisans, money dealers, smugglers, pirates, racketeers, barefoot traders etc) with a potential to have a decisive impact upon the economic future of the province.[74] Finally, as at independence, post-war Mozambique faces a delicate economic and politico-military situation, characterised by conflicting priorities about how to meet diverse needs with scarce means, and in the last instance, the dilemma will be resolved by the balance of social forces.

Conclusion

This analysis has attempted a sociological interpretation of war and economic change, linking events, details of economic activities of real individuals to the structures within which they operate. Violence appears to have been the midwife for the emergence of a specific kind of capitalism, a hybrid arrangement, which has taken root in trade rather than production. The war released the masses' latent entrepreneurial potential, forcibly entrenched entrepreneurial ethics. This has catalysed the process of capitalist expansion at a rapid pace rare under normal circumstances, or even in times of purely economic crisis. At a theoretical level, this development challenges populist approaches that emphasize the resistance of an assumed communalistic traditional society, and its concomitant "moral economy", to market related values. The supposedly conservative have become quasi-capitalists only constrained in their expansion by lack of capital and technical know-how.

The main conclusion that can be drawn from these developments is therefore that war should not be considered purely in terms of disaster. Rather it must be viewed in its dialectical relation to society as a social process capable of inducing simultaneous deconstruction and reconstruction, destroying some markets and creating others where non-existed, ruining some while making others obscenely rich. The major mechanisms responsible for this uneven distribution of the benefits and costs of war were the social positions of the particular individuals within the economic structure and their unique individual experience of war. Social position determined the extent of vulnerability to, and capacity to cope with, the effects of war, while the individual experience of war meant that some lost more than others through direct or indirect effects of war, and the impact of this loss affected their social positions.

Notwithstanding the obvious negative economic effects of war, the evidence of vigorous entrepreneurialism, creative innovativeness and entrenchment of hard-working ethics, should leave no-one in doubt that what we are witnessing is an unprecedented liberation of the hitherto arrested potentialities of many a Mozambican. The war, by breaking asunder the fossilised structures of the old bureaucratic system, which had stifled the initiatives of the local population, enabled the disinherited to take the initiative and demonstrate what they can do in the absence of state constraints. The grass-roots war-economy provided a functioning distribution system so conspicuously lacking in the official economy. Were it not for the illicit trade and smuggling, Mozambique's people would be suffering even more acutely for lack of food and essential commodities. The challenge for post-peace reconstruction is therefore to create conditions conducive for the fullest realization of this potential, as well as to offer alternative opportunities for those engaged in counter-productive economic activities.

Notes

1. M. Tafirenyika, "Peace in Mozambique: Post-Ceasefire Situation and Returning Refugees", Paper presented at the conference on First Country of Asylum and Development Aid in Malawi, Blantyre, 8-14 June 1992.

2. See Janet MacGaffey et al, *The Real Economy of Zaire: the Contribution of Smuggling and other Unofficial Activities to National Wealth*, London, James Currey, 1991.

3 Lonhro's farming and mining interests in Mozambique are extensive, and this largely explains its former Africa Regional Director, Tiny Roland's personal involvement in the peace process; many other business people and entrepreneurs, for similar reasons, have also been involved in brokering for the peace.

4 Economist Intelligent Unit, *Mozambique Country Profile: Annual Survey of Political and Economic Background, 1991-2*, London, 1992.

5. At one point the cost of maintaining Zimbabwean troops in Mozambique became a controversial issue in Zimbabwe, with opposition politicians, Edger Tekere in particular, condemning it as an unnecessary burden on the economy.

6. P. Ratilal, *Mozambique: Using Aid to End Emergence*, Maputo, National Commission for the Emergence, 1989.

7. Ibid.

8. Ibid.

9. Ibid.

10. Ibid, pp. 1-7.

11. Frelimo Fifth Congress, *Mozambique: Documents (1), Statutes and Programmes*, Maputo, Frelimo, 1989.

12. Roberto J. Tibana, "Mozambique Commodity and Policy Shocks: Terms of Trade Changes, The Socialist 'Big Push', and the Response of the Economy (1975-1986)", Oxford University, Centre for the Study of African Economies Working Paper Series Number 18, 1994

13. Ibid. p. 2.

14. Ibid.

15. Ibid.

16. Cited in Saferworld, *The True Cost of Conflict*, London, Macmillan, 1994.

17. Tibana, op. cit.

18. Saferworld, op. cit.

19. Ibid, pp. 88-9.

20. Ibid p. 89.

21. Ibid.

22. Ibid.

23. Ratilal, op. cit., p. 24.

24. World Bank, *Restoring Rural Production and Trade,* Washington, World Bank, 1990.

25. Frelimo, op. cit.

26. Anne M. Pitcher, "Recreating Colonialism and Resurrecting Marx?: Joint Venture Companies in Northern Mozambique", paper submitted for the Journal of Southern African Studies, 20th Anniversary Conference, York University, 9-12 September 1994.

27. Keith Hart, "Informal Income and Opportunities and the Structure of Employment in Ghana", *Journal of Modern African Studies*, Volume 11, Number 1, pp. 61-89.

28. Ibid., p. 67.

29. See among others, Eleanor Preston-Whyte and Christian Rogerson (editor), *South Africa's Informal Economy*, Cape Town, Oxford University Press, 1991.

30. See ibid., p. 15.

31. Ibid., p. 15.

32. Peter Worsley, *The Three Worlds: Culture and Development*, London, Weidenfield, 1984, p. 210.

33. Janet MacGaffey, op. cit., p. 9.

34. Alejandro Portes and John Walton, *Labour, Class and the International System*, New York, Academic Press, 1981.

35. Ray Broomley, "The Urban Informal Economy: Why is it Worth Discussing?", *World Development*, Volume 6, Number 9/10, pp. 1033-9.

36. David Beach, "The Zimbabwe Plateau and its Peoples", in David Birmingham and Phyllis Martin (editors), *History of Central Africa*, Volume 1, New York, Longman, p. 239.

37. Ken Wilson, "Cults of Violence and Counter Violence in Mozambique", in *Journal of Southern African Studies*, 1992a, Volume 18, Number 3.

38. John Gribbin, *In Search of Schrodinger's Cat: Quantum Physics and Reality*, Reading, Black Swan, 1994.

39. In some extreme cases, remote rural peasants in response rural areas who had been cut off from the modern economy by the war had to survive on wild fruits and roots for food, and barks and leaves for clothes.

40. John Gribbin, op. cit., p. 2.

41. Quotation from a displaced person; it was hunger that forced him, like many others, into action as a barefoot entrepreneur.

42. Provincial Department of Labour.

43. Private companies tended to practice sex discrimination, preferring male to female workers because, according to the Provincial Director of Labour, payment of a full salary on a 2 months maternity leave and provisions of 30 minutes every four hours for breast-feeding as stipulated in the Labour Act undercut their profit base.

16. Interestingly, denouncing the demonstrations by the Harare women for rises in the price of bread, the responsible Minister advised the women to form their own cooperatives and make their own bread if they wanted the price to go down.

45. Some women in Mudzingadzi bairro, Chimoio, said they had their firewood transported by rail, but they had to bribe the rail-men.

46. As shown in Chapter 5, peasant ideologies have embedded in them mechanisms for environmental protection to deal with such problems.

47. A few weeks before, 7 people in a tractor carrying maize bags had been murdered and their goods looted. It was not clear whether this was an act of

MNR rebels or social bandits, who earn their living through the barrel of the gun.

48. Some of these drivers never drove their trucks in the city, at least during day-light, for fear of being arrested for the unroadworthiness of their vehicles.

49. Interview with Provincial Director of Planning, August 1992.

50. David Keen, "War as a Source of Losses and Gains", paper presented at *The Third World After the Cold War: Ideology, Economic Development and Politics*, Queen Elizabeth House, Oxford University, 1995, July 5-8.

51. ILO/JASPA, *Employment in Africa: Some Critical Issues,* Geneva, ILO, 1988.

52. These three sectors were the most rapidly expanding sectors of the economy. With the rise in demand for accommodation by international agency personnel, house building and renting became a very lucrative business. A few Zimbabwean companies have already ventured to capture this market, and in the process, created employment. Related to this, the rise in the number of tourists visiting the country has meant investment in transport will guarantee quick returns.

53. A Zimbabwean army captain, Captain Nleya, died mysteriously in Bulawayo when he allegedly threatened to expose senior army officers involved in the poaching and racketeering.

54. Italians and Germans, as well as Zimbabweans were the ones most cited.

55. See Allen Isaacman and Barbara Isaacman, *Mozambique: From Colonialism to Revolution*, 1900-1982, Hampshire, Gower.

56. For a detailed discussion of the formation of assimilados, see Ibid.

57. See Eddie Koch, "Slave trade still booming business" in *The Weekly Mail*, Johannesburg, June 5-11, 1992 and Paul Stober, "Seeking a better life, she was sold for R200" in Ibid., p. 9.

58. According to the boy, after escaping back into Mozambique, he had seen the man who had abducted him - by luring him into going for a fishing trip - with another man. It was not clear whether this other man was a potential

victim or an accomplice. The case was reported to the police, which could not help.

59. Ronderigo Deus' case is a typical example of this problem. Unwilling to see the money he had saved during his three years in the former east German just evaporate without return or profit, he decided to rent a modern shop (ie concrete, electrified) in partnership with a local guy in Bairro Pedaco. However, within less than three months Deus had to abandon the whole idea when the business started hitting the rock. When he first realized that he was losing more than he was gaining, he accused his local partner - who he without delay ditched out of the partnership - of misuse of funds and giving his friends beer free of charge. But when things failed to improve, he accused one of his female shopkeepers (he had two, one for night and the other day shift) of fraud and dishonesty and instantly dismissed her. But this still did not reverse the rapidly deteriorating situation; the owner of the shop wanted his monthly rent, the government its sales tax, and the electricity department its electricity bills. When the final desperate attempt to get a huge loan from friends to save the shop failed, he simply surrendered the keys, but much poorer than before he entered into business.

60. D. Rimmer, "The Effects of Conflict, II: Economic Effects, O. Furley (editor), *Conflict in Africa*, London, Tauris Academic Studies, 1995, p. 306.

61 Ibid.

62. Clements, contribution to the amateur anthropological association (triple a) e-mailing-list on-line debates, 1995.

63. Anne Pitcher, op. cit., p. 1.

64. Ibid p. 1.

65. J. Alexander, "Political Change in Manica Province: The Implications for the Decentralization of Power", draft research paper, Oxford University.

66 Cited in, Howard Williams, *Kant's Political Philosophy*, Oxford, Blackwell, 1983, p. 3.

67. D. Rimmer, op. cit., p. 307.

68. David Keen, op. cit.

69. Hernando de Soto, *The Other Path: The Invisible Revolution in the Third World*, New York, Harper and Row, 1989.

70. See Alejandro Portes and John Walton, *Labour, Class and the International System*, New York, Academic Press, 1981.

71. Jean-Francois Bayart, *The State in Africa: The Politics of the Belly*, London, Longman, 1983.

72. See T.L. Maliyamkono and M.S.D. Bagachwa, *The Second Economy in Tanzania*, London, James Currey, 1986.

73. The term originated from French military history. With scarce medical resources, French generals were faced with the dilemma of choosing who to give first priority in treatment between those who were mortally wounded and those less seriously wounded. They decided to save the latter, on the grounds that this would further the objectives of the campaign as these men, unlike the former who were likely to die anyway (after having wasted medicine at that), could quickly recover and return to the battlefield.

74. In Northern Mozambique, Pitcher notes a similar process of class formation in which an agrarian bourgeoisie is emerging as a result of large-scale privatization of state land; "the land is not going to small producers but to large commercial and agricultural interests and government officials". See Anne Pitcher, op. cit.

75. See Goran Hyden, *Beyond Ujamaa in Tanzania: Underdevelopment and an Uncaptured Pesantry*, London, Heinemann, 1980, and his *No Shortcuts to Progress*, London, Heinemann, 1986.

4 War and political change: Issues and perspectives

Introduction

The dramatic alteration of the political economy documented in the previous Chapter has generated ambiguous and even contradictory attitudes and impulses among the people of Mozambique. Social upheaval and displacement has broken the ties between people and their traditional and cultural bearings. In the political arena, the combined effect of the collapse of the state, the crisis of hegemony and the institutionalization of violence has produced changes in ideas, values and attitudes among various social groups, the main discovery being that the dispossessed are also on the march. The political and social vacuum consequent upon this disintegration of traditional norms and codes of conduct have forced the dispossessed to adapt new forms of voluntary association and identity. Entering into voluntary associations and organising on specific practical issues such as mutual aid and economic cooperation, they are indeed engaging in what might be called the 'politics of the invisible'.

The main objective of this Chapter is to explore the dynamics of the 'politics of the invisible'. It focuses on the major political and ideological issues of the period, and stresses that one cannot separate the ideologies of the time from the fact of war nor from the influence of globalization. Against a changing and confusing background, the Chapter seeks to explore the relationship of war political economy to tenacious struggles for political freedom, primarily as seen by the participants. Through the eyes of the people involved, especially the dispossessed, the analysis tries to understand broader changes in society and the significance of the changes to their lives. The underlying premise is that people's perceptions significantly influence how they act in shaping their own history. The main thrust in this discussion is therefore on examining the nature of people's changing political

127

perspectives on war and society and how they have organized and articulated their interests. Their political perspectives and moral and counter moral arguments, it will be argued, are related to the on-going (latent) power struggles at the family, community and national levels.

A framework for understanding social and political change

To comprehend fully the social and political changes unfolding in any society, and their significance to the people concerned, it is necessary to consult the people. As Peil aptly pointed out:

> Until one can appreciate the background of their attitudes and motivations and the nature of their beliefs about the world and what is becoming of it, prediction of the course of events is impossible.[1]

In a similar vein, and with respect to West Africa, Zolberg argued, "the real test of the nature of authority in West Africa ... can be provided by a systematic examination of the beliefs of the followers. This alone can reveal whether and on what basis they are willing to obey".[2]

Thus, in exploring the perplexing human themes and political issues which have fired the Mozambicans' cultural imagination and divided their political thought, explanations and interpretations suggested by the interviewees will themselves provide the raw material from which this analysis draws its conclusions. They will also be looked for in the realms in which they were not verbally expressed. The successes and failures of the dispossessed have provided the dynamic of the 'moving social whole', which in turn has defined the parameters of their changing life and attitudes.

To understand the basis of these subjective values and actions, and to give 'voice to the voiceless', the discussion has to move between three levels of analysis: one that describes the setting; another that documents moral sentiments, political debate and perspectives, aspirations and nostalgia; still another that explains or critiques the narratives or perspectives and their contexts. The assumption is that 'the state of public opinion' engendered by structural transformation also influences political and economic development. As Max Weber argued, "events establish values and predispositions, and these in turn affect later events".[3] Even Engels, the co-founder of Marxism went even further to state that while the economic situation is the base, the various elements of the superstructure - moral codes, ideological belief systems and values - also exercise their influence upon the course of historical development and "in many cases preponderate in determining their form".[4]

Thus rather than emphasize either material structure or political superstructure, it is the *dialectic* between them that is emphasized. Dialectically, the changing subjective perceptions of the participants in many ways influence structural changes, as well as the choices and possibilities that Mozambique confronts as the transition process unfolds. Since these values and perceptions are constantly redefined and reshaped in a broader context of struggle for freedom and power, the discussion is necessarily based on a contradiction; reflecting their contradictory situation, the dispossessed have exhibited ambiguous and contradictory ideas and practices. This reflects the diversity of the realm of ideas and values.

Like the rest of the study, it is also situated within an holistic analytical framework which treats systems of domination and control as the primary or core sectors of society. These systems and their interrelations are conceived not as fixed, but as changing. Similarly, their mental images - the ideas - are likewise subject to change and transformation; they are therefore not encapsulated in rigid definitions, but are developed in their historical process of formation. In the following discussion we examine communities of displaced people to see how the historical formation of their political consciousness is related to their everyday living conditions.

The social and political context

The weakening of the state, a break-down of the moral bindings of the traditional society, deteriorating material conditions, a rise in crime, a decay of the ideology of the governing class, have given rise to a state of generalised restlessness and political flux. Summing up the situation, a Roman Catholic sister said: "No-one seems to care ...and it is always the poor who suffer most in such transitional confusion".[5] Although violence has become the mark of the day, people still love and care for each other. Also, without denying that the poor 'suffer most', it has also to be understood that they do not have much to lose. More important, by participation in the dialectic of control they can, and have, improved their position. What is important is therefore to understand the dialectic of forces pulling people in different directions and forcing them to exhibit certain types of behaviour.

Chimoio is a divided city, divided between the two worlds of the rich and the poor. On arrival in the city, displaced peasants joined the army of low paid wage workers who lived in the periphery of the city in mud-pole-and thatch huts. The elites, party and state functionaries, professionals and commercial entrepreneurs, occupied the flats in the city centre and the surrounding villas. This 'political class', the politicians and civil servants, is seen by the dispossessed as the real power in society. There appears to be a

129

feeling of (latent) hostility between these two major groups. The dispossessed resent the privileged elites for not caring for them and not sorting out the country's problems. On the other hand, the elites were not only contemptuous, but afraid of the hungry who they saw as a nuisance and a threat to their privileges. Many members of the elite pass time shuttling around the city in flashy cars and pampering their insatiable appetites in posh hotels.

The insecurity of the dispossessed of Chimoio has also been reinforced by the difficulties in adapting to a new (urban) social milieu and this has often resulted in alienation. The dispossessed are partially integrated into urban life and the previous bulwarks of their communal life are threatened as they have never been before. But also the extension of money relationships and the promotion of the acquisitive spirit have freed the dispossessed, to a limited degree, from the stultifying communal ethics and restrictions of feudal and other pre-capitalist systems.

The new (capitalist) ethics are very much adulterated and amalgamated with survivals of the former economic conditions, both pre-capitalist and 'socialist'. This interplay of the old and the new is a dialectic which invests cultural heritages with quite new significance: traditional values and norms are adapted to modern demands. Ironically some changes have enhanced rather than destroyed traditional values, such as the belief in superstition, the connection between wealth and prestige and the re-consolidation of the power of traditional authorities. Likewise, some changes which Frelimo desired but failed to achieve are occurring spontaneously now; progress in the emancipation of women, though in a different form, is one such example.

In addition, the dispossessed were also culturally and economically differentiated before arriving in the city. Some were richer peasants owning rural capital while others were poor peasants or unemployed or farm labourers and yet others had artisan skills. These factors, as shown in the previous chapter, influenced individual and collective survival strategies, and people's decisions on whether or not they were prepared to go back home after the war. Finally, the dispossessed communities were ethnically and socially heterogenous.

For instance, people from the same ethnic group, especially those from faraway regions such as Nampula or Maputo, lived together and helped each other. They also kept their rural connections alive through risky visits and feeding money into the rural economy. As a part result of this, ethnicity, now being simultaneously undermined and strengthened by new forms of association, still remains a strong basis for identity, and often more a divisive than a unifying one. The persistence of pre-colonial culture has been maintained. This is, as Worsley pointed out with respect to the 'Third World' in general, "by no means simply an expression of conservative, backwards looking traditionalism".[6] It is partly a reflection of the resilience of rural forms of association and identity.

Reflecting their contradictory situation, the dispossessed have exhibited ambiguous and contradictory practices and ideas. This has hampered the development of their voluntary associations into larger political forces. Nonetheless, the evidence gathered suggests that in general terms, the dispossessed have a distinct political perspective and culture. This political culture is inextricably interlinked to that of the hegemonic social groups, who intend at all costs to maintain their power, prestige and perquisites. Although the disenfranchised may not be well informed about all details concerning the war, the functioning of the state machinery, or the official debates behind the structural adjustment programme, they have a shrewd understanding of these issues and have, in some instances, effectively positioned themselves politically.

Material conditions and everyday life in a peri-urban muddy suburb: The case of Bairro Pedaco (Centro Hipico)

Bairro Pedaco (the official name is Centro Hipico, but the residents call it Bairro Pedaco) was one of the newest and most densely populated accommodation centres in Chimoio city.[7] Located to the south-west of the Provincial capital on the left side of the Beira-Machipanda road, it provides home to hundreds of people with varying degrees of poverty, a multitude of horror stories and terrible memories. The majority of its inhabitants settled there during the late 1980s and early 1990s. New arrivals were flowing in as late as August 1992. As peasants poured in from the country-side and as new accommodation centres and markets proliferated, the environment deteriorated alarmingly. There is dreadful overcrowding and hygienic conditions and living conditions are miserable. Though Chimoio is far cleaner than say Maputo and Beira, the public services provided in new accommodation centres such as the one under consideration here are pitifully inadequate.

Ethnically it was a largely heterogenous community, with the majority of the people coming from the Shona-related ethnic groupings of Barwe, Teve, Ndau and Manyika. Social stratification was not very marked as most of the people had been impoverished by the war, some kind of 'levelling effect'. Their diverse survival strategies were, however, upsetting this 'levelling'. Though the age and gender composition of the community was quite broad, children, women and men of all ages, women tended to be a majority. In fact, single mothers, who were among the poorest and most vulnerable groups in the community, comprised a sizable proportion of the population.

Eking out a marginal and precarious existence, they lived (and some are still living) in mud and grass-thatch huts so over-crowded that if one catches

131

fire the whole *bairro* (suburb) could be wiped away. The size and type of the huts depended on a number of factors which included size of the household, length of period of residence and the wealth of the family. Larger and long settled households tended to have larger and more huts, while smaller and new ones, especially those headed by women, had smaller and fewer. Eating patterns also varied, with the relatively better off families having two or even three meals a day. They would have tea and bread (mainly home-made) or cassava in the morning, and thick maize meal porridge with a relish of dried fish, green vegetables or wild life meat for lunch and supper. The poorest families had at best one meal a day. Usually this would be maize meal porridge with salt or cassava and sometimes boiled green papaws as well as many kinds of wild fruits. At worst they would have nothing. As one resident put:

> We are suffering too much here. No-one drinks tea nor eats rice anymore these days. It's always yellow maize meal [which comes as food aid, and is considered inferior to white maize meal]. People are getting thinner and thinner. For example, although there are problems in Zimbabwe, you can't see a person as thin as I am. They are also getting darker/blacker because of selling charcoal in order to survive.

In spite of these difficulties associated with uprootedness and war, the disinherited, as both consumers and producers, have continued to reproduce their cultural life, providing entertainment for themselves, performing traditional rituals and praying (see next chapter). But generalised poverty has led to a rise in social friction, which is manifested in the rise in violence, wife battering and divorces, cases of sorcery and witchcraft and the weakening of traditional solidarities. In short, the afflictions that have re-visited the Mozambicans were the classic riders of the Apocalypse - drought, famine, war, pestilence and death.

People have reacted variously, as they always do: some are praying, some are robbing, some try to help, most would flee if they could, others have abandoned themselves to debauchery on the theory that there would be no tomorrow (see next chapter). On balance, the dominant reaction has been fear and a desire to save one's own skin and that of the closest ties, if possible. Life as well as death seem to be viewed with disgust; many people vacillate between hope and despair. Below we examine how all these diverse aspects of social life have interacted in shaping the political outlooks of the dispossessed of Chimoio.

Depictions of love and harmony in a violently changing society

One astonishing thing that draws one's attention in moving through the war torn city of Chimoio is the overwhelming outpourings of love and generosity from war weary Mozambicans. For instance, it was not unusual for passengers to contribute towards the fare of another passenger without enough money, especially if the person was old-aged or disabled. Also, it was not uncommon for us (my research guide and me) to be invited home, where we were warmly received, by people from all social groups.[8] Also as many people acknowledged, even though many are weighed down by poverty, they still help each other, particularly when there is special need as in the case of sickness or attack by the rebels. In the case of sickness, the neighbours, especially if they belong to the same religious sect or ethnic group, would fetch fire-wood and water, as well as help in household work.

This kind of cooperation was most remarkable when it came to helping victims of Renamo attacks. As a young man who survived an MNR attack in a *bairro* in the periphery of the city, Sete de Setembro (7th September) testified:

> They attacked around 1:00am in the morning (in February 1989), firing shots through the door. We squatted in the corner, and when they passed to the next house, we came out and fled to the city naked. They fired again four shots when we were coming out of the house. I was hit in the elbow, fell down, but got up and picked my child in one hand and my radio in the other, and continued running. When we got to the city we were given clothes by some women and blankets by other people.

Such cases of communal solidarity, lent credence to the observation that there is hope in the despair, comfort in desolation and some beauty in the terrible situation.

In spite of the awful misery the war has caused, the dispossessed have also continued to entertain themselves and to dance; this is aptly captured in the title of Urdang's book, *And Still They Dance: Women, War and the Struggle for Change in Mozambique.*[9] With uncertainty, and even pessimism, the mark of the day, some kind of '*Danse Macabre*' (Dance of Death), became its most vivid expression. In Chimoio it is performed 'everywhere': at home; at all-night beer-drinking parties in the shanties; in the city pubs and hotels as well as night-clubs; and regularly at the Feira Popular (Fepom - an enclosed place where trade fairs are held with a dozen pubs, some open air). At these places, and in a desperate search for happiness, they dance (and fight) all night long as if it were their 'last dance'.

133

For example at Fepom, kids as young as seven, many of them orphaned, drink, smoke and dance. Young girls below fifteen also smoke, drink and dance and are 'available' as sex workers to sooth the lusts of all social categories of men. Some youths peddle real and fake emeralds (thick green glass), drink and dance. Visibly starved soldiers dance in their uniforms. Young women in their flashy wear donated by the West also dance to attract the attention of (scarce) men for 'sex for money'. The store-keeper plays his sound system imported from the South Africa or former East Germany on maximum volume to attract more customers.

The elites drink beer, eat roasted chicken or beef and, as one observer put it, 'change women like shirts'. Some unemployed youths, desirous of that life-style, but unable to attain it, occasionally vent their frustration as horizontal violence against other marginals, victims of the system. Violence, against and over women in particular and many other minor issues such as accidentally stepping on one's toe when struggling to get into a minibus, has been a major concern for many.

The institutionalization of violence, the crisis of hegemony and regeneration

Violence, as an anti-thesis to depictions of love that abound in the everyday lives of the dispossessed of Chimoio, is increasingly becoming the norm rather than an exception. Its institutionalization, on the one hand, corresponds to the weakening of the state. On the other, while in many cases causing psychological traumatization, violence has also been socially and culturally regenerative.[10] For instance, it brought out the best and worst in people - affection, comradeship, heroism and self-sacrifice as well as cruelty, greedy, selfishness and endemic violence - as well as fired the imagination of artists, poets, musicians, cartoonists, etc.[11] It is worth noting here that, peoples' murals, that is paintings and scripts on the walls of many walls of the huts of the dispossessed in Chimoio - Mozambicans in general are a very artistic people - tell the of history of war, society, personal relationships, hope and frustration in a more touching way than in most contemporary scholastic work; this in itself is another form of cultural struggle. More important, in response to violence subordinated social groups, women and youths for instance, have been forced to organise. As pointed out in Chapter Two, various groups of people have organised themselves into self-defence militias.

Violence has manifested itself in many different forms at various levels of society. At the national level, the more dramatic and shocking cases of violence, common in their own way, speak only in their silence. These include among others, cases such as a young kid whose left eye was blown off by rocket launcher shrapnel; a young woman, who now has been forced become a commercial sex worker, with shrapnel fragments in her thighs; the miserable war amputees at Marforga mission in Gondola; the ghost suburbs characterised by dilapidated houses, mango or papaw trees and tall grass in the periphery of Chimoio; and charred remains of burnt trucks by road-sides and a burnt goods train near Inchope.

At the family level, wife battering and brutality against children have been the most common forms of violence. There have also been cases of violent wives forcing their husbands out of the home.[12] Such kind of violence has forced some children to abandon their families, or even worse, the disintegration of the family. Many single mothers cited violent abuse by their husbands as one major factor for their separation. One typical example of violence against women which we witnessed in Bairro Pedaco in May 1992 clearly illustrates the extent to which violence has been institutionalised and accepted as normal by people. The story was as follows.

The previous night the husband had not turned up at home. Apparently, according to the neighbours, he had slept with another woman he had picked up at a *padoro* (all-night traditional beer drinking party, which are an integral feature of life in the peri-urban slums). When he came back the following morning, still drunk and moneyless, he started pounding his wife, a weary mother of six after she had asked him where he had slept. The neighbours were afraid of interfering in 'internal domestic affairs'. Similarly, local officials of the Mozambican Women's Organisation (OMM), who in the past would have intervened to effect some justice, could not intervene either as they are increasingly being marginalised and ignored in the new political scenario. With no-one to stop him, the man continued to vent his violent frustration against his by then profusely bleeding wife until the arrival of close relatives who were called by neighbours. What was most astonishing was the apparent reluctance of the neighbours to interfere and stop, as would have been the case in a rural community, an obviously unmatched fight in which the man was mercilessly battering his wife. When we asked the neighbours why they had not intervened to help the woman[13], one of them pointed out:

Life here [in over-crowded quasi-urban slums] is different from that in the rural areas. We are strangers [in the sense of people not belonging to the same clan, village or totem etc] and everyone has to mind his own business. No stranger can intervene in family affairs - you have to call the relatives. If you try to intervene the man might turn against you. So we will only call the police when he kills her.

This incident, which is by no means exceptional, highlights a number of important factors. First, the fact that the neighbours could not help reflect the extent of the break-down of community ties and the acceptance of violence as a norm ('we will call the police when he kills her'). Second, and as evidenced by the rise in the proportion of single female headed families (see Chapter Six), if this man's violent behaviour persists, then the end result will be a divorce and the disintegration of the family, with many other consequences.

Other forms of minor violence abound, daily. Fights between and among youths, usually over money, has become quite common in pubs and at the markets. One incident of a street fight which we witnessed between two young girls over a skirt in Bairro Mudzingadzi (north east part of Chimoio city) illustrates this point. Reflecting the way in which poverty can cause friction and enmity between erstwhile friends, the fight broke out when one of the girls refused to return a skirt, which she was wearing, and which she had been lent by the other. Unlike in the above case where neighbours could not help, and also showing the dynamic co-existence of violence and love, one elderly women from the crowd offered to give the poor girl a dress so that she could return the skirt in question.

Another form of violence that has become common is the practice of public flogging introduced by Frelimo. In its present spontaneous adaptation by the dispossessed, it often results in grave bodily harm or even death. Typically this kind of violence involves extreme degradation and humiliation. For example, in one such outburst of aggressive behaviour, a youth was beaten by a huge crowd, which was excitedly shouting *ninja* (thief in slang), all along the way to the police station for petty theft. Needless to mention that fights among young men, especially over women and/or money, as well as armed robberies have become a regular feature of the social disintegration and anarchy in Chimoio.

In addition to such minor forms of violence, there have also been incidents of major outbursts of violence in Chimoio which have been of great concern to many. Ironically, one such incident involved an army unit, the supposed 'keepers of the peace' and law and order. The incident occurred at Fepo in August 1992 when a group of soldiers, after taking a few beers, went on a rampage beating anyone they came across at the centre. According to eye witnesses, including some of the victims, the soldiers, who had just come from a dangerous trip of escorting convoys to Tete and the Malawi border, asked to be given some privacy while drinking their beer. The bar-tender complied and asked all other civilian customers to leave that specific pub, which they did.

After a while, when the alcohol started taking effect, the soldiers started moving about with beer glasses. The bar tender asked them not to take beer glasses outside the room. The soldiers replied by beating him up, according to an eye witness "when people started gathering to see what was happening the soldiers turned against the crowd". In the mayhem that ensued - according to one observer, "Mozambicans love incidents"[14] - a number of people were injured, and the fighting ended only when another army unit, called by one of the local businessmen, came in to arrest the 'soldiers who had gone wild'. Although this case is rather extreme, it illustrates the level of lawlessness and the extent to which violence has become endemic. Hoile, in his review of *The 1992 Africa Watch Report on Mozambique*[15], cites other major incidents of mass murder in which Frelimo soldiers and foreign intervention troops may have been responsible.

Generally, many people have endured terrible ordeals that will remain imprinted in their minds for a long-time to come. These include among others: the MNR attack survivor cited above, who also had four of his relatives, all of them soldiers, killed in action - one in Mukosa, two in Guru and one in Musoridzi, all of which are districts in Manica Province; a father who had visited one of his surviving son in Chimoio from Macate, who said that one of his sons, who was a Renamo *mujiba* (auxiliary), was shot dead at point-blank range by a Renamo soldier for no apparent reason; and the young woman, and mother of four, who said they had slept in the bush several times for fear of MNR attack, and that some of her relatives were captured and others murdered - an uncle who used to sell bananas to villagers [resented rich peasant] who was cut into two pieces, and a grand-mother's sister who was also cut into many small pieces (and cut several times in the head) and then put into a bag. Such remembered ordeals, and many others and their traumatising effect, are the most enduring bitter legacy of the war.

As is evident from the above, violence has stripped man and women bare of their social sustaining relationships, dissolving relatively stable societies into a chaos of elementary principles. Violence, in its extreme manifestation as this, pays tribute to a process that robs man and women of their dignity and society of its moral bonds, and discredits old standards: it is a process of cultural convulsion and political uncertainty in a context of poverty and resilience. Poverty has given rise to a great deal of direct frustration and aggression in the day-to-day lives of members of the dispossessed, both children and adults. For instance, there is more frequent use of physical punishment by poor parents, which tends to increase rather decrease aggressive and violent behaviour. A new culture, a culture of resilience in crisis, with love and violence as its core elements, is fast sinking roots. In the next section we examine the popular responses to these changes and the type of political cleavages that are evolving with them.

Diverse and changing perspectives on war, society and politics: *'Nyaya yacho ndeyekutongana ...'*

A common expression on the lips of many is the reiteration that society today with all its ills and aberrations, flounders blindly in a terrible morass; 'it's war', they would say, with humility and dignity. In the words of a leader in Maforga Mission in Gondola, "the whole society is ill". Another middle-aged lower middle class man cynically characterized the situation thus: "I am called Pvatahuara, because [it means, in slang?] everything is spoiled". Yet another resigned young woman put it more fatalistically: "It is written in the Bible that towards the end strange things (such as the general social decadence, drought and incurable diseases) will start happening". Thus for many like these people, the diseased society, with decaying structures and values, some loathsome, seem to be veering from economic ruin to a final crazy lurch which may see it disappear over the gaping precipice to complete destruction.

One of the commonest remarks on war that could be heard from virtually every social group in Chimoio was: 'We are tired of the war. It has been going on for so long'. But this was the end of the consensus. When it came to whether or not the occurrence of the war is a matter of blame, and if so, who is to blame, and to questions of what should have been done to avert the war and its consequences, the diversity of perspectives is as perplexing as it is contradictory. For instance, among those who believe it is a matter of blame[16] some blame South Africans or Renamo while others blame Samora Machel himself. The table below shows the diversity of the reasons of the war as perceived by the interviewees.

First, it should be noted that the large proportion in Table 4.1 of those who said they did not know the cause of the war, actually reflects the pervasiveness of fear within the civilian population. Many people were simply reluctant to comment on politically sensitive questions for fear of reprisals. As one illiterate young woman, refusing to have an interview put it:

> We are afraid. I will not say anything. Everything that happens here gets known within the neighbourhood very easily (implying that talking to us might get her into trouble). This (the request to have an interview) is frightening. In February a whole family was beaten by Matsanga in a nearby locality as a result of talking to strangers. In Beira some people died of maize poisoning, and here many others have died in similar ways. We are afraid to talk to strangers.[17]

Table 4.1
Reasons for the war as perceived by the dispossessed*

Reason of War	Percentage of sample
Government policies	21.5
Ethnicity	17.0
Power struggle	10.5
Other (or a combination of the above)	16.0
Don't know	35.0

Table 4.2
Proportion of people who wanted to vote*

Want to vote	Percentage of sample
Yes	70.0
No	8.5
Don't know or not decided	12.0
Other (eg vote on condition)	9.5

* These statistics, though they provide a rough guide, should be interpreted with caution as, for reasons mentioned in the Introduction, the sample (102 people) was smaller than was desirable.

This kind of fear bears testimony to a system of rule based on exclusionist politics and terror tactics to subdue the dominated population. In the case of this particular woman, once she was assured that we were not state secret agents nor Renamo spies, her suppressed expressiveness burst out exhibiting great knowledge about, and bitter resentment of, the current political and social processes.

Without mincing her words, she summed up the cause of the war thus: "*Nyaya yacho ndeyekutongana. Uyu ne uyu anoda kuita 'president'*. (It's a question of rule and struggle for power. Both [Chissano and Dhlakama] want to be the president)." Like 70 per cent of the sample (see Table 4.2 above) she wanted to vote although, like two thirds of the interviewees as opposed to about 5% who knew more than six political parties, she only knew Frelimo and Renamo. But the problem was, she said:

> The leaders lie so that they live well while we suffer. They get rich through lies, while the *povo* (the mass) gets worn out by hard work. This is why many people no longer want to attend meetings. For example, even church leaders (like politicians) get money from the people to buy cars.

Nonetheless she acknowledged that Frelimo tried 'a little bit': "It brought equal rights and respect for Black people. During the colonial era there was nothing like that". As such, "those Europeans (the Portuguese) - who used to beat people - should not be allowed to come back". She was also explicit in her condemnation of Renamo:

> No, he (Dhlakama) can't be president. He is too power hungry and ambitious. For example, the more concessions he gets (from Frelimo) the longer his list of demands grows. In any case who does he want to rule when they are massacring people like this?

Such political awareness, also evidenced by the eagerness of many to vote and participate in politics (see Table 4.2 above) partly reflects the efficacy of the word of mouth in transmitting information, especially since the press and radio are not accessible to many poor people.

Through word of mouth, in which news from the radio, papers or even rumours is rapidly spread throughout the whole community, the level of political awareness has been rising. This awareness was particularly remarkable with respect to the keen interest with which people followed events in Angola in particular, as well as the former Eastern bloc and the world in general. It is perhaps the awareness of the Angola situation that accounts for why the majority of those interviewed said that the demobilised soldiers should be given first priority in jobs and housing lest they start another war.

In fact, the fear of another war is quite widespread, and this partly explains why even though self-repatriation is still going on, many families prefer to send one member of the family, usually a male, to survey the situation first before they all go. As a Renamo attack survivor, who had found work in the city declared: "Even if this war ends [August 1992, before the cease-fire], I will never go home, because another war might start again".

Unlike this man, the above cited woman's greatest ambition is to go back home and start farming on a commercial basis, but the problem is in her words:

First many fields have been mined[18], and many people have already been amputated or killed. Second in Sena, because the soil is heavy, you need a tractor to engage in profitable farming ... but we don't have the money.

The question of mine-clearing, estimated to take anything up to ten years, will be a nightmare for the post-election government. As implicit in her argument, if the peace is to hold, providing initial capital to the dispossessed to reconstruct their lives (a tractor in her case) should be an urgent priority task. As she remarked with specific reference to the rebels:

It may be a good thing to give them first preference in jobs and housing. Since they are used to getting free food and clothes, they may become bandits, if they suddenly find themselves marginalised.

Indeed, there is a real danger that if the demobilised soldiers are not offered something worthwhile, and if popular aspirations are not met, frustration and disillusionment might easily degenerate into violence, as is already evidenced by the rising problem of armed robberies.

Commenting on the then crucial question of ending the war, she pointed out: "We are all losing in this unnecessary war. It should be ended through understanding and mutual exchange of ideas". Although, like many people she believed that the devastating drought was due to God's anger for the bloodshed she, unlike many others who believed in praying to end the war (see next chapter), argued that 'praying cannot end the war'. Also on the crucial question of the appropriate relationship between traditional authorities and the modern state, an issue that was central to the war, she suggested a more pragmatic combination of the two thus:

Young people (party secretaries) rule like 'bandits' - for personal gain. On the other hand, the village elders lack the necessary sophistication of managing a modern society. It is therefore 'better' to combine the two (systems - the traditional authorities and the modern state system) and share ideas.

> Young people on their own are 'shit'. They don't know anything about past traditions and customs. Young people should leave some of these matters to old people, and let traditional authorities rule the country-side.

Talking about change and contrasting the present social decomposition with the dignified human communities of the past, she pointed out:

> The world is changing. We now only talk about the war. There is no more respect and dignity. Some women are becoming prostitutes because of suffering. For instance, in the past if I was divorced I would go to my parents' home and get the hoe and work in the fields.... This (the social crisis) should be resolved by the elders, because it is *they* who are perpetrating it. Working men, for example, sleep with young girls the age of their children. Similarly, mothers simply accept goods brought home by their daughters without asking them where they have got them from.
>
> Things are difficult, and if you find something (acquired through prostitution) in the house you don't ask where it has come from. You just consume it. In the past if a girl got pregnant before marriage, that would result in serious problems for both the girl and the mother - the girl could be chased away and the mother mercilessly pounded by the father. But now, because of the war and the generalised poverty, everything has changed.

No doubt, as this woman points out, there has been profound change, change which is simultaneously a matter of blame, a cause of inspiration as well as nostalgia for different people.

One other example, though not an exception, of a person for whom all these changes are a matter of blame is provided by an old man in his late fifties, a Sena from Sofala Province. He had lived most of his life in the periphery of Chimoio city. For him, all the problems were the "fault of our leader (Samora Machel) who started the war". In his words:

> Our leader who always said *a luta continua* (the struggle continues) caused the war. He never listened to anyone. Many people perished, as old people were given guns in the hope of defeating Matsanga".

Having been disillusioned by Frelimo, he thought Renamo, the only other party he knew apart from Frelimo, could rule the country better than Frelimo since, "they know where Frelimo has gone wrong".

We have no faith, because the politicians are crooks. They lie. For example when Frelimo was fighting its war, we gave them our chickens and food because they had promised us better life after independence. But where is it? ... Therefore we will take the middle way (in voting) because you cannot know the sex of an unborn baby.

As with this man, uncertainty - 'you cannot know the sex of an unborn baby' - has forced many to take 'the middle way', and a wait and see attitude. But at the same time they are making some efforts to hedge against that uncertainty. In the early days of Independence, he pointed out: "Frelimo tried hard to help us, but now it no longer cares for us. Real happiness" he continued, " we have not yet had it...Chissano's powers come from the *povo* (the ordinary people), and he must therefore ask them want they want".

Commenting on the contested question of traditional authorities and the modern state technocrats, he pointed out:

Good rule depends on the individual's intelligence (or wisdom). Young or old men can both rule well or badly ... and the stripping of traditional chiefs' powers by Frelimo was *boa* (a good thing).

Traditional rituals should be performed to appease the ancestors he added. But the problem is that "no-one knows how to perform the rituals anymore". Pointing out the link between war and drought within the neo-traditional and religious ideological framework, he said that drought and famine were due to war: "God does not give rainfall and food to people fighting against each other, because with vegetation cover (from rainfall) and energy (from food) the fighting will go on for ever". As pointed out in the Chapter Two, and as is implicit in this man's argument, drought played an important role in bringing about peace. Like many other Mozambicans in a similar situation, he saw drought and famine as a punishment for the senseless bloodshed, and a deterrent to continued fighting. But unfortunately, as he pointed out, "those who eat (enough), who know how to write", are the ones who control the institution of war, though not all its outcomes.

Drawing our attention to the tensions that arise between host and dislocated populations, he complained of having lost his farming land to displaced people who had built their houses on it thus:

Now I have only one small field left, which is not sufficient for my family's food requirements. I could not refuse them (the displaced people) a place to build houses.

143

His main concern was therefore for the war to end so that he could start farming, on an individual landholding basis as he, like the above cited woman and many others, believed cooperative/collective work causes confusion. In fact this preference for individual over collective work/property is quite widespread. It reflects how 'socialism' has manifested itself in Mozambique, and hence shaped the ordinary people's conception of socialism. For example, of the 102 people interviewed, 41 per cent said they preferred capitalism, 23 per cent a mixed economy, 18.5 per cent socialism while 17.5 per cent said they did not know. Here it is important to stress that, as should be clear from Chapters One and Two, although Frelimo claimed to be attempting to implement socialism, in reality the system that transpired was essentially a variant of capitalism, namely, state capitalism.

Reflecting the contradictory demands for a less constraining state and the need for a government that can solve problems, he went on to point out that since people are squabbling against each other because of poverty, it should be the government's priority to open new companies after the war. This, in his view would also solve the problem of moral decadence and social decay which was caused by 'over-crowdedness'. Further, he also believed that first preference should be given to demobilised soldiers, because if they are neglected they might go back to the bush and start another war.

In short, this wise old man's political discourse, in particular his demand that leaders should ask people 'what they want' and that the government should open new companies underscores the need for leaders to learn from the people as a precondition for any effective re-democratisation process. For such marginalised, but critical observers, by silencing the people Machel committed a crime against his own people. For one youth: "If he (Machel) had not died (in an unexplained plane crash in South Africa in October 1986), he would have been tried for his crimes".   Like the above men, Anatolia, a twenty-three year old separated mother of two did not have much to be excited about and did not think the war would ever end. Not hiding her disillusionment and mistrust of politicians she said: "We hear on the radio that the war is about to end. It's lies. They have been saying this for so long now". But she added: "Let it end so that some people can go back to the countryside". Pointing out ethnic domination of politics by the Southerners as the main cause of the war she said:

All the leaders, in the firms and government, are from Maputo. The people from there don't go to war. The Senas, Tewe and others are the ones who go. They are troubled. Renamo wants all this to end. But those from Maputo are refusing. If they agree, the war could end.

Renamo wants people to live their lives as they wish, whereas with Frelimo if you bought a car, house or open a shop, they were taken away by the government. All that was the work of that 'little idiot' (Samora). That's why he died - he was finished by the South Africans -, because if you are cruel you won't live long.

In addition to viewing nationalisation as 'cruelty', she also believed that:

Frelimo cannot rule the country. It has failed. They are thieves. They know nothing except stealing from the coffers to build houses, buy cars and videos. For example, Texta-Afrika (a state-owned clothing factory in Chimoio - the largest employer) is about to be sold, because it has gone bankrupt. They stole the money. We workers suffer (work) for nothing. How can then the war end?

She went on to add that, like many others idealizing the glories of by gone days: "Only the Whites can do it (efficiently manage the economy). During the Portuguese era, everything was available. But later, in response to further questioning, she admitted that:

The Portuguese also troubled us. Since they did not have cars, they used us as porters to carry them on a *machila* (a sort of sedan chair in which the Portuguese would sit in with two people in front and two in the back carrying it). They also introduced *chibalo,* forced labour. Frelimo put an end to all this.

Crediting Frelimo for creating the Mozambique's Women's Organisation (OMM) and introducing the emancipation of women, she said:

In the past there was repression between the sexes. Now there is equality. That is good... But I am being repressed by my former husband because he is refusing to sell the house, so that we can share the money.

Nonetheless, she openly stated her support for the rebels thus: "I will vote for Renamo because I am suffering. Frelimo wanted European things, but they don't know how to do it". The real problem according to her is that: "A person does not want to see another person enjoy. They want to see you suffer." This intrinsic evilness of humankind, she added, is the main cause of repression and corruption. Her dream is therefore to leave Mozambique for the United States, because "in America people live well and there is no war". But realising the high odds against realising her dream she added: "I will die here in Mozambique, because I don't have the money".

Therefore her more realistic ambition is first to built a two-roomed brick and asbestos house in the city for herself. Second, after the war, she wants to buy a farm, which will be worked by employed labours. But the problem is, she points out:

> I can't find a place to build the house (with savings made from previous employment at Ifloma, a state owned timber factory between Chimoio and Manica town) because the responsible authorities want a bribe first. But I don't have the money to both bribe someone and then buy the place.

As she points out, in the current liberalisation of the economy, corruption and nepotism have become the high road to wealth and power; in an effort to hedge against the uncertainties of the future, in which they might lose their jobs, the elites have resorted to official corruption. The rise in official corruption, 'the politics of the belly'[19], has forced many people to long for change. Some people believe Renamo could be the answer.

As Dida, a twenty-one year old young man who could not finish his secondary education due to the war argued:

> Renamo rule may make things better, but only if they come with Whites, who will open companies so that we find jobs. If they come on their own, it won't be better. In fact it could be worse, because Dhlakama himself is not educated.

His forty-two year old brother in law concurred, advancing an argument which seemed to flout common sense:

> Things are much better now (because of the war). Matsanga has tried. There is no more repression and restriction on movement. You can travel easily as the every-5km-roadblocks have been removed because the soldiers (who manned the road-blocks) are tied down in the battlefield. They introduced road-blocks from the first day of Independence [an exaggeration?]. Why? They knew they had left some of their 'comrades' [who later, according to his interpretation, constituted the nucleus of Renamo] in the bush. They were together with the those who started the war.

Thus for him, not only are some of the consequences of the war positive, but the war also had local roots: it was started by those other 'comrades' who remained in the bush because they were not happy with the way things were being 'handled' (by Frelimo) during the run down to Independence. These 'comrades', he pointed out, "later went to seek military and logical assistance from South Africa". Making explicit his support for the rebels, he added:

It is difficult to support Dhlakama while you are here (Chimoio city - under government control), and difficult to support Frelimo when you are there (his home area, Buzi which was under rebel control). There are many people here and there who support him.

He, like his brother in-law, was very bitter about the changes which he attributed to socialism and corruption. Mercilessly lambasting Frelimo for corruption he asserted: "It did absolutely nothing. It taught people thieving, because the *'chefes'* (leaders) do not work for the *povo*, but work for their pockets".

The crisis, for him was evidence enough that:

Socialism does not work. We used to walk on bare feet in socialism. The problem in socialism is that all stores/shops are owned by the government ... and the director loots everything. There must be change. Things are already changing.

Comparing socialism with capitalism, in the Mozambican context, and exhibiting an understanding of the basic laws of supply and demand he went on:

In capitalism [since the liberalisation of the economy in 1986] prices are too high. But if more shops are opened, prices can go down. We therefore need more shops for competition.

It appears the philosophy of individualistic entrepreneurialism is being well received and is sinking roots steadily. Rejecting charity aid, because it enriches the *'chefes'* via corruption, he asserted:

We don't want to be helped. We can help ourselves. We just want the war to end so that people can do something for a living. Aid - they want to get rich through us. For example, many times trucks that ferry food aid for distribution in affected areas return half full. What happens to the food? They claim they have given it to the people, when in actual fact they sell most of it. People only get left-overs.

In any case free food hand-outs can never be sufficient for your family. Being fed like a dog! For instance, if you fail to hear your name during the role-call for food distribution, that's it. You will get the food the following month.

While some like this man still highly value their dignity, have pride in themselves and have high future expectations, others have had to renounce

147

their dignity and honour just for food. As he aptly points out commenting on the resurgence of religious revivalism:

> These new converts and their churches don't pray (to) God. What they want is food and clothes. Donations of food, blankets and clothes from overseas are distributed by the churches.

He also believed that, since both God and the ancestors were angry about the bloodshed, people should do proper praying "to God first and then later to the ancestors". He concluded his discourse in politics and social life thus; "Things will be alright when people have enough to eat".

This displaced man is certainly happy about some of the changes war has brought about and has high hopes of going back home and 'eating well' as soon as the war ends. But for many others, as for a single illiterate mother of about thirty, "it's just living - living, and partly living". Lorena, a separated fourth wife of a polygamist lived precariously in a small hut so close to a gorge that if the gorge flooded it could easily be swept away. Exhibiting great uncertainty and a sense of resignation about the future she said: " I cannot say what I will do when the war ends. We don't know how we will live. Many will not get there. They would have died". Amidst terrified screams of her traumatised child, she added:

> Hunger has changed many things. Surviving strategies are different. Each person knows how he or she has to survive.

But nonetheless, although she blames hunger she also blames the individual (especially the parents): "It (being or not being a prostitute) depends on the individual". As implicit in her argument, both the individual and society are to blame for the current crisis. Even the supposed victims are also accountable. However many have chosen to lay blame squarely on others' shoulders and depict themselves as unjustly victimised.

People's leadership character profile

Seeing the crisis in terms of personality and in what amounts to a 'character profile' of the leaders, some people specifically blame Chissano for the worsening economic conditions and the crying inequalities in the distribution of wealth. For instance, among ordinary folk the current hardships are of Chissano's making who unlike, the 'kind', 'warm-hearted' and 'populist' Machel, is said to be 'hard-hearted', 'quiet' or 'detached' and perhaps, 'more intelligent'. Machel was admired for his charisma and his militant approach to solving problems, though others still, like the above cited woman who saw his 'nationalisation' as 'cruelty', hated him.

Nonetheless, while some admired Machel for his charismatic populism, others disdained his militarism and the tendency to giving long speeches in which he ended up largely talking to himself. Yet others still had little, if any, respect for him and his ideas. As with Machel, not all people dislike Chissano. For some, like a young expatriate women teacher in Maputo: "That quiet and intelligent young man has worked extremely hard for this country..."[20] In a similar vein, a middle-aged man asserted that; 'it is only fools who do not appreciate what Chissano has done for this country ... He has performed miracles.[21] By and large, many people did not seem to think highly of Dhlakama, who they considered 'uneducated' and 'aggressive'. They were others, though, with a spirit of vengeance who admired him for his movement's destruction of Frelimo hegemony.

Part of the problem, and a dilemma in coming up with a people's character profile of Machel and Chissano as well as Dhlakama, is that the ascendence of Chissano to power coincided with the implementation of the structural adjustment programme. Many people identify the Economic Rehabilitation Program (PRE) with Chissano and socialism with Machel, and hence attribute problems associated with these systems to the two leaders respectively. But in reality the PRE deal had already been under negotiation before the death of Machel in October 1986; although personalities matter in politics, it is important to stress the enormity of constraints imposed by social and global structures on individual leaders' capacity to effect change through policy.

Many people face a dilemma on saying which is better, Samora's 'socialism' or Chissano's 'reform'. On the one hand, while under socialism there was virtually nothing on the market, and people had to queue for almost everything, people had money and rationing ensured that at least everyone was guaranteed of basic necessities. On the other hand, under the economic reform programme, shops are full of food and other consumer goods, but people starve to death because they do not have the money to buy the food. As a primary school teacher put it:

It is like when you want to cook mealie-meal, but you can't get both the water and the mealie at the same time. You put the water on the fire first, and start looking for the mealie. But by the time you get it, the water is finished - and so you can not cook your meal. In the past there were no clothes. Now the clothes are there but they are too expensive. It's no better: a person with one leg is in no better situation than one without a hand because they are both disabled. Maybe it's worse.

In short, the impact of economic reform has been ambiguous, and it has given rise to a serious dilemma: it is a difficult choice between the 'tyranny' of the state or that of capital.

"Where is the Independence?"

The diversity and conflict of perspectives on the 'changes that are influencing change' was most dramatised in a heated and emotional political debate between members of one family that I witnessed as a guest. The mother, a middle-class women in her late forties, and abandoned by her husband, argued that the whole country has been messed up by Frelimo. She started thus:

> During colonialism things were not so difficult. We used to eat, dress and live well. You could buy a piece of cloth for 100Mt (now just enough for a cigarette). Now you need 20, 000Mt for the same piece of cloth. Life has become so difficult.
>
> Frelimo should not have fought the independence war. Where is the independence? Is suffering independence? Dhlakama will end all this. He will bring back the Portuguese (who have money for investment).

She was supported by her 26 year old daughter, the first born in a family of six, and also separated from her husband. She suddenly got into some kind of instant frenzied propaganda campaign for Renamo. She declared (several times): "Dhlakama is the best!", and that, as another man had put it earlier in Beira: "Matsanga will win". Furious and shaking with anger, her brother, then an unemployed twenty-four year old young man, replied:

> You are mad. You are talking nonsense. Dhlakama is *malandro* (rogue). *Muito mal* (He is bad and evil). He has caused so much misery and deaths. It is the destructiveness of 'his' war that has caused the shortages and the rise in cost of living.

At that point his mother interjected: "What caused the war?", implying that it was deteriorating living conditions that sparked off and fuelled the war in the first place. The egg and chicken question of what caused the other, the war or the economic crisis, they are locked in has dogged and divided scholars and local and international officialdom alike.

The debate continued, but their opposed positions could not be reconciled as the son went on to attack Dhlakama accusing him of fighting for parochial personal ambition:

150

This is what lazy and uneducated people do. When they fail to progress in life - through hard work - they seek to cause confusion and chaos.

Defending Renamo violence against civilians, the mother pointed out: "It's war (meaning it was unavoidable or inevitable). When a witch enters into a house what does he do?", to which she replied herself, "he kills a child (not the parents) in order to grieve the parents. [It hurts most that way]".[22] Similarly, Renamo, the witch in this analogue, kills children (ordinary people) to hurt the father, Frelimo.

Some see nothing much to admire in either Frelimo or Renamo or their leaders, and give a more balanced perspective. For example, a secondary school leaver unemployed youth from Dombe pointed out: "Both Frelimo and Renamo *querro comer* (want to eat)". For him, as for many others, both these parties are instruments of political entrepreneurs who have chosen to militarise their factional struggle. Yet some, like the extremely frustrated youth who had served in the army, went even further to make rather unwarranted assertions such as: "Real good rule is impossible because we are all Black... I have not yet seen anyone well able to rule the country - from Machel, Chissano and Dhlakama himself". Clearly, a deep-rooted distrust and contempt of politicians as scheming men bent on fulfilling their parochial interests, and the consequent resentment of the state, is fast gaining ground among significant sections of the popular sector. In other words, what is unfolding is a crisis of legitimacy, in which the values of significant segments of society no longer fit with those of the hitherto dominant group.

The crisis of legitimacy

The crisis of legitimacy of the state arose following the emergence of sharp cleavages among groups which, because of the expansion of the political space, are now able to organize around different values than those previously considered to be the only acceptable ones. Once solid working social and political premises are being made obsolete by the rapid movement of events. Thus while the statue of Samora Machel in Maputo and war murals in other cities such as Chimoio still retain both heroic and triumphalist feelings, they now seem to belong to a bygone age, and are lost in the welter of contemporary discontents and scandals. Seeing life as harsh and brutal, in which only the fittest can survive, the dispossessed have made their own murals. Most of these people's murals are about love, good neighbourliness, poverty and suffering, violence and war.

Thus if the value of particular ideas and accounts of the world is to be judged against the benchmark of history rather than philosophy, then the political discourses of the dispossessed are a more important guiding narrative than the high flown phrases of the manipulative political gladiators. Sayings of the dispossessed like 'things should change', 'the unrighteous state of affairs should never have been permitted to occur', 'making the country a better place to live in', 'they (the leaders/politicians) have got so much to say', 'we want leaders who learn from the people' etc are from this viewpoint more valuable than the elites' petty factionalism and squabbles. Such critical comments are more likely to mobilise people towards some version of ethical or socially responsible action. However, in the current hysterical transitional process and struggles for political freedom, economic justice as well as power, one must make a sharp distinction between what the people say, their real organisation and real interests, between their conception of themselves and what they really are. Below we look at the methods and problems of the 'politics of the invisible', focusing mainly on primary and occupational associations.

Formal and informal participation: the politics of the 'invisible'

The disinherited of Chimoio, in refusing to submit to institutionalised violence, have had to practice an alternative politics based on practical issues. This alternative politics is manifested in the rise of localised voluntary associations which suspend sectarian and political differences in pursuit of shared aims, such as spiritual security, cultural improvement and self-help and self-repatriation initiatives. For instance, although the majority of those interviewed (65 per cent) were not actively in any organisation, 30 per cent said they were. As with the grass-roots war economy, this politics has its own organizational rules specific to it, and involves risks as well as generating tensions.

The emergent social classes - economic, political and professional elites and the dispossessed - are locked in permanent conflict, which they fight out in various ways. Only through their voluntary associations were the dispossessed able to overcome some of the difficulties that arise from the failure to form an active and coherent class. Some such social organisations are quite powerful and well organised and can exert considerable pressure on the state.

Some of the associations of traders at markets scattered all over the city, although they are primarily economic, have taken on political functions when necessary to influence the government to moderate the regulations which they see as hindering business. For example, central city market traders, who are relatively well organized (and informed about the market), have engaged in continuous discussions with the local authorities to keep the rent low - and they have often been successful.

Similarly, market traders forcibly relocated from the city centre, where they had erected a market overnight, to a site in the 'concrete city' periphery, managed to get some concessions. First, the authorities, at least some of them who saw the traders' improvised stalls of sacks and poles as a disgusting sight in the city, wanted the traders to be moved completely out of the city. As a result of the resistance of the dispossessed, this did not happen. Instead they were relocated to a place not far away from the city centre, which as evidenced by the popularity of the market, is still convenient for business. Second, the traders had to be guaranteed that they will not pay any rates (although there were fears that soon rates/rents were to be imposed) before they could move to the new site. Thus in short, though not always successful, these traders have managed to achieve small victories in their struggle for survival. In similar ways, some other voluntary associations have exerted pressure on the government and/or organized themselves.

Some youth organisations, such as that of the unemployed returnees from Cuba and former East Germany, have been able to articulate and organise their interests in a more or less coherent way. For example, these youths kept on demanding that the Provincial Labour Department find them jobs or provide them with initial capital so that they could start their own enterprises. They wrote letters and petitions to the Director, sometimes threatening chaos. Similarly, low paid primary school teachers have organised and agitated for wage increases, just as unpaid soldiers have demanded, often violently, their wages.

The military as well as well as the *Antigos Combatantes* (the War Veterans' Association), and demobilised soldiers are powerful interest groups. For example, in July 1992 the *Antigos Combatantes* managed to force the Provincial Governor to promise them immediate redress of their grievances after they had 'captured' the offices of the power supply authorities and switched off electricity for the whole city.[23] Women's organisations have also been relatively effective in articulating their interests vis-a-vis the state. For example, in the same month, members of the Mozambique Women's Association (OMM) demonstrated in the city complaining against continued deterioration of living standards and reneged government promises to redress this. Earlier in March, and in a similar enactment of the dispossessed's politics of confrontation with the state, women of Beira had taken to the streets to protest against inadequate government protection against MNR attacks.[24] These politically active organisations were creations of the state. As such, though they seem to have attained an autonomy of some kind, their actions have to be seen in the context of a conflictual-paternalistic relationship with the state.

There have also been a wave of strikes in the Province, against low wages but mainly for unpaid wages. An extreme case was that of the workers at a chicken farm near Chimoio who threatened to remove the roofing of the firm's buildings if their demands were not met. In the present strategic conjuncture, the workers, not only in Mozambique, but world-wide have suffered a major drawback. In the case of Mozambican workers, lacking experience in democratic practice, they have been unable to take advantage of the opening up in political space to organize and defend their interests. The following example of a failed 'uprising' by workers at one of the Chimoio city hotels illustrates this point.

Workers at Flor de Volga hotel are among the most underpaid, earning 40, 000Mt (about 8 pounds on the black market) a month, which is an equivalent of five meals at the hotel or just two nights in an inadequately furnished room. Sometime in February 1992 the workers held a meeting in which they discussed their poor wages and working conditions, especially the resented 48 hours on duty. They agreed to have these grievances redressed, but the problem arose when it came to confronting the management about this. Out of the twenty eight workers, less than twelve finally confronted the management, which in turn, as the others had feared, threatened them with dismissal. The pay was not raised. For workers employed by small petty-traders, the situation is much worse, and as the market is saturated with unemployed youth the employers can almost arbitrarily set the wages and the terms of employment.

But in such circumstances, the workers, and the disinherited population in general, engage in what might be called the 'politics of the invisible'. As George Orwell pointed out in 1948, "in a world dominated by the powerful, the weak (must) break the rules or perish".[25] Indeed at the above hotel, and in many similar situations, the poor did break the rules to survive. Workers helped themselves generously to hotel food, which they took home to feed their families. They also did laundry for clients for a payment. One worker even went to the extent of letting in clients, at concessional prices, without giving them receipts and pocketing the money.[26] Many other people in similar situations have used such individual strategies as well.

In other words, in the context of a declining formal economy, spontaneity provided a crucial safety valve for frustration; it created employment and the ethics that have developed with it legitimate the emerging *inequality* and thus defuse the development of a revolutionary consciousness. As argued in the previous Chapter, the grass-roots war-economy provided elites with unprecedented opportunities for wealth accumulation.

For example, and also reflecting the ways in which this group's Western values are transmitted to the dispossessed, owners of TVs and videos, especially returnees from former East Germany, are making a big killing on the children of tribulation by charging them to see Western videos. Even beggars, like Agy, a seven year old beggar who lives on the street but tries hard to find money to attend these video sessions, have been subjected to these values and norms. Although living in world apart materially, the lives of the elites and the dispossessed are inextricably interlinked, and their changing political perspective influence each other.

Like the dispossessed, the elites are not an homogeneous group, and their allegiance to either Frelimo or Renamo is also varied. Not surprisingly, it is from the frustrated elements of this class that the most vocal criticism and open opposition of both Frelimo and Renamo has come. Within the last few years various factionalist parties, now numbering nearly two dozen, have emerged from this social category making equal claims to adherence to democracy. But ground underfoot by the social system of which it is a part, and detached from the mass of its followers, most of the new political parties created by this group appear to be of no consequence.

The picture is complicated by the existence of another 'third force', the international agencies and their personnel. International agencies, bilateral and NGOs have exacerbated the process of class formation through creating a class of pampered technocrats in the relief and reconstruction industry. This has resulted in friction and competition for status between these new 'assimilados' and the political elites as well as the commercial class. Some of the NGOs, such as the Marforga Mission in Gondola which is said to be operating without government permission (see next chapter), are openly hostile to the government.

Generally, although there have been attempts to develop an understanding between the government and the NGOs, suspicion, mistrust and even contempt still remain a major feature of their tenuous relationship. As Hanlon[27] shows, the government has reason to mistrust the NGOs and to argue, as some Chimoio officials did, that the NGOs are undermining its capacity. On the one hand, as the Redd Barna and Italian Cooperation officials in Chimoio pointed out, the NGOs complain of government inefficiency, bureaucratic red tape and corruption. A Roman Catholic sister also remarked: "They like confusion, because it offers them opportunities for corruption". In a similar vein a UN official attacked Frelimo and Machel in particular thus: "The Mozambicans did not deserve him (Samora Machel). They don't deserve this".

In short, in no period do we therefore find a more intense 'war of words' characterised by a confused mixture of high-flown phrases and innuendo, actual uncertainty and clumsiness, enthusiastic striving for innovation and deeply-rooted domination of the old routine, and of apparent harmony of the whole of society and profound estrangements of its elements. In this transitional confusion or 'the Mozambique national confusion' in the words of a young Mozambican journalist, some revel in their vision of the wide prospects that change has opened before them and engage in serious business of wealth accumulation, while others reflect on their misfortunes and miseries and yearn for the by-gone golden days.[28] Yet others still lament that this unrighteous state of affairs should never have been permitted to occur. What is unfolding is therefore a crisis of legitimacy, in which the values of significant segments of society no longer fit with those of the hitherto dominant groups.

Summary and conclusion

Implicit from the foregoing, a number of variables determined people's perspectives on many issues. The major variables included peoples' experience of the war, education (which is related to social status), sex, age and exposure to the outside world (through working abroad or neighbouring country, living in urban areas or access to the media - mainly a radio), and even ethnic background. As one of my research guides pointed out, "not all people had the same experience of Portuguese repression nor of the independence war", and of the recently ended war. Some have been impoverished by the war, while others have gained from it, and this has shaped their attitudes.

The formerly privileged yearn for the good old days, while the poor realize that the old days were as bad - if not worse - because revolutions do not occur in a paradise and yet others still see no difference between the present and the past as both has suffering as their major feature. A brilliant young Mozambican journalist cynically characterised this situation as, "Mozambique national confusion". In fact, *confucao* (confusion) - like *corrupcao* corruption) - as they call it, has become a popular theme in everyday social discourses.

The existence of divergent even contradictory perspectives among people belonging to the same broad social group shows that, while classes and class struggle constitute the main force behind change, similar class position does not necessarily entail similar social identity. Although people are aware that society is changing and is divided into groups that would not converge, they still feel part of the same society. Life in the various associations - religious, mutual self-help - people joined could be richly satisfying, but in ways that inhibited rather than promoted class conflict. Groups and classes live and let live, in some kind of love-hate relationship.

The networks of subordination, manifest in paternalism and patron clientelism, have, 'cross cutting classes', muted the development of class consciousness, and hence the persistent disorganisation of the under-classes. Consequently, class identity and class conflict, were less important to many. Instead it was the more traditional notion of 'the people', who, in a curious paradox, thought of themselves and their society in so diverse and different ways.

The developing divergent conceptions of the family, society and politics, and the appearance of new subjects, new collective identities, has enlarged the sphere for the operation of politics, and new constituencies for change. But these have not been easy to organise into any single and cohesive political will. The very proliferation of new sites of social antagonism "makes the prospect of constructing a unified counter-hegemonic force as the agency of progressive change, if anything harder rather easier".[29]

Consequently, there is no coherent political or ideological position binding either the under-classes or the new elites. Rather, there is a haphazard assortment of ideas, both progressive and retrogressive, parochial and insightful, shared by most. The disinherited, like the new elites, do not have a single voice. For some, the war has been violent and creative. Yet for others, it has been a pointless and bloody carnage which has given rise to anarchy and even repression. Amongst others still, it has inspired dire prophetism and religious revivalism (see next chapter). In short, we have before us a contradictory situation in which what constitutes the basis for high hopes and a (perceived) bright future for some, simultaneously heralds a dark era for those who now languish in nostalgia for the golden bygone days or are simply fatalistic. Some see themselves as active agents of history challenging the status quo, while others have simply resigned to 'follow your leader', 'we are the ruled', 'the leaders know' attitudes. This diversity of the realm of ideas and values shows the dispossessed have no single voice; giving voice to the 'voiceless', therefore requires a greater degree of openness, sensitivity and respect for views that might not necessarily coincide with one's own.

In conclusion, the unfolding transitional processes have therefore no necessary and inevitable political trajectory already inscribed in it. The political future remains undecided, open-ended. The collapse of the ideology of authoritarian populism - 'regressive modernisation' - which had underpinned the development strategy since Independence has been accompanied by the displacement of the old party elite (non-reformers, to be specific) from its position of economic dominance and civic leadership by a generation of unrestrained entrepreneurs, and the 'new *assimilados*'. The disinherited, marginalised from public and institutional life, have withdrawn from covert politics and engaged instead in an 'alternative politics' of the invisible. This 'alternative politics', one of the few positive 'unintended social consequence of war', reminds us that history is neither God-given nor predetermined but is there to be actively made and remade in a process of collective struggle by men and women.

Notes

1. Margaret Peil, *Nigerian Politics: The People's View*, London, Cassell, 1978 p. 1.

2. Cited in A.R. Zolberg , *Creating Political Order: The Party-states of West Africa*, Chicago, Rand McNally and Company, 1966. p. 145, by Ibid. p. 1.

3. Cited in Max Weber, *The Methodology of the Social Sciences*, Glencoe iii, The Free press, 1949 pp. 182-185, by Seymour M. Lipset, *Revolution and Counterrevolution*, Oxford, Transaction Books, 1988, p. 21.

4. Fredrick Engels, "Letter to Bloch, Karl Marx and Fredrick engels, *Selected Works*, Moscow, Progress Publishers, 1985, p. 682.

5. Interview in Chimoio

6. Peter Worsley, *The Three Worlds: Culture and World Development*, London, Weidenfeld and Nicolson, 1984, p. 215.

7. Bairro Pedaco was chosen because, though not the largest, it was comprised mainly of 'newcomers' to the city who had abandoned their homes due to war. The largest *bairros* such as Bairro Cinco and Bairro Sete de Abril were extensions of *bairros* that already existed before the war, and as such some of their residents had not been displaced from their homes by the war.

8. One old man received us thus: "You are God's messengers. If I don't welcome you I would have rejected God". Insisting that we have some food at his place he said, "What I eat is what you eat (meaning we must share the little he had). If you refuse, I would not have sinned". Interview Chimoio, Bairro Pedaco.

9. Stephanie Urdang, *And Still They Dance: Women, War and the Struggle for Change in Mozambique*, London, Earthscan, 1989. This book, and the reality of the situation it depicts, in part, inspired me to form DANDARO Frontline Vibes, which through sound power, seeks to explore to the fullest the dialectical mix of music and dance, entertainment and education, emotion and motion as a way of re-charging afflicted communities, *riddimwize*.

10. In Namibia and North Ireland violence has also been regenerative in some ways. Comment by Patricia Hayes, Research Fellow, Cambridge University.

11. Many cartoonists, musicians and poets have depicted the violence of war in their works in different ways. See among others, Chris Searle, *The Sunflower of Hope: Poems from the Mozambican Revolution,* London, Allison and Busby, 1982, and L. Magaia, *Dumba Negue: Run for Your Life, Peasant Tales of Tragedy in Mozambique,* Africa World Press, USA, 1983.

12. This is an interesting area of research. In our random sample there was one divorced Christian man who cited violence as the reason for separation.

13. We almost got into trouble ourselves with the man when we tried to convince him to resolve their dispute peacefully.

14. A chat with Peter Fry, an experienced researcher on Mozambique, in Harare, September 1992.

15. Africa Watch, *Conspicuous Destruction: War, Famine and the Reform Process in Mozambique,* London, Human Rights Watch, 1992.

16. Many people, largely because of fear of dangers, simply said they did not know the cause of the war, and did not want comment on whether anyone was to blame.

17. It was only after (a known) passer-by read our credencial (credentials) and re-explained who were that she finally agreed to talk.

18. According to United Nations Report, US$13 million will be needed to clear the mines in Mozambique, "United Nations Presents", *Zimbabwe Television* (ZTV), 25 June 1994.

19. For a discussion of the notion of 'the politics of the belly', see Jean-Francois Bayart, *The State in Africa: The Politics of the Belly*, London, Longman, 1983. The 'politics of the belly' is indeed a universal phenomenon in capitalist societies where rituals of extravagant consumption, for example in formal halls, high table, parties etc, is the norm.

20. Interview in Maputo, March 1992.

21. Interview in Maputo, March 1992.

22. The analogy here is that Renamo attacks civilians (the child) to prove the weakness of the government (parents) in protecting the people.

23. The city was cut off from electricity until quite late in the night (about 10:00 pm.).

24. During this period there was a spate of killings in the margins of the city of Beira.

25. See George Orwell, *Nineteen Eighty Four*, London, Harbour Publishing, 1960.

26. At the time I left he was in prison for this crime. Apparently he was 'sold-out' by his colleagues.

27. Joseph Hanlon, *Mozambique: Who Calls the Shots?*, London, James and Currey, 1991.

28. It can be note here that the end of the war has also changed the fortunes of many. For example, Zimbabwean traders who had capitalised on the crisis suddenly found themselves with no business as Mozambicans became increasingly self-sufficient. Similarly, some private aircraft companies which had provided air taxi services are increasingly finding it difficult to break-even since the opening of some roads which were unusable during the war.

29. Stuart Hall and Martin (editors), *New Times: The Changing Face of Politics in the 1990s*, London, Lawrence and Wishart, 1989, p.17.

5 Religion, war and politics: Religious ideology and power in a changing society

Introduction: Religious practice and analysis as a contested terrain

Hand in hand with the changes in economic organisation and political power configuration documented in the previous chapters, there has been a marked resurgence in religious revivalism. In Manica Province this religious activism has taken the form of neo-traditional worship[1], Catholicism and Pentecostal Protestantism all co-existing in competition and synergy with one another. The phenomenon of religious conversion and belief is not unique to Mozambique, but is occurring "on a grand scale ...in Africa and ... throughout the world'.[2] In the literature the significance of this religious revivalism in the context of economic crisis, social breakdown, and war in the case of Mozambique has been interpreted in widely different ways.

According to Ranger,[3] the earlier approaches of the mid 1950s attempted to portray African religious movements as a precursor to anti-colonial nationalism.[4] Few of these hypotheses stood the test of the time as religious movements continued to proliferate in the post-colonial era.[5] This prompted a re-thinking of the politico-religious interface. There was a shift from the earlier position that churches arose particularly in zones of intensive colonial oppression to an attempt to understand them "as responses to cultural and psychological tensions and not as expressions of political antagonism".[6] But, as Ranger notes, these attempts to depict religious activism in Africa as either "purer than or inferior to political activity are no more convincing, however, than previous notions that they were essentially part of the sequence of anti-colonial nationalism".[7] Too sharp a distinction is drawn between cultural and political, symbolic and instrumental, "a false dichotomy ...which has serious consequences for research".[8]   The 'fresh approaches' have therefore been not as much concerned about *whether* the African religious movements were 'political', as with what *form* their religious and political activity took.[9] For

161

example, with specific reference to the spread of Christian fundamentalism in Africa, Gifford argues that it does not act as a spur to Africa's development: "On the contrary, it leads its adherents to downplay the importance of development, to dismiss it as irrelevant, or even positively to turn their backs on it".[10] On the basis of research on 'born-again' Christians in Nigeria, Marshall arrives at a radically different conclusion: religious conversion is "experienced as a liberating and empowering personal re-birth, and ... the new spiritual power possessed by the born again individual cannot be disassociated from the 'practical' power to transform his/her social and economic world".[11]

In Southern Africa in general religious activism has been seen as a powerful political force in the transformative process unfolding in these societies.[12] In *Guns and Rain*, Lan has demonstrated the role of 'traditional' religion in Zimbabwe's guerrilla war.[13] Commenting on the 're-treat to neo-traditionalism' in Manica Province in Mozambique Roesch argues that:

> ... people in Mozambique use religious discourses to explain their current problems and situations, and ... in doing so they mystify the economic and political forces that have shaped their current reality. While such mystification may serve reactionary political objectives, it does not do so necessarily... In the Mozambican case, however, such religious mystifications do often serve the reactionary objectives of 'traditional' political authorities who oppose democracy, defend hereditary authority and are concerned to re-instate their lost political powers and economic privileges.[14]

As is clear from these divergent positions, the relationship between religion and politics is a complex one. The complexity partly derives from the wide range of social meanings carried by religious movements and their multiple significance in different phases and in different times.

This complexity and ambiguity demands that the subject be approached with fear and respect; fear of being unable to render adequately the whole rich complexity of this social and cultural life, and respect towards what so many have built up, lived with and suffered from and loved. Whether true or false consciousness, religious belief needs to be treated seriously. What people believe in does matter for "it is the beliefs themselves which provide the means whereby people negotiate the personal, social and political conditions they experience and through which they may even be empowered".[15]

This chapter seeks to identify the specific social conditions that make groups give to their historical situation a religious interpretation. It will not deal with the internal organization of power in the religious movements nor with their institutional structures. To seek to cover them in one chapter would be to risk a mere listing. The emphasis will instead be on the changing relationship between religion and politics, and in particular the role of religion in overcoming tensions that arise from social change. It will be argued that in Chimoio religious activism has simultaneously contained a potentiality of protest as well as of conservatism. Thus the extent to which religion is or is not a political force for change is issue specific and cannot be ascertained *a priori*. The task is therefore to identify and disentangle the nature of the forces at work in shaping the way in which people position themselves religiously.

The chapter is divided into four broad sections. The first section briefly deals with the relationship between religion and politics in the pre-colonial, colonial and post-colonial periods, emphasising the changing nature of the relationship. The second is an inquiry into the reasons for conversion, and addresses the interrelated questions of 'why' people are converting, 'what' they are converting from and 'what' they do when they convert. The third section examines the political practices of a few selected religious groups, highlighting their implications for the contested state civil-society relationships. The final section summarizes and ties together issues raised in the discussion.

Religious ideology and power in pre-colonial societies

Centuries before the arrival of Christianity in Southern Africa, African traditional religions[16] often constituted a very important force in society. They exercised a strong influence on the educational, medical, cultural, economic, social and political spheres. The political domain, as Jules-Rosette notes, "has traditionally been defined and reinforced by sacred symbols and beliefs that are fundamental to the communities involved".[17] In the Shona pre-colonial political systems of present day eastern Zimbabwe and central western Mozambique, religion was, in fact, the major "integrative factor"[18]; it had the crucial role of sustaining and maintaining the individual and society.

Though there was a degree of cultural heterogeneity and variation in the way power was constituted among the Shona 'clusters' of Manyika, Ndau, Tewe and Barwe, it was difficult to draw a line between the religious sphere and these other areas of life in these societies. Religion, military forces and foreign relations were the three most important facets of the state which had to be carefully handled by the chiefdoms, for each had the potential to destabilize the state. In the Barwe community before and during the uprising of 1917, for instance, the spirit medium exercised great influence on the chief and society.[19] In the Shona rebellion of 1896, the spirit mediums themselves organised armies and led them into the attack on the Portuguese.[20]

The structure of religious meanings was constructed as homologous to the social and political structure, with the former giving expression to the latter. The religious hierarchy reproduced the earthly power structure, and it was based on the concept of a High God/Supreme Being (*Mwari, Musiki* or *Murungu*) and its concomitant practice of ancestor veneration. At the apex of the religious hierarchy was the Supreme Being, considered a deity, that is a supernatural being from whom one expects spiritual and material benefits. Below him were the ancestors, the spirits of the deceased who were not Gods themselves but were believed to be in *kumatenga* (heaven), and to directly communicate with God. Represented by popular belief as an immanent presence, the ancestors were consulted, primarily through the chief and religious advisers (usually possessed by the royal spirits), in times of crisis, famine and war.

Next in line were the evil spirits or demons (the avenging spirits of the grieved deceased, variously referred to as *chikwambo, ngozi* or *mfukwa*), whose souls, either because of their evil deeds while still alive or because of their 'anger' at some injustice, roam in the wilderness. These malevolent spirits of sinful or grieved ancestors were the cause of many evils - as punishment - such as spirit possession, and sometimes induced illness or even death if their demands were not met. Nevertheless, they needed the living (to perform the appeasement rituals) and the living (especially the family of the grieved spirit who would get compensation from the families of the accused) needed them too. Recourse was usually taken to the *n'anga* (traditional healers) or the spirit mediums in dealing with these 'restless' spirits. This moral scale included not only the deities, but also the sum total of all living beings since each one occupied a special position in this temporal/spiritual space.

Interlocking the heavenly/spiritual with the temporal/earthly hierarchy were the chief and spirit mediums. The latter had the power of rain-making (through performance of certain rituals) and performed religious ceremonies, which were an expression of social relations underpinned by religious meanings. These ceremonies made the status quo seem natural and right, and consequently ensured its perpetuation. Next in line were the chief's lieutenants, the royal council, traditional healers and kraal heads, whom the chief consulted and to whom he delegated some of his functions at a local

164

level. At the base of the pyramid, were the ordinary people bound to the political aristocracy both by links of economic interdependence and by religious ideology.

This hierarchy was, however, not rigid and fixed. Instead, there was group mobility, and this was largely mediated by the vicissitudes of wars with neighbouring kingdoms. Also, the king could enjoy absolute powers only in theory: in practice he could be autocratic only so long as he retained the consent of the people. As Bhila comments with respect to the Manyika:

> His [the king's] reliance on the kinship network for running his kingdom effectively checked his powers. The king could not afford to defy or ignore the wishes of his people.[21]

Thus, while entrenching the dominant power structures, religion also provided a check against arbitrary use of power by chiefs. In fact, in some instances religion did indeed provide the basis for revolt especially when there were disputes on succession/ascendence to the throne.

Traditional religion, revolt and change

Traditional religion and spiritual authorities, as was to be the case later with Renamo and Zimbabwean guerrillas[22], played a crucial role in inspiring and co-ordinating anti-colonial resistance. According to Ranger, the Makombe revolt of 1917 was "initiated by the traditional religious and secular authorities".[23] Also the fact that the rebellion broke out in Barwe "was as much due to the greater strength there of traditional institutions as to special grievances of the WaBarwe".[24] Some revolts within the kingdoms were inspired and guided by such religious agents.

One illustrative example is the case of Chief Kanda's accession to the chieftaincy in Gorongossa district in the mid nineteenth century.[25] According to his grandchild, Chief Kanda settled in Gorongosa in 1860 having come from Manyika[26] (in the western frontier with Zimbabwe, in present day Manica district of Manica Province). When Kanda arrived in the area, "searching for greener pastures, people were not sleeping in their huts for fear of wild animals - hyenas, lions etc - which were preying on their animal stock and human beings".[27] As bearer of a spirit medium and with supernatural powers, he performed some rituals to appease the ancestors who had set loose the animals. He also concocted some magic which 'weakened' the animals and stopped them from eating people. Suddenly he became popular with the people, who became his religious followers and whom he provided with healing and 'vaccination'. Since part of the (or his) explanation for the anomaly was that the incumbent chief had erred in his religious duties, he was automatically made chief and religious leader of the chiefdom.[28] Since then his descendants constituted the dynasty that ruled the chiefdom until Independence in 1975. Religion thus offered, as now, different groups the necessary means and religious/moral basis for opposing domination and control.

To recapitulate, the chief was, in the moral sense, seen to occupy the intermediate position between God(s) and the living. But since the political and economic system was based on dominant/dominated power relations, unequal access to land, and tribute exchange relations, it was the whole structure of power, of which everyone formed a part, which was sanctified and legitimated by religion. Inevitably, therefore, the implantation of Christianity transformed the structural elements and the relations established between religion and politics; it also offered opportunities to social groups marginalised in the traditional system to 'reinvent' their future.

The implantation of christianity and its impact on traditional religion and politics

Christianity arrived in Mozambique in the sixteenth century. It was not the first alien religion to appear in the country. Several centuries before Islam had been introduced by Arab traders, mainly in the northern provinces of Niassa and Nampula. Since in central and western Mozambique Islam was never effectively established among the indigenes, our focus will therefore be limited to the relationship between Christianity and traditional religion.

There was, and still is, a vast variety of Christian Churches and movements that have emerged at different times in history. Their relations have been characterised by rivalry, competition and conflict. For example, as early as the 1880s the Catholic Church and the Protestant missionaries in southern Mozambique (Inhambane) were already locked in an intense rivalry, characterised by innuendo, spiteful and sarcastic remarks directed by each to the other.[29] As in other parts of Southern and Central Africa, independent churches offered another opportunity for workers and peasants to vent their hostility against the traditional hegemonic structures, the colonial order and the hypocrisy of the established Christian churches. Virtually all independent churches traced their origins to the separatist church movements (Zionist and Ethiopian) in neighbouring South Africa and Southern Rhodesia.

However, unlike now when most of the alien religions are brought by foreign missionaries and religious crusaders, then the Mozambican migrant workers themselves were central in the construction of a new religious discourse; in the neighbouring countries they found refuge in churches, and when they returned home, they either organized branches or formed autonomous sects modeled after their South African and Southern Rhodesian counterparts.[30]

The state, traditional religion and christianity

Christianity, as it manifested itself in Mozambique, was a religion of conquest. Catholicism was the official religion of the state and the state's ideology was manifestly religious. The strong connection between the political and religious systems manifested itself on the plane of symbolic function and on that of organization. On one level the missionaries (Catholics in particular) sanctified the colonial state's conquest and subjugation of the indigenes, and on another the state exercised jurisdiction over the religious institution, ensuring it political protection. The missionaries built schools to train a submissive technocratic stratum to run the state apparatus. There were, however, tensions and conflicts between the state and the Church emanating from different priorities and the struggle for hegemony.

The tensions arose precisely because colonial rule in Mozambique was based on two irreconcilable ideologies. On the one hand it depended on Christianity which saw its mission as freeing Africans from the bonds of superstition and mysticism, and on the other on traditional religion which gave authority to the chiefs in the system of rule. The ideology of the colonial state was therefore profoundly ambiguous: simultaneously encouraging the locals to perform their traditional rituals and also supporting the Christianity which sought to suppress these religions.

The attempt to suppress traditional religious rituals and beliefs led to clashes with chiefs whose authority rested partly on their control of these rituals. Thus to enhance the image and legitimacy of their newly appointed *regulos* (chiefs), and colonial rule, the Portuguese went to great lengths in supporting and participating in African traditional rituals of succession. For example, according to folklore, throughout the colonial era the Portuguese authorities in Chimoio generously assisted in the yearly traditional ritual ceremonies performed on top of the then sacred mount Cabeca de Velho, situated a few kilometres north-west of Chimoio city. Similarly in Barwe the Portuguese participated in the social custom of baptizing the chief with *madzimanga* (holy water), which was brought from Sena by a Portuguese official.[31]

African traditional religions were therefore not completely destroyed. Instead they were a factor in defining that transformation. Their transformation was accompanied by the 'Africanisation of European institutions'. Also the relations between the religious, the political and the economic fields remained intact. By the time of Independence traditional religion was still a force sustaining the organization of economic and political power in the countryside.

Neo-traditional religions, christianity and the post-colonial state

Since Independence, the relationship between the state, traditional religions and the church have been sensitive. There has been a particular mistrust of the traditional religions and the Catholic Church, both because of their close relation with the colonial state in the past, and because of their ambivalence towards the rebels. The confiscation of Church property as part of the nationalisation drive led to tensions between the clergy and the state. Finally, the dissemination of much misleading propaganda about restrictions on religious freedom further complicated the situation.[32]

In principle, Frelimo's position was that religion is a private matter. In reality, however, unlike the Zimbabwean guerrillas who (interestingly like Renamo) relied heavily on traditional spirit mediums in their war of independence, Frelimo's socialist programme did not naturally accommodate traditional or Christian religions; traditional religions were dogged by 'feudal obscurantism'; Christianity by its disarming philosophy underpinned conquest and subjugation. According to Fry, "almost all that was 'traditional' was to be suppressed under such slogans as *Abaixo o feudalismo, Abaixo o obscurantismo* [Down with feudalism, Down with obscurantist ideas]".[33] In particular, Frelimo opposed spirit possession, exorcism by traditional healers and those practices which perpetuated the idea of the chief's greatness. These were opposed in the context of communal villages; what peasants chose to do outside of the villages in the bush was of less concern. Ceremonies in honour of family ancestor spirits were not repressed.

Geffray finds, with respect to Nampula, that the uncompromising approach to traditional religion and institutions was a major incentive for the local population to turn its back on the Frelimo state.[34] According to some frustrated Christian leaders Christian worship was also suppressed, Church property was confiscated and many Christian leaders were persecuted and sent to detention camps, euphemistically dubbed re-education centres.[35] The point is, whether or not these allegations are true, the state has generally been viewed as anti-religious. Thus one often heard angry outbursts like: "You [the authorities] who used to say *abaixo Deus* (Down with God), make the rain fall".[36]

More important, there were significant regional differences in the way the state dealt with both organised and individual religious practices. This was due, as Otto observes:

not only to differences of opinion amongst the leadership on this question, but also due to the fact that the local Frelimo officials responsible for implementing government policies were usually themselves peasants, who were often reluctant to enforce central government directives against fellow peasants.[37]

Consequently, repression of religious practices varied in degree and kind from one part of the country to the other. Thus, for instance, in the Lower Limpopo River Valley some people's homes inside communal villages functioned as churches, with most local authorities choosing to ignore such practices.[38] Similarly, although organized Christian services were banned inside communal villages, people were often free to build churches and to worship outside the villages.

Thus, notwithstanding the Frelimo state's high-handed attitude to religious worship, religious belief and even practice, were never eradicated; it simply went underground. When Renamo appeared on the stage, claiming to be fighting a 'war of the spirits' for religious freedom, what had been forced underground re-emerged with a vengeance that has dazzled even the Mozambicans themselves. This is aptly captured by a common remark among many a Chimoio denizen: "*Machechi acho azowandisa. Mamwe acho ndeekunyepera*" (There are too many new churches. Some of them are false [prophets]). Indeed there has been a remarkable religious resurgence in political activism, manifested in the proliferation of churches and 'places of religious worship' in the peri-urban slums of Chimoio.

War, religion and politics

Renamo has elevated traditional religion and Christianity in its war to win the 'minds' of the people. It has used spiritual symbols and mediums and has distributed bibles to its combatants[39], as well as encouraged them to attend sermons in the bush. The practice of leaving churches and mosques untouched amidst the wreckage of a town as an integral element of its mobilizational strategy has added a political dimension to religion as a social force. This, combined with the invasion of the country by western Pentecostal Churches, and the liberalization of the economy, is the immediate background from which the adherence or non-adherence to religious ideas has to be understood.

The data presented in this section were gathered through a combination of interrelated research methods.[40] These included: opinion survey on religious beliefs and practices; questioning believers (and non-believers) on their religious histories and the basis of their religious orientations; interviews with religious leaders or agents; and critical participant observation in the form of attending religious services and sermons. However there were a number of constraints encountered in the gathering of the data which warrant that its results be interpreted with caution.

One difficulty was in drawing a clear line between 'past' and 'present' religious affiliation or orientation. For instance, some interviewees' affiliation to a particular religious denomination was merely passive. Particular examples being those who said they were religious simply because they were born into a religious family. Some had moved (and are moving) between so many religious denominations that they could not remember the dates of conversion from one to another nor the number of religious groups they had been members of. For simplicity, in this analysis the term 'past' refers to the decade before the date of the interview (that is, the period before 1982), and the results given below should only give a rough impression of the trends and tendencies.

Contrary to appearances of an increase in the proportion of religious believers, actually there has been an overall decrease. For example, out of the 72 people (admittedly a narrow base to generalise from) interviewed on their present and past religious affiliation, 20 per cent consider themselves atheists, as compared to 12.5 per cent who had been atheists in the past. The corresponding figures for neo-traditionalists and Roman Catholics has been a decline from 25 per cent to 17.5 per cent and 15 per cent to 10 per cent respectively. This partly reflects Frelimo's success in secularising society and establishing a scientific outlook, and partly the effects of urbanisation and cosmopolitanisation, both compounded by the war.

While neo-traditionalist and Catholic membership is declining, that of Protestant churches has risen from about 30 per cent to 35 per cent. The more public profile and activism of the latter seem to be responsible for the apparent, but misleading, impression that there are now more believers than before. What appears to be happening is that, although a larger proportion of those who have abandoned Catholicism and neo-traditionalism have become atheist, many people still consider themselves to be believers. Most have joined Protestant Churches. Thus though there has been a small overall change in the population of people who consider themselves believers, there has been substantial movement within the religious movement itself, with many changing from one denomination to another with amazing rapidity.

Another interesting trend to emerge was that people belonging to the same social groups and facing the same social situation, have adopted different, and even conflicting, religious orientations. This diversity of religious responses and beliefs gives rise to a number of questions: What has led these people to make the religious choices they made, whose consequences on themselves and their social milieu they have little control of? Why have they adopted radically different approaches as a way out of the crisis? Finally, what is distinctive about Protestantism which has led it to attract more followers than its rivals?

Age, class and gender in religious orientation

There appears to be a correlation between religion and age, class and gender. At the risk of over-simplification, the aged seem to be still worshipping traditional religion. The decline in the proportion of neo-traditionalists seems to reflect the changes in the population structure, which is now largely youthful. The bulk of the membership of the locally based religious groups comes from the poorest social strata. That of the Roman Catholic consists of the relatively well-off, those who can still afford to have wedding ceremonies and to buy fashionable clothes for Sunday services. The decline in its membership, in particular the rise in that of Protestantism and atheism, perhaps reflects rising poverty. Most of the atheists are relatively educated and wealthy young men, some of whom have been outside the country. Conversely, the bulk of the believers are poor women, especially in locally based religious movements or certain Western based ones which are involved in channelling and distributing food aid, a and a significant proportion of whom have children but no stable partner. In virtually all religious groups women predominate numerically. What then are the 'distinctive' opportunities or possibilities that churches might be offering to women, and not to men?

Women and christianity

Most religious doctrines advocate the submission of women to men and their confinement to the domestic sphere. Logically, women would have little reason to join these religious movements which protect the status quo. Contrary to this logic, however, women have vigorously protected certain elements of doctrine and the distinct, though perhaps somewhat contradictory opportunities these create. It seems the key to understanding this counter-intuitive reality, as Lehmann suggests, lies in inquiring "into the relationship between what happens to and with women inside the Church and what happens to them outside, in their homes and at work".[41]

As elsewhere in Africa, it is particularly in the sphere of marriage, family and sexuality that one finds Christian doctrine and practice not only transforming the position of women quite dramatically, but doing so in ways that are highly attractive to young urban women.[42] Strong religious commitment provides women, especially younger women, with strategies for escaping the all too pervasive phenomenon of being forced to exchange sexual favours for things which they feel, and which society promises, should be theirs by merit. The condemnation of adultery and fornication as sin for either gender, for instance, offers women the possibility of a stable marriage. This is one of the most strongly emphasised aspects of living a 'Christian life' and, as Marshall notes, "although it may be one of the least adhered to, the mere fact that it has such prominence in the discourse constitutes a powerful resource in the hands of women."[43] In the context of family break-down, the rise in prostitution and the epidemic of AIDS, the stress on marital fidelity is radical. There is a great deal of discussion in popular discourse that if one wants a 'steady' spouse, the church is the place to find one (see the case of Maforga Mission below).

The way in which marriage and the family is viewed by these churches demonstrates striking innovations which hold distinct advantages for women. First, it is the nuclear family and not the extended family which is emphasised. This undermines the authority of the in-laws over married women. Although the woman is subordinate to the authority of her husband in the home, it is clear that he has an obligation to respect her and treat her with consideration. Emphasising equality in a Christian marriage, a pastor in *Ijreja Evanjelica Cristo* (Jesus Lives Evangelic Church) put it thus: "Woman was created neither from man's head nor feet, but from his side. She is therefore neither above nor below, but equal to man". Such religious teaching can offer women an opportunity to construct a space in which they can move with relative freedom and dignity. It allows them to gain a measure of control over their sexual and family lives, and "from there use their positions to gain more influence in the sphere of labour outside the home".[44] The remarkable religious conversion of women, as shown below, is therefore neither 'false consciousness' nor merely reflective of the efficacy of 'religious marketing'. It is instead a pragmatic and rational response to a concrete situation, and an attempt to transform that situation.

The religious conversion experience

An inquiry into reasons for conversion should begin with an interrogation into why people are converting and what they are converting from. As already noted, different people have different reasons for converting. Eonomic decline, however, and the struggle for material survival forms the backdrop of the conversion experience. The disintegrations and conflicts within an urban society, catalysed by the war, and the oppressive and debilitating ways in which individuals are 'inserted' in that struggle are most significant. In a context in which the struggle for power at every level has become a 'zero-sum' game, and in which other bases of resistance in civil society are absent or repressed, religious conversion became a pragmatic act of individual and collective reconstruction; people had to wield the little power and influence they had as a matter of survival. Believers contrasted the hopelessness,

172

sinfulness and destructiveness of one's past and security, hope and empowerment belief offers in the social reconstruction project.

In addition to these socio-economic factors there is a multitude of personal, psychological and cultural factors that account for the increased *activism* of the believers. Different people have become religious for a variety of reasons ranging from the search for healing and desire for community, to fear of the 'miracles' that are happening and the felt need for redemption. The sense of guilt (for not praying in the past, for example), and the need to conquer it individually and collectively has been a major force in turning many to religious belief. To some, religious conversion has been a form of 'survival strategy', in both the purely economic and broader social senses, helping them establish useful connections and alliances. Yet for others still it has provided a rationale and explanation for their social situation. For religious elites, religious conversion has been a 'holy avenue' to the accumulation of wealth and power. Yet others still considered themselves believers simply because they were born in a religious family. The causality and effect nexus is not a straight-forward phenomenon; there is a multitude of contingent and specific personal considerations that have determined religious involvement and commitment.

The most often cited reason for converting into neo-traditionalism has been a strong belief that the present calamities are a punishment by the ancestors and spirits for abandoning and neglecting them. Illness, drought and the unnecessary blood letting are explained as an expression of wrath by the dead for not performing traditional rituals to appease and thank them (for life and protection). One typical case of such beliefs leading to conversion is that of a displaced family which had to leave the relative (material) security and safety of their refugee camp in Zimbabwe.

The family had been captured by Renamo in Barue district, had escaped and fled to Zimbabwe. But the had to leave Zimbabwe where 'life was much better' in order to perform the appropriate rituals to appease their grieved ancestors who were causing misfortune and illness to one of the family members, a daughter- in-law. According to the oldest woman in the family (and its de facto head, as women tend to gain more power and authority as they grow old - see next chapter), her mother-in-law, the ill young woman had 'hysterical fits' (epilepsy) which could not be treated at the clinic, as the nurses could not see anything wrong with her. The later consulted a *n'anga* (traditional healer) who told them that she was being haunted by the avenging spirit of her deceased grandfather, who had not been properly buried when he died (during the beginning of the war). As the old woman put it:

> The *n'anga* advised us to brew some beer, perform a traditional
> ceremony at which a sacrificial offering was made to lay the deceased's

173

spirit to rest. But the *n'anga* emphasized that all that had to be done in Mozambique, since the deceased was a Mozambican, his ancestors were in Mozambique and he had died on Mozambican soil. This is why we came back.

But the problem is not over yet; first, no-one knows exactly how to perform these ritual anymore. We last had such rituals long back - after Independence it was difficult to perform the rituals publicly. Also we are very poor, and don't have the money to buy the required items. Also, because of drought and war, we don't have the *rupoko* for brewing the beer, the animal to sacrifice nor the money to buy them.

The family believed that without doing what the traditional healer had instructed the possessed young woman would not recover. It was clear that she was mentally disturbed and spoke with considerable difficulty. Consequently they were busy trying to raise the money to perform the ritual.[45] Interestingly, the family had practised traditional religion before but had stopped, in the words of the elder women, "during the period of *abaixa o obscuntarismo* (down with confusion)".

A similar case, which reflects the power of traditional religion and its conflict with Christianity, is that of an extremely desperate couple at Matsinye resettlement camp whose life has been "ruined by the evil spirits". Paulino Adjuni was a former junior officer in the army, later a successful craftsman and recently a popular Christian leader. He was the first born in his family, and according to tradition he was supposed to perform traditional burial ceremonies at his father's death, and thereafter preside over family affairs. But having converted to Christianity soon after leaving the army, when his father died he buried him instead in the Christian way - a memorial service and prayers. Confirming the objections of some of his brothers and village elders' predictions, a few years later the avenging spirit of his father 'rose from the dead' and started haunting his family. As he puts it:

Ini zvandoionesa yatarira chaiyo. Nhamo haibvi pane imwe chokwadi. (I have really suffered many drawbacks. Problems do not want to leave me. First it was misfortune in business. My sales (of handicrafts) declined as customers refused to buy my goods. Then it was my children. Three of them got ill, and one died. Now it's my wife ... she is so ill, and she can't even walk.

We prayed and prayed, but it didn't help. Now all my brothers are blaming me and turning against me. That is why I am now trying to raise some money (by cutting firewood for sale) to consult a traditional healer, and perform the ceremonies.

174

But unlike the previous case, where the concerned had believed in traditional religion, for him traditional religion is all about evil spirits: "Once we perform these rituals, and our problems are resolved, I will go back to the Church".

In both cases, it is important to note the crucial link between the living and the dead, which is the central notion at the heart of African traditional religion and philosophy. The dead are an immanent presence, and they continue to influence the daily lives of the living. As the above cases and many others show, neglect of the dead and failure to give them due recognition caused affliction, misfortune[46] and illness - at least according to the healers and diviners. The living remember and convey respect to their past and the dead, and the latter provide protection and guidance. Thus for many, as one devout traditionalist put it: *"Hazviiti kukanganwa midzimu yedu* (It's not possible to forget our ancestors)".

More significant in its religious and political scope is the mysterious happening in Dzembe locality (in Chimoio district). According to the headman of Dzembe, Katize, strange things had occurred in his area following a violation of some sacred traditional rule by a young village man.[47] The accused young man had violated the traditional norms and practices by cutting down trees in a cemetery, a traditionally sacred place. While he was cutting down the trees a mysterious being suddenly appeared in front of him and while still dazzled, chickens started 'shooting' up from the ground. The whole community was terrified and dumbfounded by this miracle. The chief, who had been recently re-installed, sought assistance from the party. The party, owing to it's historical hostility to traditional beliefs and ideologies, was ill-equipped to handle this case, and only asked the chief to come back later. The chief was, however, advised by a former colonial policeman (who through his participation in succession ceremonies knew of the procedures to follow) to go back and collect contributions from all the villagers and prepare traditional beer. With the guidance of a traditional healer or spirit mediums, they would then hold a ceremony at which the offender would publicly repent.

A number of important points emerge from this mysterious incident. First, it is clear that the occurrence of an unnatural phenomenon beyond the comprehension of ordinary people prompted a mass recourse to tradition. The fear (of the unknown) that the incident induced among the villagers strengthened the belief in and grip of superstition and mysticism. That fear, ironically, also strengthened the power of the religious agents, the traditional chief, spirit mediums and traditional healers in particular. These alone, because of their strategic position in the politico-religious temporal/spiritual hierarchy, could offer an interpretation of, and solution to, the mystery.

One must ask how these villagers envision the sacred and the secular, and what symbolic challenge they perceive themselves as making. It seems the appeal of traditional religious belief lies in the way it successfully reduces the inexplicable to the explicable and the unfamiliar to the familiar, thereby stabilising the relationship between the individual, society and nature. It offers a meaning to life: the mysterious event is perceived to have happened because of the violation of the norms governing this relationship. As with the popular interpretations of drought, the behaviour of nature is explained in terms of (human) agency, and the unfamiliar forces of the wild are reduced to the familiar explanatory category of personal/social relations. These misdeeds of the living (agency) that cause the miracles of nature can only be re-dressed by performing the appropriate rituals.

Neo-traditional religion has provided a mechanism for effecting this reconciliation. Such changes in the religious symbolic meanings in order to cope with the crisis of a war economy stand as testimony of the dynamism of African traditional religions, contrary to a fixed quality which the term 'traditional' usually connotes. Seen from this angle, the recourse to traditional religion is therefore an innovative response to a social crisis/demand.

The second point that emerges relates to the political significance of the resurgence of traditional religions. The failure of Party officialdom to respond immediately to the incident seriously dented its legitimacy in the eyes of the local people. With Party and state elites unable to comprehend this mystery, the villagers had to resort to their own means to solve the problems of their own affairs independent of the former. To this extent, neo-traditional revival should be seen as a crucial force in the expansion of the sphere of the civil society vis-a-vis the state.

At the same time, however, traditional power seems unable to exist without alliance with either official or Renamo power (see below), or even both. In the above case for example, the chief had to go begging to the Party officialdom not only for assistance in resolving the miraculous incident, but also for food to feed his starving people. Similarly in Gaza Province, the bearer of the spirit of Mungoi had to get Party approval before starting her work on establishing a peaceful zone - to which thousands of peasants flocked - protected from Renamo atrocities.[48] Thus traditional religion, in particular its agents - spirit mediums, traditional healers, and traditional chiefs - are less an alternative source of (emancipatory?) power, than a balancing, modifying or complementary one. It is subject to its limitations and constraints from the state, but is also able to challenge the state system and, to both justify and resist Renamo violence as shown in chapter two.

To sum up, the resurgence of neo-traditionalist activism has not constituted a retreat from 'popular politics', as Roesch contends, but rather has actually strengthened traditional healers, chiefs and people in a political struggle against both the modern state and Renamo violence. Adapting to cope with new social demands, neo-traditional religion has been a potent force in the matrix of politics in Mozambique. It has played a crucial healing function, both for illness and social trauma. It has also helped people develop and accept a new set of multi-faceted concepts about the nature of the world. Finally, it has been an effective strategy for the dispossessed in negotiating for their survival amidst a vicious war.

Nonetheless, it is not clear whether this development has actually empowered the poor. The glorification and call for a return to traditional rulership in some quarters of Frelimo[49] must therefore be taken with caution: it could well be a return to an old order in which the traditional authorities accumulate power and wealth while the peasantry remains immersed in poverty and superstition. As in the colonial era, the greatest challenge to neo-traditionalism, in addition to state secularism, has come from Christianity, its arch rival, to which we now turn.

Contemporary christianity

Contemporary Christianity in Mozambique, its form, content and political articulation, has very much been shaped not only by the war, but to a large extent by the world-wide Pentecostal explosion. The impact of this explosion, transmitted mainly by Western based evangelists and their local agents, is manifested in the proliferation of Christian Churches (or 'places of worship') of various orientations all over the peri-urban suburbs of Chimoio city. In almost all the new residential areas the church, dwarfing into insignificance the mud-pole-and-thatch huts that surround them, has become the most prominent and common building.

Though the churches vary in membership size, organizational sophistication and institutional structure, they all emphasize spiritual redemption and salvation. Nevertheless, the picture of contemporary theology, preached to and absorbed by Mozambicans, is difficult to figure out, not least because of the conflicts within the movement for Christian re-awakening itself. The main cleavage is between the Catholic and the Protestant Churches, though within the latter there are also fissures. In their competition over membership, and hence the construction of hegemony and wealth, each has presented itself as representing the truth and offering the surest way to salvation. These divisions and counter-accusations of 'adulterated' Christendom, 'false prophecy' etc. among these religious denominations has resulted in considerable confusion among the new converts, some of whom have been changing churches with an amazing rapidity.

As with neo-traditional religious worshippers, Christians interviewed claimed to have personal and socio-political reasons for believing. Some even claimed to possess divine understanding/faith, to know something or be committed to something beyond the comprehension of non-believers (see below). In many cases the very same reasons that have forced some to worship traditional religion are the ones that have led others to enthusiastically embrace Christianity. One touching, but by no means exceptional, example of how the quest for healing prompted conversion to Christianity is the sad story of a young woman whose affliction resulted in the breakdown of her marriage. The story also highlights the intermixture of traditional religious belief and Christianity.

According to her husband, the woman was possessed by an evil avenging spirit of a deceased person (*chikwambo* or *ngozi*) who had been unjustly killed by the woman's uncle. The woman's family had been advised by a traditional healer to pay compensation to the relatives of the deceased in the form of a sacrificial animal, a goat, and a huge sum of money. Both had to be presented at a ritual ceremony organized to put to rest the aggrieved spirit of the deceased. But due to poverty, which had been worsened by the war and the economic crisis, the woman's family could not afford to pay the compensation.

Consequently, the woman continued to be haunted by the evil spirit which, according to her husband, seriously interfered with their sexual life. At the suggestion of a 'saved and born again' believer, she decided to join a religious sect whose prophetic leaders claimed to have the (healing) powers to dispel demons from their victims. Unfortunately for the woman, her husband could not live up to the strict code of moral behaviour that the sect demanded (prohibiting smoking and drinking). As a result her illness continued, further straining their relationship before its final collapse.

From this story, according to the diviners, the woman's problem had its roots in the sphere of traditional ideology. But because of economic constraints, namely her family's inability to perform the rituals as advised by the traditional healer, she had to turn to Christianity for healing. Economic factors and illness, which are closely interrelated, are here therefore the major reasons for this woman's decision to become a Christian. Later, because her suffering did not recede when she joined the Africa Zion Church, she switched to the African Apostolic Faith which she believed to be 'true Christianity' that could 'save' her.

Another young separated woman in her mid twenties similarly testified that becoming a Christian "helps in many ways". She had joined the Chigubhu religious sect, a locally based religious movement which combines elements of African traditional dance and Christian religion, following her separation from her husband who was married to three other wives. Indeed membership in some religious movements, such as the Chigubhu, does help in many ways; as for this woman and many others, it offered a sense of community, empowerment and fostered love.

Community, empowerment and religious conversion: The case of the Chigubhu religious sect

The Chigubhu religious sect is a typical example of popular grass-roots religious movement, whose exaltation of 'wild brotherly and sisterly dance' has earned it rebuke from mainstream established Churches as well as the state. The latter, as in neighbouring Zimbabwe, accuse the sect of promoting promiscuity and the break-down of family life through its nightly uninhibited dance (to drums) and prayer sessions in which "brothers and sisters freely intermingle". But for the believers, dance and prayer is not only the most important expression of 'brotherly and sisterly love' - it is the only way one can achieve genuine communion with Jesus Christ, and be saved.[50]

Membership in such a religious group not only fosters love and communion with God, but it also guarantees caring and material support in times of need. As Amaria, a single mother and member of the sect, pointed out:

We help each other in times of need.... When I was ill a few months ago they (other members) visited me here, bringing with them firewood, water and some donations, maize meal powder and sometimes money. It really helped me, otherwise my son would have starved to death.[51]

The sect, like many other religious groups, is therefore playing a vital social service function, which is important given the state's inability to provide these services. Participation in the sect's activities also fosters a sense of belonging and community, and thereby shapes the process of re-defining the relationship between the individual and society. More important, one finds a surprising degree of egalitarianism in the congregations. Calling each other 'brother' and 'sister', members appear to have put aside, to some extent, the traditional respect for social status, age and gendered inequality.

Like other religious groups, the bulk of the membership at one 'place of worship' (unlike established Churches, the prayer sessions usually take place on open ground) came from the poorest sections of society, mostly single middle-aged women. Also, as is almost the norm with all Christian religious groups, while women were far more numerous than men, the official leadership of the sect resided in the hands of the latter. But it appeared, through informal processes, women had influence over the male leadership,

179

and in some cases even set the agenda for the congregation. In short, membership of such religious communities, as one other sceptical believer and an enterprising young man in his late twenties, put it, "saves, materially and spiritually". Becoming a member of such religious movements thus expresses individual and collective attempts to reconstruct the social world.

Such a quest for a humane social world has led some to continuously move between different denominations searching for 'true' Christianity and genuine love. The case of a former pastor in the Assembly of God (Africa) who left the sect to become a pastor in Igreja Evangelica Cristo Vive (Jesus Lives Evangelic Church) clearly illustrates this point. In his own words:

> I was a pastor in the Assemblies of God since 1977, after I had just been demobilised from the army [which he had served in from 1972 as a guerrilla in the war of Independence]. But I left it in the mid 1980s because I wanted a church which encourages real love, not one that operates like an *'empresa'* (firm or enterprise), as the Assembly of God did.

Elaborating on his notion of 'real love', he argued that it was the leaders' lack of love and respect, especially for freedom fighters who had brought independence, which caused the war:

> The leaders turned their backs on freedom fighters who had brought them to power. Some of them (the freedom fighters) have become Matsanga [local name for Renamo]. They want to live well too [implying that is why they went into the bush].

For him, both Chissano and Dhlakama did not have real love for their people: if he was in the position of the former he would 'agree to give up the Presidency' and, if in that of the latter, 'give up the struggle for power'. Since, the genesis and prolongation of the war was due primarily to lack of love, "people should pray...and the country will progress and develop".

Emphasizing the importance of prayer, he made an interesting comment on the relationship between war, drought and God:

> If there is rainfall, the war will not end because there will be lots of food and vegetation cover for the belligerents to continue fighting. By causing drought, God wants to destroy these things [food and cover], so that the war ends.

Indeed this is a common belief among many believers and preachers, some of whom make explicit reference to the war in their sermons and preachings.

180

For many religious movements and believers, such as the Holy Spirit Church, the changes that are taking place are evidence of God's power and anger.

The holy spirit, sin, redemption and prosperity

In a purposefully charged, but very short, Good Friday sermon one preacher at a Holy Spirit Congregation, subtly attacked the political elites and prayed for those unjustly arrested to be released. Making it clear that those who had made the arrests - not the arrested[52] - had sinned, he shouted to an electrified audience: "Even those with sin as dark as charcoal will be forgiven, if they repent".[53] Many had braved the cold of the night waiting to hear the sermon, which was occasionally interrupted by women who became hysterically 'possessed' and started talking in tongues.

Exhibiting his strong sentiments against the political elites and gloating over the collapse of their power due to the war he later pointed out idiomatically:

> Nyaya dzinotongwa nedzimwe nyaya. Kushata kwezvimwe ndokunaka kwezvimwe. (Problems are solved by other problems. In every cloud there is a silver lining)

He was arguing that the problems Frelimo had created by its persecution of religious believers had been solved by another problem, the war. This apt idiom not only captures the religion-politics dialectic, but that of the whole social process unfolding in the country: looked at dialectically, some problems seem to have presented themselves with elements of their solutions embedded in them. But his attack on "those who want to get rich without sweating for it" as having caused the war, may well also apply to him.

His life style, his relationship with his followers as well as the 'voice' of the 'street radios', suggested that he was also getting 'rich without sweating for it'. For instance, his house, a spacious seven-roomed, asbestos-roofed and brick outfit, was an island in an ocean of mud-pole-and-thatch huts in which most members of his Church lived. Further, he had a 'small business' and a commercial farm in Manica district, in addition to a car. It was clear that his salary as a junior civil servant was by no means sufficient to acquire these assets. Unsurprisingly, in his sermon he emphasized that it was every Christian's obligation to contribute donations to the Church. More revealing however is his condescending relationship with his followers, as well as the social class of his close associates.

Typically, especially for young pastors, after delivering the sermon he went around the Church briefly talking to people who were preparing to sleep inside and outside the Church, before disappearing. He did not conceal the fact that, in his flashy suit and tie, he could not imagine himself sleeping outside on the ground with his fellow believers - most of them in rags - as part of the ritual of Easter ceremonies. Instead he decided to go to the exciting night life at Feira Popular (popularly known as Fepo).[54] At Fepo pubs open throughout the whole night, and all sorts of vices, drinking, prostituting, drug taking and dealing, rackets etc. go on with no-one seeming to care.

The irony of it is that, while the poor women and young children were freezing in the cold night, the pastor was having a nice time at Fepo, drinking (soft drinks), warming himself on the fire, and devouring some roast chicken. The pastor looked more at home in the company of non-religious people than with his apparently 'blind' followers, whom he is separated from not only by age, but by class as well. As a capitalist entrepreneur, this man of the bible was trying hard to barricade himself against poverty and hunger. But at the same time he was also probably inflicting it on others by underpaying his workers (who work in his recently opened shop and at the farm) as well as by 'stealing' from the poor who donated the little they had to the church.

Clearly, there is a strong connection between religion and money, with the former being 'a holy' avenue to wealth accumulation, and hence power. Money has been wedded to religion and this seems to be becoming the norm. As one ill old woman, and a non-believer, bitterly remarked when asked why she had not joined any religious group in order to get some help:

> It's all the same. At the clinic they want money. The traditional healers want money too. In the church, they also want money all the time. Where can I get the money from?

This recurrent phenomenon is particularly pronounced especially among foreign 'professional' preachers who have invaded the country. One typical example is the 'Jesus Lives Ministries' crusaders who are moving from place to place in the central region of Mozambique spreading the gospel.

Jesus Lives crusaders, the Prosperity Gospel and After-Life Salvation

The Jesus Lives (Gospel Reach Tent Ministries) have their headquarters in Germany and offices in South Africa and Zimbabwe. The preachers, two women and seventeen men, were well pampered youths from Zimbabwe. They seemed utterly insensitive to the material conditions and plight of those to whom they preached. For example, at one of their camps in the outskirts of Chimoio city[55], they led a conspicuous life that sharply contrasted with that of their Mozambican counterparts. They had lots of clothes and food, only left-overs of which they would give to the hungry souls who had assembled to hear the word of God.

One of them, a youth in his early twenties, openly admitted that he had joined the crusaders because, like most of his colleagues, he had failed to get a job in Zimbabwe after completing 'O' levels.[56] Although (like many others who did not come) he was afraid of the war, he was not regretting having volunteered to come to Mozambique:

> There are so many opportunities of prospering in life while here. Everything - food and clothes - is cheap here. Mozambicans do not know the value of money. For instance you can get a shirt for just 2000Mt (the equivalent of a bar of soap from Zimbabwe).

For him, it is the economic opportunities of getting cheap second-hand clothes (donated by European Charities) for resale in Zimbabwe that is the most exciting part of his experience in Mozambique. Like other such Churches, preachers teach that a key aspect of prospering is giving to God first: "if we give and to the extent we give, God will reimburse us".[57]

The leader of the group, an overweight man in his late thirties, even went further to praise the Mozambicans for their humility, meekness and openness to the word of God. Contrasting them to Zimbabweans, and drawing a Biblical analogy he said;

> The Zimbabweans, like the Pharisees in the Bible, are arrogant, self-praising and 'full of I know' (attitude), whereas the Mozambicans are, like the Galatians, humble, polite and open to new ideas. God blessed the Galatians and punished the Pharisees for their boastfulness...It is much more difficult to spread the gospel in Zimbabwe than here. Here people are thirsting for the word of God, and the spiritual uplifting it brings.

This kind of gospel has obvious socio-political effects. It tells the people of Mozambique, among the poorest in the world, that material prosperity will be provided by the 'blessings of God'. It encourages people to accept their earthly miseries, as 'sinners who don't deserve justice', and instead seek mercy.

For example, the leader of the group bluntly said that helping the Mozambicans materially was not their objective. Quoting the Bible again he said, "Man does not live on bread alone", and that it is the spirit/soul that needs to be saved. Dismissing the counter-argument that 'man cannot live without bread', he insisted that, as a Christian, he would simply pray for a starving man, rather than bother with giving him food.

It is this disarming emphasis on the spiritual and after-life-salvation that has been the main target for criticism of religious philosophy by concerned observers. But paradoxically it is also the element from which religious philosophy derives its strength. As a young mother of four, put it in explaining the current crisis and her reasons for conversion:

> It is written in the Bible that towards the end of the world all these miseries will happen. War, hunger and suffering are all signs of the coming doom.

The appearance of these signs and a sense of sinfulness combined to strengthen her resolve to become a dedicated Christian. War, suffering and drought are all seen as punishment for sinning by God, and "if people prayed, the war and these other plagues could end".[58] But when poverty, sickness and famine are attributed to God's plan, there is of course no need to discover economic, social or political causes for them. As this speaker illustrates, the remedy becomes prayer, not social analysis, political activity, or development.[59] By bringing various groups of people together, religious ideology has engendered and fostered relations of dominance and domination.

The cases of the preachers of the Holy Spirit and the Jesus Lives Churches mentioned above amply demonstrate this point. Judging from their life styles, associates, relationship with their followers, and their general attitude to politics, war and society, they seem to be leading a double life. On the one hand they mesmerize believers by their preachings, promising them heavenly salvation if they repent their sins, and on the other they have a nice time with sinners, and sinning with them too. While entrenching their power they preach the virtues of submissiveness to their followers. Attacking such false prophets Bob Marley sang: "I feel like bombing the church, now that I know the preacher is lying".[60] As will be shown below, it is this kind of hypocrisy and indulgence in what they preach against that has driven many others into atheism and scepticism about religion.

Nonetheless, the mere existence of religious groups and religious activism has had the effect of expanding the possibilities establishing elements of civil society. Some religious groups have in fact adopted a more public profile, and engaged in activities that are more explicitly political. Consequently some groups have been the subject of controversy among politicians and scholars alike. It is the *practice* of these religious groups, and not their claims to being apolitical, that is crucial to our understanding of the political significance of religion in a changing society. In the next section we briefly examine the 'political' activities and practices of three radically different religious groups, the Roman Catholic Church, the Maforga Missionaries and Brother Elijah's Honour God (God Honourous, as he pronounced it) Movement.

Religious practice, politics and power

The Roman Catholic Church

The history of the Roman Catholic Church has been manifestly political.[61] Its relationship with the state has vacillated in a love-hate fashion. As already noted, during the colonial era the Church enjoyed the protection of the state to which it provided legitimacy and for which it trained technocrats. During the anti-colonial struggle, this relationship was strained as the Church proffered some half-hearted support to the cause for liberation, a move that earned it less harsh treatment (than other religious groups) when Frelimo took over power. Its property was, however, confiscated thereby undermining its institutional capacity.

With the spread of the war, the Church gradually reclaimed its credibility by involving itself, at various levels, in bringing the belligerents together to end the war. The role of the Vatican in encouraging and sustaining the negotiation process, which took place mainly in Italy, is well enough known not to be repeated here. While the Church has tried to present itself as neutral, some sections of the Church have been viewed as avowedly anti-Frelimo and pro-Renamo. A case in point is the Church's Beira diocese led by Bishop Gongalves, "a mediator with sympathies for one of the parties".[62]

These accusations of 'sympathies for one of the parties' have been linked to a recent row over the Bishop's insistence that Church services be conducted in Ndau, instead of Portuguese, to a largely Sena congregation. The Ndau language issue has been interpreted by those opposed to it as a symbolic support, and hence promotion, of Renamo. Most of the latter's top leadership are Ndaus and the movement's major language is Ndau.[63] The Bishop has dismissed all criticism as the work of Frelimo spies who have infiltrated the Church to destabilise it. In Chimoio, where many adherents seem aware of the Church's role in the peace process, language is not an issue as mass is usually conducted in Portuguese by white priests.

The main issue of contention between Frelimo and the Church seems to centre around the return of church property seized by the state after Independence and used for schools and other services.[64] The return of this property, under pressure, has contributed "to further degradation in state provision and popular alienation"[65]. It has conversely, however, enhanced the image and status of the Church which now has more resources at its disposal. For instance, the Church is now able to feed about two hundred children daily under the programme to combat malnutrition. Additionally, it now provides basic health care and trains women in hygiene and midwifery.[66]

As in the rest of Africa, the involvement of the Church in development has been considerable, not just in traditional areas of schools and hospitals, but in rural development in general. For example, through its development agency Caritas, the Church has been sending agricultural extension officers trained in Zimbabwe to set up rural development projects in Sussundenga District. They dig wells and bore-holes and teach soil conservation farming to local people.[67] The Church's involvement in the rural areas has been hampered by the war. In the words of one of these officers:

> Definitely we want the war to end so that we can go to the rural areas and build churches and schools. But war is a (dirty) business. Many people are making money out of it, and are therefore not interested in ending it - they will lose their jobs. The poor want to stop it [the war] and live in peace, but *they can't*. The real problem is lack of education. Education is the answer.

Implicitly attacking state authoritarianism, the official pointed out:

> Today people are still thinking in authoritarian structures ... and it's only *fear and helplessness*. It will take a long time to restore the initiative that has been knocked out of the people by decades of being told to move, do this or that.

This concentration of power and control of society were (incorrectly?) attributed to Marxism, which had been proclaimed the official ideology by Frelimo. Taking a position not dissimilar to that of Liberation Theology, this radical theologian concluded:

> I find many things in Marxism quite relevant to our time and in line with Christianity. As Bishop Helder Camara said: "When I give hungry people food you call me a saint, but when I ask why they are hungry you call me a Communist". It is the same here - you get yourself in trouble with the government.

The dominant state ideology is seen as having stifled the initiatives of the poor. The Church's urgent task is therefore to empower the poor, through education and love, so that they can fight for their rights. Without going into details about the internal workings of power within the Church, it can be noted that it is hierarchically structured and has a clear division of gender roles. Its claims to 'empowering the poor' and its commitment to egalitarianism seem therefore to be based on a flimsy foundation, and could be seen as a veiled attempt at the construction of hegemony.   Challenging

186

this hegemony, some Fundamentalist and Protestant Churches have attacked the Catholic Church for promoting 'false' Christianity. It has been attacked for accommodating traditional practices and rituals such as funeral rites and ceremonies to rest a departed spirit as well as for its liberal code of conduct which permitted beer drinking and smoking. But interestingly, it is precisely this 'liberalism' that led some of its members to prefer it against other churches with stricter moral codes. But in being permissive, the Church has also discouraged away some would-be-converts: many members of Protestant Churches pointed out precisely this liberalism as evidence of the hypocrisy and falsehood of the Roman Catholic Church. Next we look at one such religious group, the Maforga Mission, whose activities have been a subject of intense controversy.

Maforga Mission: Anti-state or pro-people?

Maforga Mission, is situated on a farm a few kilometres east of Gondola town along the Beira highway (its workshop and training centre for women is in Gondola town). It was established in the mid-eighties by a white couple, the Perkins. The Perkins, both 'born again' Christians, took over the farm from a German baroness[68] in order to establish a centre to distribute food aid donated by Christian organisations based in Zimbabwe. It was through one such Christian organization, 'Youth With a Mission' which recruits youths from all over the world, that the Perkins started getting involved in missionary work in Mozambique. Mrs Perkins had been involved with Churches in South Africa where she studied and taught for seven years, before going to England where she painted and "made a lot of money".

Assisted by short-term volunteers from the West,[69] the Mission's activities include provision of basic health care, training for women and disabled men in knitting and sewing, care for the elderly, the disabled and orphans, and provision of food and clothing. Sometimes they feed up to 400 and treat up to 1 000 people a day.

The Mission has been attacked left and right by both the government and non-governmental organisations (NGOs) as well as by other churches. It is criticized for operating illegally; engaging in activities that contradict overall government policy with respect to 'concentration of peoples; using food aid as a bait for membership recruitment; alienating children from their culture; and most seriously, collaboration with Renamo. According to the Provincial Director of Planning, the Mission was not registered with the government nor did it have the permission to operate there. Venting his frustration, he complained: "They don't seem to recognise us. They just do what they want... Well it's a question of money and power". Corroborating the

187

Director's complaints, the Chimoio-based United Nations Field Representative mercilessly attacked the Mission thus:

> Where in the world can an organisation just come like this and start working without the knowledge and approval of the government? It's ridiculous! They are capitalising on the government's weakness and the country's crisis ...(to advance their hideous agendas). If it was in another country, like Zimbabwe for instance, they would have long been arrested or kicked out.

Outlining the specific 'crimes' the Mission had committed against the government, he continued:

> It is illegal, and professionally unacceptable, for a private organisation to run a clinic for incubating pre-maturely born babies, as the Mission does. This is the responsibility of the Ministry of Health. Further, by concentrating large groups of people on one place, the Mission is violating government policy.

The government's policy has been to discourage the 'concentration' of large groups of people, the rationale being that this would create a 'dependent population' unable to support itself. It seems the government is worried that the concentration of large groups of people, apart from providing an easy basis for organised opposition, will further highlight its own weaknesses: when the NGOs depart, it is argued, the burden of supporting these groups of people will squarely fall upon the government.

The Mission has also been criticised for using food aid as a bait for recruiting membership. Commenting on the general resurgence in religious activism in general, and making specific reference to the Mission, the Frelimo Provincial Secretary explained:

> Is that real genuine (Christian) believing and worshipping when some churches force people to become members as a condition for getting food?...If your neighbour goes to church and comes home with maize mealie-meal, will you not also go to feed your starving children? We will see, say three or five years after the war when people become self-sufficient again, whether this trend will continue. Only then can we be certain whether or not this is genuine belief and true Christianity.

Other NGOs, citing the above complaints, have also attacked the Mission. According to a Redd Barna (a Norwegian NGO) official, "the activities of the

Mission have tarnished the image of all NGOS, as now we are all suspected of having hidden agendas by both the government and the locals".

The Mission has rejected all these accusations. Refuting the accusation of 'illegality', the Missionaries pointed out that, for them as Christians, it was more important to save lives than to waste time and resources negotiating through a byzantine and corrupt bureaucracy for a permit when people are dying. Denying contradicting government policy and using food aid as a bait they said:

> Giving aid is not our main objective. We did not invite the children - the government sent them or they simply came on their own. We started the programme of teaching women to knit and sew because they kept on coming to us seeking help. After starting with one or two people, all of a sudden we had fifty - and at one point ninety. Just because of sheer numbers - at one point 700 to 1000 came to get medical treatment and food here - it becomes something.

That people had come voluntarily was corroborated by many people interviewed at the two sites of the mission. A young single woman, who was learning knitting at the Gondola workshop testified:

> I had been moving from place to place for the last decade since being first displaced in Barwe in 1982 before coming here. When I heard (through the grape vine) that there were white people helping people, I decided to come. They received me well.
>
> When I came here I was suffering. There was nothing in the rural areas. I used to eat wild roots and tree barks. It's much better here. We now are eating mealie-meal, and are learning new skills. We pray to God to guide and strengthen these kind people, our real leaders.

An amputated old man said that even if the war ends he will not leave the Mission, as his children were receiving food and education at the Mission. Many more said they thanked God for bringing these 'good Samaritans' and that they came 'voluntarily'.

Another accusation which has been levelled at the Mission is that it is alienating children from their culture by taking them from their homes. Stressing that their objective was not to take away children from their culture Mrs Perkins pointed out:

> All over the world people are getting to change. But here young people are not equipped for the changing world. We have got to equip young

189

children so that they make right decisions that will be good to their lives and family.

While there is no doubt for the need to equip young people to confront, and even command, the changing world, it is not clear whether the Mission is best placed to undertake this noble task.

Explaining how they are equipping the young for the 'new times', one of the missionaries gave a few examples of young people who had been disciplined and reformed. One was of a pretty thirteen year old girl who had come to the mission as a destitute. After a while, the girl started slipping out to see a boyfriend. As punishment, they sent her home where her mother was losing the battle with poverty. Not surprisingly:

> She [the girl] started getting thinner and thinner, and eventually she came back again and behaved herself beautifully. She repented, and [as a reward?] we gave her responsibilities to look after the kitchen. Later she fell in love with a teacher here, and we organised a brilliant wedding for them. Now they are living happily ...We want to give our girls a moral background.

For the Mission this is one of the many success stories. But, one would wonder whether feminists would look sympathetically at the 'arranged' marriage: the emphasis on 'proper marriage' and the position of women within it could well be seen as a reversal of the limited gains that women have gained (see next chapter). In addition, and highlighting the imbalance of power relations between the Missionaries and their followers, food is used as a mechanism for control. The Mission, unlike locally based sects like Chigubhu, is hierarchically structured and based on patron-client relations. For instance, virtually everyone at the Mission referred to Mrs Perkins as *'Patrao'* (Boss/Mistress). To many she was a real God-sent messiah, providing almost everything, thatch grass, clothes, food and medicine etc. As my research guide aptly remarked: *"Iye ndiye Mwari wawo, nekuti Mwari ndiyeka anoita zvakanaka.* (She is their God, because God is he that does good)". While undoubtedly there is an unequal power relationship between the ordinary people and the Missionaries, most of the people interviewed exhibited a great appreciation of the assistance they had received from the Mission.

The most serious critique of the Mission relates to its alleged links with Renamo and South Africa. The allegation, for the critics, was substantiated by the 'attack', capture and subsequent release of the Perkins (and their colleagues) by Renamo in 1987. The Perkins and an American nurse and her young baby were captured by Renamo on 13th May 1987, and stayed with their captors in the bush for about three months before being released in Malawi. According to Mrs Perkins, before their final capture, they had been attacked nine times by the rebels, but by God's grace had survived.

On being released from captivity in Malawi they made a press statement which was interpreted as "too political" and sympathetic to Renamo by both the Zimbabwean Central Intelligence Organisation (CIO) and the Mozambique government. The statement was:

> They [the Renamo] had treated us to the best of their abilities. They never deliberately harassed or tortured us.

After being flown to Zimbabwe, they were taken to Goromonzi maximum security prison where, "contrary to earlier promises of VIP treatment we were tortured by the CIO...We had a much more horrible experience in Zimbabwe than we had in the bush". Three weeks later, after "seeing a vision of God asking [them] to come and help the dis-privileged", they went back to Mozambique to continue with their missionary activities.

Denying any political objectives or connections with any political movement Mrs Perkins explained the nature of their dilemma thus:

> We don't want to be politically involved. But it's difficult to work with the government. You never know what they want and where you stand. The other problem is that, both the right wing and the left wing want us to say things that support them and attack their foes. We understand their accusations ... and I am sure we have made mistakes. We are learning all the time.
>
> [With respect to ordinary people], there is always that barrier all the time. People have learnt not to trust whites. Nobody trusts anybody else here. You try to build a relationship of trust, and being open and honest to people, but people are not trusting. You discover that the intelligent guy is a Frelimo spy trying to catch you out.

From the mission's perspective the major problem in the country was that: "There is no direction and self-discipline. Any society like that is open to any kind of exploitation - spiritual as well as material. And the country will get poorer and poorer". The main reason for this 'directionlessness' and corruption is, she aptly observes, that "no-one seems to have anything, and no-one can be trusted with anything". As mentioned in chapter three, official corruption has become a major survival strategy for elites trying to hedge against an uncertain future. More important for the Mission, corruption and war are the work of Satan and evil spirits: "...the thing behind the war is satanic, although God is behind everything. ... There are spiritual things behind it ..., a lot of evil forces at work". But through prayer Christians can swing the balance:

> If the people really believe in God and trust, those evil things would not have the power that they have. Whatever you say about the war, there is only one thing that you can do. Pray and forgive one another. Many times we have bowed down and prayed and things have worked.[70]

There was no just element in the war, and it was a pity that "everyone is trying to kill them (Renamo)", she added.

The Mission's struggle against 'Satanic' forces, sinfulness and selfishness has led it into a hostile relationship with the government as well as with some of the supposed benefactors of their projects, and with other churches. Hinting at the conflict within the religious movement, Mrs Perkins attributed the 'sinfulness' that has gripped the country to the activities of other churches they do not recognize as 'true' Christians. Attacking the Jehovah's Witnesses first she said:

> We don't recognize the Jehovah's Witnesses as a church. Their doctrine that only 144, 000 people will go to heaven is blasphemous. As Christians we believe in the Trinity, and that Jesus Christ died for our sins and is our only saviour.

Turning to the Roman Catholic Church, she attacked it for elevating people and worshipping saints, such as the Virgin Mary. By so doing, she argued, "they have added something to the Bible, which is blasphemous". The Mission has tried to establish links with other smaller churches by encouraging their members to participate in the Mission's activities. But this could be seen as part of an overall strategy to either gradually absorb these churches or eventually convert their members into the Mission's religion, all this in an endeavour to outmanoeuvre its rivals.

In short, notwithstanding claims to being apolitical, the Mission's activities have a political significance, and this has evoked both condemnation and admiration from differentially located social groups. A most glaring example of the awe, revulsion as well as admiration that religious doctrines have received is 'Brother Elijah's God be Honoured' ("God Honourous", in his own words) movement, which has dismissed all other religious groups as liars and false prophets. Below we examine how this spontaneous, structureless but fear inducing movement has emerged and asserted itself on the political arena.

Brother Elijah's God be Honoured movement is a relatively recent phenomenon. It may evaporate or mature into a powerful force to be contended with.[71] As it stood at the time of the interview[72], Brother Elijah's 'movement' was a one-man movement, with no structures, no permanent members nor a permanent place of worship. Instead 'Mukoma' (Brother) Elijah, whose proclaimed mission was to 'save the chosen few', single-handedly moves from place to place preaching (sometimes to no-one), prayer-healing, and most often lambasting the politicians for corruption and causing the war. His attire was weird and frightening: a white gown and a pair of white trousers (both turned brown with dirt), a short walking stick, a huge spear-like cross with glittering silver metals and red pieces of cloth, and an animal skin bag (with fur). Partly because of this, he usually draws huge crowds of people wherever he walks in the city. While most of the people following him seemed to be just curious, surprisingly a considerable number of them really believed that he was a messenger from God.

When we first met Brother Elijah, he was in front of the Chimoio City Council offices furiously shouting at no-one in particular thus:

> *Munhu haikona kubira vanhu. Yese irikuitika iyi ndeyekubira vanhu.* (A person should not steal from the people. All that is happening is looting from the people.)

For the bewildered spectators and the officials alike, this was the climax of strange things that had been happening in the city.[73] One other passer-by, shocked, referred to him as '*outra guerra*' (another war). Others dismissed him as a mad man. But after talking to him he turned out to be quite normal and to have a clear sense of mission. He said that he was on a sojourn to Beira, where he wanted to meet some of the few people who would be saved in the impending doom. He had only come to Chimoio city to claim his demobilisation allowances, being an ex-combatant who had fought in the Independence war.

Two women who greeted him said that they used to worship with him in Messica (Manica District) in the Zion City Mozambique Assemblies of God. According to him, he was brought up in the Catholic Church, but had converted to his present prophetism after seeing a vision of God in 1989 asking him "to spread the gospel and warn the sinners that the day of judgement was imminent". Since then he had devoted all his time to preaching, healing, and even attempts to bring about reconciliation between the warring parties.

193

For example, during the previous few weeks he had been praying to stop poisonous cassava from killing people in Macate. This was later corroborated by people from the areas. According to Brother Elijah, the cassava had become poisonous due to the sinfulness of man, and the 'spoliation of food' was one of God's punishments. Similarly in Dzembe, where God had demonstrated his wrath by unleashing crocodiles to feed on people, he had prayed for God's mercy to stop this. Also in all the places that he passed through, he advised people to stop preparing their fields for the rainy season as there would never be any rainfall: people had sinned too much and God was withholding rainfall as punishment.

Arguably, as in 1981 in Nampula[74], people were dying of cassava because, due to severe drought, they were eating it without sufficiently drying it. Similarly, perhaps crocodiles were preying on people because, as smaller rivers were drying up due to drought, people were forced to fetch water in bigger pools and thereby became more vulnerable to crocodiles.[75] The drought itself was probably caused by global climatic changes. Nonetheless, the important point is that many people believed in Brother Elijah's prophecies of doom.

For example, when he started preaching loudly in the Independence Square Park right in the city centre, he was joined by an ever-expanding group of people. Continuing with his theme of 'unforgivable sinfulness', he shouted:

Inyasha dzaMwari kutendeuka. Kutadza kwanyanya, hakucharegerereki. Musavangwadza, vanofanira kufa. (It is the Lord's mercy to become born again. There has been so much sinning that it cannot be forgiven. Don't alert them (the sinners) - *they must* die.

Making a specific reference to his attempts to end the war he said that he had written a letter to both Chissano and Dhlakama, *wanaMambo wehondo* (the war-lords/kings of war), to come and talk to him on a mountain in Messica that God had designated for talks to end all the wars in the world. But:

The war-lords refused to listen - they did not even bother to reply to my letters. Consequently, a hell of fire is coming soon to devour the whole world. In Zimbabwe and Mozambique only fifteen people will be saved in each of the countries. The saved will go to Iraq and Azai [Azania?].

When I go back, I will leave the Bible and start selecting those who will be saved.... No-one will get into heaven before I, the first and last prophet - alpha and omega - arrive. I will be standing at the first gate (of the three gates that one has to pass through before getting into heaven) and Paul and Jesus will be at the second and final gates respectively.

194

The preaching was interspersed by songs of redemption, in which he led the singing. When the crowd had grown to about a hundred (six times more than would go to heaven from Mozambique), he asked the people to kneel down facing east, with women on the right-hand side and the men on the left respectively. He shoved away, with his spear-like cross, some young girls who had burst out laughing at his instructions. When everyone had knelt, he started praying, repeating the prayer 'Our Father who art in Heaven' three times, with some modifications. After the prayer he ordered everyone to stand up, and started answering questions from the people.

The most important questions centred on the symbolic significance of his unusual cross and its various pieces of cloth and metal. Making reference to Chapter 22 of Revelation, he explained how the top part of his cross, which was shaped like a seven pronged spear, symbolised the fire and war that will devour the world. Below it, and just before the actual crossing of the cross, were two triangular shaped out-carvings, which he said represented the two countries, Mozambique and Zimbabwe where sin had become so pervasive that it cannot be forgiven. Just at the centre of the lower out-carving, was glittering silver metal, which he said represented the Biblical bright star that guided the three wise men from the east. The red clothes, were the 'matches' that would be used to light the fire that will devour the world.

Not surprisingly, some people simply dismissed him as mad. One of them was a soldier, who was silenced thus: "I don't speak to the dead. He who says Jesus' messenger is a madman is the one who is mad." Others criticised him for his shabby appearance, to which he replied that he would not bath nor change his clothes until he had accomplished his sojourn, and that in any case he would not dare touch unholy waters in an unholy land. Yet others still thought he was a beggar, and they mockingly offered him some money. He rejected it saying; "Your money is debased, and I cannot accept it". He added that he was not a destitute, and instead that he had three 'full granaries' (in heaven). He produced and showed people a tattered (first class) nurse's certificate, and told them that he was not concerned about earthly riches as evidenced by his giving up a professional job. Later, however, he accepted money from a few women who had insisted that he should accept it as it was in appreciation of his spiritually uplifting prayers and illuminating preachings.

The most surprising thing which left many dumbfounded and unsettled, was a confession by a man from among the crowd that what he was seeing now was exactly what he had seen in vision in a dream a few days before. The only difference, he said, was the walking stick - it was much longer - and that the person he saw was Jesus Christ himself. The 'prophet' assured him by saying that he had left that particular walking stick - with many others - at the top of the mountain from which he operated. As to the question of whether or not he was Jesus Christ himself, he said he was not, though later when the crowd had dispersed, he confided to me that (he believed) he was. Explaining the reasons for not acknowledging publicly that he was Jesus Christ he said:

> John, Paul and even Jesus Christ himself did not go around telling people who they were. If I tell people publicly who I am, I will alert them (the sinners). We don't have to alert them. They have to die.

It was difficult to disperse the crowd after the prayers and preachings. They seemed to want more, and he had to repeat 'may God bless you' several times. Finally, when the crowd was dispersed, save for a few children who were so fascinated that they could not leave, he asked his new 'witness' to carry his cross for him and walk along with him. After walking for a while, they stopped, knelt and prayed facing the east, with the other man still holding his cross. After the prayer and before parting, he told the other man that he was blessed and would be one of the few that will be saved if he kept his faith.

Until my departure in October 1992 Brother Elijah had become a permanent presence in Chimoio city, and a subject of much controversy among politicians and ordinary people alike. His preachings of impending doom due to unforgivable sinfulness unsettled many hearts, while his uncompromising verbal warfare against the politicians disturbed them. Although not coherently articulated, his religious-political statements had a resonance among the general citizenry, who formed the bulk of his listeners. The authorities tried to pretend that his prophetism was of no consequence and dismiss him as one of the psychopaths (alienated men) who roam the city - some of them virtually naked.

As a Roman Catholic Sister pointed out, "the important thing is that people follow freely. No force or coercion is being used". The fact that people have 'followed freely', shows that Brother Elijah's prophetic messianism, regardless of whether it is true or false, seems to provide a vision of an ideal community life (that is free of sin), and a (desirable) critique of the political status quo. This vision and critique has shaped the actual perceptions and life experiences of believers and non-believers alike, and this seems to have made Brother Elijah more of a 'prophet' than a 'madman'. What impact this movement will have on the community and political awareness is hard to say. His presentation of national politics in terms of religious conflict may be a powerful avenue of mobilisation for the community, as can be seen from the tendency to view relations of domination and subordination in terms of spiritual warfare.

By emphasising the disarming philosophy of spiritual salvation, like other religious groups, the movement runs the risk of losing its emancipatory appeal. Its vengeance ('they must die') and claim to a monopoly of religious

196

truths has not only confused many would-be believers, but has had the opposite effect of driving them into atheism, and even debauchery. As pointed out earlier, though still much smaller than that of believers, the proportion of atheists seems to be rising much faster than that of religious believers. Consequently, any treatment of religion in Mozambique would not be adequate without giving consideration to the atheists, their reasons for disbelieving and their perceptions of and relationships with believers.

Atheists: Religious rebels or mere spectators?

Marx believed that religion was the most extreme form of alienation. The emancipation of individuals should therefore begin with its critique.[76] Attacking religion as a 'fantasy of alienated man' and an indirect recognition of the individual through an intermediary, he rejected the idea that the world was created.[77] Instead he argued that man was his own creator: "Atheism, is a denial of this unreality... a denial of God and tries to assert through this negation the existence of man".[78] It was therefore inseparable from humanism, and was only a stage on the path to communism; only in communism will the individual recover his/her alienated self and develop full consciousness. Marx stated his position:

> The criticism of religion ends with the doctrine that man is for himself the highest being - that is, with the categorical imperative to overthrow all systems in which man is humiliated, enslaved, abandoned and despised.[79]

Like many other Marxist-Leninist regimes, Frelimo's project of secularizing of society was largely based on such a conception of religion. The contemporary rise in atheism has been shaped by Frelimo's deliberate strategy, education, urbanisation and the war.

In Chimoio atheism has manifested itself in the form of scepticism and cynicism about religious belief and religious believers. Atheists have observed the diversity of religious movements and the acerbity of their disputes, and decided that all alike were pretending to possess knowledge which was in fact unattainable. As with religious belief, the personal and social reasons for disbelieving are diverse and tend to correlate with gender, age and class. Though not exclusively, relatively well-off young men tend to constitute the bulk of this social category.

The perceived inadequacies of religious belief and the moral bankruptcy of believers, which have become apparent at many points, have been the main factors in determining this sub-category's choices. Unfulfilled religious hopes;

197

frustration with the 'turn the other cheek philosophy'; the apparent contradiction between the life styles of self-proclaimed believers and their religious rhetoric; and the utopianism and fatalism of most religious groups all have combined to produce a move in the opposite direction by the disenchanted. A few examples will suffice to illustrate these observations.

Alberto, a young man in his early thirties who owns a welding machine, was born in a Roman Catholic family, but he has now ceased to be a Christian 'due to increasing poverty and suffering'. In his own words:

> How can we go to Church when we are suffering like this? It does not help....We also want to drive cars and buy houses.... We will start going to Church when we are living well.

His friend, a non-believer as well, assented thus: "*Takanamata kare* (We prayed in the past)", cynically meaning they no longer feel obliged to pray as it does not make any difference. Alberto had been forced to leave his wealth in the rural areas (in Buzi) following specific threats from Renamo which wanted them because his brother, whom Renamo eventually murdered, was connected with Frelimo. It was despair and frustration at the unjust threat to his life - he himself did not sympathise with Frelimo - and the consequent loss of property, that dented his faith in God.

Another extremely cynical young man who had just returned from Germany, dismissed religious worship thus: "*Ndezvekunyeperana* (It's about lying to each other)". Making specific reference to Christian religion, one middle aged man actually blamed it for the current social malaise. He lamented that, "it is this blind belief in and worship of foreign religions that is contributing to confusion and chaos". An intelligent and pragmatic young woman pointed out the inadequacies of religious philosophy in redressing real problems thus:

> *Kunamata kuti tipedze hondo nada. Hondo inopera nekutaurirana.* (We cannot end the war by praying. It is only through negotiations that it can be ended).

Others condemned Christianity from purely ethical considerations. For example a young man and Frelimo activist criticised Christian love as 'false' believing it to be a product of fear: "Christians love their neighbours because they are afraid of going to hell". The Christian who loves because of fear, like one who abstains from theft because of the law, would be wicked if he were not restrained by the thought of hell-fire. He tried to elaborate his ideas in a paper entitled, "The Man Centred Principle", written in almost incomprehensible English. In a similar vein, another former military commander and senior member of Frelimo attacked Christianity saying that it causes 'submissive mentality'. In a typical Nietzschean[80] fashion, he argued that Christianity destroys the strong and their will-power to fight the enemy (Renamo).

It appears the rise in atheism partly reflects the increasing desire among many Mozambicans to have a right to choose for themselves the form of belief which increases their happiness and they are most comfortable with: according to many, when religion dictates what one should think or do it becomes a greater evil than the freedom enjoyed by atheists. Atheism has not necessarily implied nihilism and selfishness, as Dostoevsky had feared when he said: "If there is no God, everything is permitted".[81] In Mozambique, neither atheists nor Christians have a monopoly of moral and ethical values. In fact, religion and atheism seem to need each other, and it is by attacking the other that each gain in strength.

Summary: The politico-religious interface

As the preceding discussion has tried to demonstrate, religious activism, both in its neo-traditionalist and Christian forms, has re-emerged with a vengeance. It has become a central ideological apparatus in the contested political arena, "a symbolic and material resource for the 'elaboration of a conceptual challenge to the power monopolies'".[82] Its driving force has been the war and urbanisation: war-related anxiety, grief, and disruption and the consequent need to re-interpret, explain and re-adjust to this reality has fostered religious activism. The war, by crippling the anti-religious Frelimo state, has provided a social space for religious ideology to flourish, and for worshippers to assert themselves in the political arena.

In addition to this there has been a religious invasion of the country by Western-based churches, which are competing for influence with a variety of locally based religious movements. The result has been a complex situation in which religion, politics and economics feed on each other in a fashion which mocks any attempts at arriving at a smart distinction between cause and effect: it appears the effect is simultaneously the cause. The specific articulation of religion and politics and economics has been contingent upon the exigencies of surviving in a war situation. Thus, while there can be no doubt that post-peace Mozambique will be a multi-religious society, the form, content and direction it will take remains to be seen.

As is evident in most of the examples cited above, religious belief and/or activism has gained momentum as a conscious politico-military and economic survival strategy or both. For instance, as with Naparama and Mungoi, the villagers of Doroe *localidade's* successful employment of traditional religious ideology to curb Renamo brutality (see chapter two) demonstrates how religion can be used as a cultural weapon for survival. Similarly, the case of

Dzembe shows religious ideology in operation as a conceptual tool to stabilise the contradiction between man and nature, and also as a weapon for local communities to wrest control of their lives from the hegemonic state. In both instances, however, religion has had the effect of entrenching the power of traditional religious elites, as against that of the ordinary people. This alerts us to the need to caution against the glorification, as Baptista seems to suggest, of neo-traditionalism.

Apart from considerations purely of security, religious activism, especially Christian, has been precipitated by the need to construct community, identity and basic necessities for survival. Religious affiliation has been important for the social value and importance it attaches to individuals' lives, as well as for the material assistance (food, cloth, caring during illness etc) and community relationship it promotes. In some specific cases, religious activity has been a channel for accumulation of wealth and graduation from poverty, as well as providing self-security, hope and consolation. In addition, religion has played its historic role of justification and compensation: it has justified wealth and poverty; simultaneously legitimating the power of the dominant (religious) elites, compensating the dominated by promises of an after-life paradise, and giving voice to the hitherto voiceless, as in the case of Brother Elijah's movement.

The overall effect of these processes has been a redefinition of the state-civil society relationship, itself the product of a dialectic and not just the simple imposition of the former over the latter. The religious institutions and values that Frelimo sought to transcend have proved to be one of the terms of that dialectic. A new synthesis has emerged in which the religious field has attained a position of relative autonomy, and indeed some leverage over the state.

Nonetheless, religious activism has yet to emerge properly as an autonomous weapon of struggle against domination. It has as yet to chart out a coherently articulated theology of liberation as has been the case in Latin America. The dispossessed have been able to use religion as an effective weapon for their emancipation only to a limited extent. Although in some cases leaders are actually prisoners of the congregation, by and large the control of religious ideology has remained the monopoly of the relatively educated and wealthy elites. This partly reflects the extent to which many forms of resistance that the disinherited create for themselves remain open to co-optation and undermining by dominant social groups. As Mosala points out with reference to South Africa, part of the reason for this "has to do with its (religion's) class and ideological commitments, especially with respect to its biblical hermeneutics".[83] According to Mosala, unless the dispossessed break ideologically and practically with the dominant biblical-hermeneutical assumptions, especially those that exalt the virtues of spiritual salvation and after-life paradise, religious activism can never become an effective weapon for emancipation.[84]

Conclusion

The rise in religious activism has been an inextricable part of the new emerging society. This new society is socially and politically pitted against the ossifying, but not yet buried, old order. Thus the decision to become religiously active is never an isolated mental act nor only limited to considerations of physical security, hope and access to basic material needs. It is a self-conscious response to a historical and social process of change, an antithesis to the forcibly secularised post-colonial social order. Viewed in this way, therefore, what is unfolding is a religious 'revolution' with multiple consequences for both popular consciousness and political power. What is remarkable is the innovativeness of religious ideology in responding to new social demands that the war and change have entailed.

The varied forms of religious engagement in politics lead us to one final conclusion with respect to the politico-religious interface. In Chimoio, religion has been at one and the same time both the symptom of a deep social malaise and a protest against it. As Marx pointed out:

> Religious suffering is at the same time an expression of real suffering and a protest against real suffering. Religion is the sign of the oppressed creature, the feeling of a heartless world and the soul of soulless circumstances. It is the opium of the people.[85]

As protest it has offered a critique and alternative to the status quo. But as an 'opium of the people' it has mystified the social forces shaping their situation, and hence stood in the way of any cure of social problems. Wedded with money, the new 'secular God', it has accelerated social differentiation and polarisation of power and wealth. Its force derives from the need to impose as stable a definition as possible upon an extremely volatile and fluid reality.

Notes

1. See Otto Roesch, "Peasants, War and Tradition in Central Mozambique", paper prepared for the Symposium, 'Symbols of Change: Transregional Culture and Local Practice in Southern Africa', Free University of Berlin, January 7-10, 1993.

2. Pepe Roberts and David Seddom, "Fundamentalism in Africa: Religion and Politics, in *Review of African Political Economy*, Number 52, November 1991, pp. 1-3.

3. Terence O. Ranger, "Religious Movements and Politics in Sub-Saharan Africa", in *African Studies Review*, Volume 29, Number 2 June 1986, pp. 1-69.

4. See among others, G. Balandier, "Messianism and Nationalism in Black Africa", in P. Van den Berghe (editor), *Africa: Social Problems of Change and Conflict*, New York, Chandler, 1965, and V. Lantemari, "Revolution and/or Integration in African Socio-Religious Movements", in B. Linoln (editor), *Religion, Rebellion, Revolution*, London, MacMillan, 1985.

5. Terence Ranger, op. cit, p. 2.

6. Ibid., p. 2.

7. Ibid., p. 4.

8. Cited in A. Wipper, *Rural Rebels: A Study of Two Protest Movements in Kenya*, Nairobi, Oxford University Press, 1977, by Terence Ranger, op. cit., 3.

9. See among others, W. Beinart and C. Bundy, *Hidden Struggles: Rural Politics and Popular Consciousness in South Africa*, London, James Currey, 1986.

10. Paul Gifford, "Christian Fundamentalism and Development", in *Review of African Political Economy*, Number 52, November, 1991, p. 19.

11. Ruth Marshall, "Power in the Name of Jesus", in *Review of African Political Economy*, Number 52, November, 1991, p. 36.

12. See Carl F. Hallencreutz and Mai Palmberg (editors), *Religion and Politics in Southern Africa*, Uppsala, The Scandinavian Institute of African Studies, 1991.

13. David Lan, *Guns and Rain: Guerrillas and Spirit Mediums in Zimbabwe*, London, James Currey, 1985.

14. Otto Roesch, commentary letter on an original draft of this Chapter.

15. Cited in S. Hvalkof and P. Aaby (editors), *Is God An American? Anthropological Perspective on the Missionary Work of the Summer Institute of Linguistics*, London, International Work Group for Indigenous Affairs, Copenhagen and Survival International, 1981, by Ibid p. 7.

16. The use of the term 'traditional' is not intended to convey the impression that these religions were static, unchanging systems of belief and practice, but is simply a convenient and appropriate way of referring to the oldest of Africa's 'living religions'. See Peter B. Clarke, *West Africa and Christianity*, Oxford, Edward Arnold, 1978.

17. Cited in Bennetta Jules-Rosette, *African Apostles: Ritual and Conversion in the Church of John Marange*, Ithaca, Cromwell University Press, 1975, by Terence Ranger, op. cit., p. 8.

18. S.I.G. Mudenge, *A Political History of Munhumutapa c 1400-1902*, Harare, Zimbabwe Publishing House, 1988, p. 119.

19. See Terence O. Ranger, "Revolt in Portuguese East Africa", in *St Anthony Papers Number 13; African Affairs*, Number 2, 1963, pp. 54-80.

20. Ibid., p. 67.

21. H.H.K. Bhila, *Trade and Politics in a Shona Kingdom: The Manyika and their African and Portuguese Neighbours 1575-1902*, London, Longman, 1982, p. 13.

22. See David Lan, *op. cit.*

23. Ibid., p. 67.

24. Ibid., p. 65.

25. Interview with grand child of the chief in Chimoio.

26. Later in 1896 the scarcity of grain forced Mutasa's son, Chimbadzwa, to leave Manyika for Barwe with 500 and their families. See H.H.K. Bhila, op. cit., p. 48.

27. See ibid.

28. The last chief in the dynasty, who was stripped off his power at Independence by Frelimo, is now an old man in Beira. Renamo has appointed the son of his brother, who is twenty-years old, as the new chief.

29. See Alf Helgesson, "Catholics and Protestants in a Clash of Interests in Southern Mozambique", in Carl F. Hallencreutz and Mai Palmberg (editors), op. cit, pp. 195-205.

30. Ibid., p. 72.

31. See Allen Isaacman, op. cit.

32. In December 1982 Frelimo had a meeting with Catholic, Protestant, Moslem and Hindu leaders to clarify some of the points of the misunderstanding and dispute.

33. Peter Fry, "Lusotropicology and the Dual Mandate: revisiting the Portuguese and British in Africa after independence", paper presented to the University of Zimbabwe (UZ) Department of Sociology Seminar, May 1991, p. 13.

34. Ibid, p. 13. For a detailed analysis of this situation in Nampula, see C. Geffray, *La Cause des Armes au Mozambique: anthropologie d'une Guerre Civile*, Paris, 1990.

35. Interview with a Holy Spirit pastor who said he knew many people who were arrested or simply 'disappeared' because of their religious beliefs.

36. This outburst, made by a female member of the Roman Catholic Church, is quite a common remark.

37. Otto Roesch, commentary Letter on earlier draft.

38. Ibid.

39.   Interviews with amnestied former rebels at Matsinye resettlement camp and in Chimoio city.

40. See the Introductory Chapter for a detailed description of the methods used in gathering and analyzing the data.

41. David Lehmann, "Women", draft paper p. 72.

42. Ruth Marshal, op. cit. p. 29.

43. Ibid., p. 30.

44. Ibid., p. 32.

45. The husband of the possessed woman was making (reed)mats, while her mother was cutting thatch grass for sale.

46. In the case of Paulino, however it appears the generalised impoverishment of the masses, which diminished their purchasing power, rather than misfortune caused by ancestors, accounts for the collapse of his business.

47. It was by sheer coincidence that I met the chief at the Frelimo's Head Quarters in Chimoio. The chief had come to report the matter and to seek help from the Provincial Party Secretary, who I had also gone to interview on that day.

48. See Gil Lauriciano, "The Spirit of Mungoi: An alternative Power or Just a Phenomenon of the War?", Special Report in *Domingo*, September 1990, Maputo.

49. Irae Baptista Lundin, of the Institute of Strategic Studies (ISRI) and the Ministry of State Administration, is trying to formulate a new policy on local authorities based on 'what was functioning on the ground'. Jocelyn Alexander, "A Summary of Letter to Terence Ranger on Papers and Discussion at the Maputo Conference", held in January 1993 - letter sent to me.

50. This is what most members of the sect interviewed at one place of worship believed.

51. The son was visibly psychologically traumatised, as evidenced by his hysterical screams when we tried to take them a photograph. Interview in Mudzingadzi, June 1992.

52. He said that he knew many people who had been persecuted and arrested (and some of whom never be seen again) by Frelimo.

53. I attended this particular sermon at the invitation of the pastor himself.

54. Popular Feirra (Fepo), is a an enclosed place in Chimoio city where festivals, especially trade fairs, are held, and there are a number of pubs and a few night clubs.

55. Their lack of fear of attack by the MNR - as evidenced by the location of their camp in the periphery of the city which has long been deserted by residents fleeing Renamo - makes one wonder whether or not, through their South African offices, they were guaranteed against MNR attack or worse still, had links with it.

56. Interview with the crusaders at their camp in the outskirts of Chimoio city.

57. Paul Gifford, op. cit., p. 13.

58. Almost all believers thought that it was only through prayer that God could forgive them.

59. Paul Gifford, op. cit., p.15.

60. Bob Marley and the Wailers, "Talking Blues", a reggae track.

61. The Church has never claimed to be 'apolitical', and the Pope and clergy have frequently commented on political questions of global significance.

62. Interview with a Roman Catholic official, Chimoio, August 1992.

63. According to an amnestied former Renamo soldier - the teacher cited earlier - on the day of his capture (by Renamo) he was beaten for answering questions in Portuguese., and they forced him to speak in Ndau. Recently, as a result of criticisms of Ndau dominance of the movement - a criticism that was never publicly accepted, at least by the movement's arch sympathizers such as David Hoile (he rejected this criticism at a public meeting on Mozambique organized by the Zimbabwe British Society in London, March 1993) - there has been an attempt to redress this by promoting cadres from other ethnic groups to leadership posts.

64. Ken wilson, *Internally Displaced Refugees and Returnees from and in Mozambique*, SIDA, Report Number 1, November 1992, p. 25.

65. Ibid.

66. Interview with the Sister in Chimoio city.

67. Interview with a Zimbabwean Catholic agricultural extension worker based in Chimoio, July 1992.

68. According to Mrs Perkins, the baroness had lived at the farm since just after the Second World. At independence she decided she was not moving, because in the past she had lost everything when governments changed: in Tanzania after the Germans lost in the First World War, and in Kenya after the Second World War.

69. For example, when we visited the place we met few white people from the West, a nurse from Birmingham (England) who is a member of the Christian Fellowship, A Japanese young man who bakes and delivers bread- in an old truck that keeps on breaking down all the time - to nearby resettlement camps, a lady teacher from England, an architect from England and a few others from South Africa who seemed to involved in the co-ordination and administration of supplies.

70. She cited a recent case in which Manica Freight would not release their food because of a mix up in paying, but after praying, the food was released.

71. According to Ken Wilson, a similar 'movement' had emerged and collapsed in Maputo in the mid-1980s.

72. Unfortunately we got to know of Brother Elijah's movement during the last few weeks of the research, when he arrived in Chimoio city on 'a sojourn'.

73. Previously, as noted in Chapter Four, demobilised soldiers had captured the Power Station, depriving the city of electricity for about nine hours, the women's organisation, for the first time, had gone on to the streets demonstrating against the government, and soldiers had gone wild at Fepo, beating and hurting a number of people.

74. Cassava roots or madyoka are normally dried in the sun for some time before they are eaten. See Hans Rosling, *Cassava, Cyanide and Epidemic Spastic Paraparesis: A Study in Mozambican Dietary Exposure*, Stockholm, Uppsala, 1984, and Julie Cliff *et al*, "Association of High Cyanide and Low Surplus Intake in Cassava-induced Spastic Paraparesis", in *The Lancet*, 30 November 1985.

75. One Mozambican suggested, jokingly, that people had become a favourite prey for crocodiles because they were walking semi-naked.

76. See T. B. Bottomore (editor), *Karl Marx, Early Texts*, London, Pelican, 1963, T.B. Bottomore and Maximilen Rubel, *Karl Marx: Selected Writings in Sociology and Social Philosophy*, London, Penguin, 1965, and D. McLellan,, *Karl Marx: His Life and Thought*, London, 1972.

77. D.McLellan, op. cit, p. 122.

78. Ibid., p. 123.

79. Ibid., p. 92.

80. For a critical analysis of Nietzsche's anti-Christian ideas, see among others, Bertrand Russell, *History of Western Philosophy*, London, Routledge, 1991.

81. Cited by Michael Novak, *A Theology for Radical Politics*, New York, Herder and Herder, 1969, p. 18.

82. Ruth Marshall, op. cit., p. 21.

83. Itumelng J. Mosala, *Biblical Hermeneutics and Black Theology in South Africa* , Michigan, W. B. Eerdmans Publishing Company, 1990, p.3.

84. See Ibid.

85. T.B. Bottomore and Maximilien, op. cit., p. 41.

6 Women, war and change: An ambiguous legacy

Introduction

Women in Mozambique in particular and the 'Third World' in general[1] have been simultaneously the most productive and yet the most marginalised social group. As Wippier observes:

> In traditional African societies women were subordinate to male authority and male dominance was buttressed by an ideology of superiority on a status system where women showed deference to men.[2]

This subjugation of women is embedded in the social fabric of society, and stems from the economic power imbalance between the sexes. Such sexual division of labour, which condemned women to the private sphere, is a social and historical construct whose terms are constantly ratified in the on-going gender struggle. In Mozambique, the war has catalysed this process of social contestation. The consequences, for women, have been ambiguous and contradictory.

More precisely, the socio-political upheaval caused by the war, has been a mixed blessing for women; it contains both new possibilities for the emancipation of women as well as seeds of their further subjugation. The collapse of rural economies as a result of the war has undermined the power base of patriarchy and the hegemony of its legitimating ideology. Traditional social support networks have also broken down. In their struggle to counter-act their vulnerabilities occasioned by this break-down, some women have attained relative economic and political autonomy from male domination. This has been primarily through entrepreneurial activity in the grass-roots war-economy. However, while some women have graduated into relatively established entrepreneurs by ingeniously manoeuvring their way in the turmoil, others have further been marginalised. Many have been reduced to 'beautiful slaves', sex workers and even social mendicancies surviving on charity. In this chapter the main objective is to find out among other things how the experience of war has affected the lives of women.

The chapter examines the following questions: what war or violence did *for* women, what it did *to* women, and what women did for themselves and to fuel the war. More specifically, it will explore the strategies women have adapted to improve their position in deteriorating material conditions. It will also try to understand why some women have been successful while others have failed in their personal and collective gender struggles. Four important points, which emerged from women's life history narratives, will be emphasized in this discussion.

First, as with the independence war, the conditions of war have challenged the relations between women and men and "created the possibility for new gender relations and new family identities" .[3] Second, these new relations have been established through women's gender struggles. Third women engaged in this struggles at various levels, for instance, through confrontation with male members of their families, traditional authorities and the state. Finally, there are also divisive tendencies and cleavages within the women's movement that has, inevitably, hampered their struggle. A combination of these factors has produced an ambiguous and contradictory situation for women. This ambiguity has been reflected in the literature, which is broadly divided into two schools.

Contesting perspectives on women, war and power

The first, the 'vulnerable group' approach, focuses on the victimization of women in war, emphasizing their special needs and vulnerabilities. For such scholars, best represented by Nordstrom:

> Dirty war tactics, elevated to a common strategy grounding many of today's wars, place women at the epicentre of conflict. Women stand as general targets, raped, maimed and murdered in the dirty war construction of terror.[4]

This approach, which has provided the theoretical underpinning for international refugee assistance in Mozambique, has its foundation in the belief that "the vulnerability or special needs of refugee women provide the rationale for the majority of refugee assistance projects".[5]

The second approach focuses on women's role in community welfare, and is based on the assumption that "the satisfaction of the needs of women and

210

ways to deal with women's specific problems will in turn contribute to an amelioration of the welfare of the refugee community".[6] Assistance to refugee women, as key providers for their families, is seen as an instrument rather than a goal in itself, important in its own right. While both approaches may prove important in some respects, they neglect important aspects of women's lives and war experiences.

The 'vulnerable group' approach's depiction of women as passive victims underplays the resilience women have displayed in adapting survival strategies that have transformed their situation. As will be argued in this chapter, through the operation of the dialectic of control, women have been active agents shaping their history. As Hanna-Anderson aptly puts it:

> This focus on women as a vulnerable group has done women a disservice. Instead of being seen as actors (often major actors) ... women are portrayed as conservative and passive, and the important role they play remains invisible to planners.[7]

Similarly the treatment of women only as integral elements of the community central to its stability and reproduction, underplays excessively the changing desires and aspirations of women.

First, by emphasizing community needs and not the individual woman's, the approach implicitly ends up legitimating the subordinate position of women and the intensification of women's role in the domestic sphere. Second, the underlying assumptions about the 'family' and the 'community' on which the notion of 're-integration' currently in vogue is based, seem to underestimate the extent to which the structure of the family and community have been fundamentally altered as an unexpected consequence of the war. 'Re-integration', depending on the kind of family and community into which women are 're-integrated', could well be a reversal of the limited gains women have made as a result of both revolution and war.

This chapter will try to go beyond the current conceptions of women as mere passive victims or instruments for community welfare. Instead it views them as conscious agents actively transforming their environments to meet their changing needs. It explores women's experiences of war, their changing economic roles and political status, emphasising issues that are of central concern to them. It will be shown that the historical construction of gender identity, as opposed to sex which is a biological phenomenon, has been linked to changes in the socio-economic base as well as features of the superstructure. By altering the political economy, the war has therefore also shaped contemporary gender struggles.

In particular, the war has influenced contemporary construction of gender identity by: (1) undermining the power base of patriarchy, thereby creating a political space for the 'feminisation' of the social; (2) weakening the patriarchal family, resulting in the rise of multiple forms of co-habitation; (3) forcing women to adapt new survival, and sometimes transformative, strategies which involve acquiring new roles which had been the preserve of men and (4) affecting different categories of women differently, a fact that partly accounts for the perplexing diversity of ideas among women. Changes in family structure and women's position within it and society at large raises important questions about the relationship between marital status and access to income, and hence autonomy.

Second, and related, what is the effect of women's access to income on their marital relations and power configuration within the household? Finally, to what extent do class and age influence women's individual survival strategy and the options available to them? In order to offer some insights into these questions, this analysis draws on women's perspectives and experiences of the war. The ways in which women talked (during interviews) about their lives and their relations with men and the political system can help us understand the significance of these processes to their lives; by highlighting what women are already doing and demanding, the significance of these changes to their lives could be better understood.

To appreciate the extent of these transformations it is important to contrast the present and the past and to know how far gender relations had changed before the war. Women's subjugation and struggles for liberation need to be placed in their historical context, for the options and possibilities of any one time and place are clearly governed by the past.[8] Mozambican women's changing political roles are a product of the past organization of their societies. Similarly, the understandings of the present are shaped by ways the past has been interpreted. Thus before examining how women have engaged in the dialectic of control and exercised (temporary?) power, the analysis briefly looks at the past position of women.

Women and power in pre-colonial and colonial societies

Women's access to power in pre-colonial times in Mozambique was determined primarily by the sex division and control of labour at the economic level, and by the ideology of patriarchy at the political level.[9] As elsewhere in sub-Saharan Africa[10], whether married or not, a woman worked with her parents, with her husband or on her own. When a man cleared the land with a matchet and fire, the woman helped in the planting, weeding, harvesting, and transporting of the produce from the field. It was the woman's job to keep the household area clean, do the cooking and care for the children. In village life the effects of sexual stratification were obvious in the education of the child from an early age. As Fafunwa pointed out with respect to pre-colonial Africa in general:

> Boys and girls began to receive separate instruction, the girls staying close to their mothers and other female relatives and the boys moving progressively into male society. In this way the two sexes began to learn the productive and social roles which they would play in adult life. Young girls were kept busy in the household looking after infants, fetching water, sweeping the compound and washing dishes, whereas their brothers were taught to look after the family's animals, chase birds from the crops and hunt.[11]

Later on the two sexes were initiated into the different aspects of their future lives by participating fully in production with increasing independence and responsibility.[12]

Sexual stratification did not simply mean the division of labour between males and females, but also meant inequalities between the sexes. The low status of women was reflected in their low participation in public affairs and in the exploitation of their labour power.[13] Patriarchal structures, which were strengthened as a tradition in the colonial period[14], prevented women from having equal access as men, to land, power, education and leisure time. As in West Africa, these structures operated primarily at a practical level through the organization of production and distribution of resources.[15] Their main tenets were supported ideologically by patriarchal values which operated at the general level as well as in women's minds. The control of the major means of production, land, by male elders enabled them to control young women and men through marriage arrangements.

Generally, women and young children were largely seen in terms of their contribution to the production process, and the products of their labour were controlled by men as fathers, husbands or brothers. This was the economic basis of bride-wealth payment, which had been elevated to ritualised practice, and the rationale for polygamous and large families. Since the size of the family correlated with prosperity - generally the larger the family the more prosperous as there were more labourers - polygamy was common, and it further entrenched the subjugation of women by men.

Even the matrilineal societies of the Makua and Lomwe in the northern provinces were far from 'matriarchy'; women did not enjoy total political and economic freedom. Although upon marriage the bridegroom had to move to the home of the bride and descent and inheritance traced through the mother, married women were under the influence of their male relatives - fathers, brothers and cousins. Among most ethnic groups in central western

Mozambique practices of forced marriages of young girls - in some cases even before the birth of the girl - and initiation rites were common. Boys were generally preferred to girls[16], and this is partly reflected in the different opportunities and roles between men and women.

In short, although women, as now, contributed a far greater share to the survival of the family, they were politically and economically dependent on men and were often forced into marriage. It is important to note, however, that women generally gained in status as they grew older, and were consulted for advice and words of wisdom. In some cases, especially if they were possessed by spirit mediums, or owned property, women actually enjoyed some power within their communities; they gained control over their sexuality and could become independent decision-makers.[17]

Later, the impact of colonialism and Christianity resulted in a more or less radical transformation of pre-colonial stratification systems. Although colonialism was felt differently in different regions of the country, its over-all effect was to entrench patriarchy and the marginalisation of women in the country-side. With reference to Africa in general, Sacks notes that, colonialism, "far from liberating women, has subjected them to Western forms of sexism, which are often more oppressive to women than previously existing social relations". [18]In the urban areas of Mozambique, and especially for women *assimilados (Black* elite women assimilated into Portuguese culture), the situation was made more complex by the intense fusion of two different cultures. While patriarchy remained the order of the day, elite women enjoyed "extra-ordinary freedoms"[19] - what Frelimo later condemned as western social decadence - associated with income and status. At independence Frelimo set itself the task of eradicating what it considered retrogressive traditional and western practices that underpinned the subjugation of women by men.

Women and the 'revolution'

Coinciding with the Declaration of the Women's Decade in Mexico in 1975, was Mozambique's independence on June 25 after ten years of armed struggle led by FRELIMO. During the independence war Frelimo had emphasized the liberation of women and considered it "the fundamental necessity for the revolution, a guarantee of its continuity and a precondition for victory".[20] In 1973 the Mozambique Women's Organization (OMM) was founded as the vehicle by which women's emancipation was to be achieved.

The participation of women in the war of independence was massive. They travelled long distances, staying away from home for many days, and "they were doing so on equal footing with men".[21] The structure of authority within which these tasks were carried out were also new. As already noted, in their normal daily lives women were subordinated to patriarchal family authority, whether it be a father, an uncle, a husband or a brother. During the war the family ceased to be the ultimate source of authority; a new authority was at work, "an authority which, when *necessary* and for the time being supported women against men" (emphasis added).[22] In this process, gender relations changed. Some women developed a conception of themselves as women: new aspirations, new goals, a new family identity was emerging.

After the war, according to some observers, women were abandoned by Frelimo and the Mozambican Women Organization (OMM) founded in 1973 to articulate women's interests. At independence Frelimo found itself in a totally new situation for which it was badly prepared; fighting a liberation war was very different from building a nation-state. Rather than popular mobilisation and collaboration with the peasantry the focus now was on the creation of national institutions and the structures of economic and political power. As Armfred notes, "the idea of peoples' power which had been developed during the war was insufficient as a political base in this new situation".[23] According to Armfred, in the rural areas of the north where the war had been fought, gender relations returned to the situation before the war as men took back even more than they had lost of patriarchal power.[24] Moreover, the extent to which Frelimo's policies were translated into practice varied over space and time, with some modifications made at the various conferences. For instance, at its second Conference in 1976 policy towards women was restructured along the lines of the classical theories of women's emancipation.[25] Later, at the 'OMM's Extra-ordinary Conference' of November 1985, emphasis further shifted from the radical tenor of the founding conference of 1973 to child care as women were exhorted to 'produce and feed fighters'.[26]

Similarly, the OMM's campaigns tended to be concentrated in urban areas, where decisive conferences were held. The campaigns were also most intense during the early years of Independence[27], that is, before the war came to the centre stage. Since the policy was implemented at village level by peasants, there were also local variations as the peasants neither completely understood the policy nor were willing to alienate their neighbours by implementing controversial policies. Overall, the "priority task" was national reconstruction and revolution, while the participation of women was only a precondition for triumph. This conception of the relation between women and revolution informed Frelimo's strategy for the liberation of women. As in other 'socialist' countries such as Cuba, Frelimo pursued a broad based strategy for improving the position of women. The strategy involved education, legal and constitutional changes to protect the rights of women, active participation of women in the labour force as well as mass organisations.

215

Work in state farms was seen as a way of enhancing women's economic independence. Women were also encouraged to attend literacy classes set up in the rural areas, and indeed a few women interviewed reported having acquired their literacy through these campaigns. Forced marriage and initiation rights were abolished (especially in collective villages). The OMM was the major mass organisation for popular mobilisation which fulfilled a variety of tasks, such as health and adult literacy, at the local level. Notwithstanding the initial success and promise, and as shown below, 'empowerment' of women still remains elusive.

Women and the OMM: The contradiction between theory and practice

The OMM, as the vanguard organization for women's emancipation had structures from national to village level in the whole country. It was effectively an extension of the party and the state apparatus. Women were exhorted to participate in the movement's activities. But as their testimonies below suggest, the movement turned out to be nothing more than a bureaucratic organization that simply transmitted orders from the top to bottom. The result was demoralisation and demobilisation of women, the extent of which is reflected in their perspectives on the role and activities of the OMM.

Women's views on the activities of the OMM range from passive acceptance to indifference and contempt, and in some cases blame for the collapse of the traditional family. For many peasant and elite women alike, the OMM and its activities were largely seen in terms of party politics. Its main function was seen as to entertain party officials at rallies, by singing, playing traditional dance, preparing food for them and cleaning the place before the rally.[28] As one young woman put it, "they taught us how to treat husbands, hygiene, dancing, sewing and cooking".

The fact that women were expected to clean the place, their traditional roles, reflects the extent to which patriarchal attitudes were still well entrenched within the Frelimo hierarchy. More important, this reveals Frelimo's failure to resolve the fundamental problem of the sexual division of labour within the household. Since women were encouraged to take on men's roles in all spheres, the allocation of such domestic tasks to women placed an excruciatingly heavy burden on their daily lives. As Urdang aptly observed:

> Half the battle for women's liberation and equality lies in the need to ensure the full participation of women in production outside the home as well as their equal access to and appropriation of society's resources resulting from such production. The other half is the need for both men

216

and women to share domestic labour and responsibilities within the household, so that women can participate in outside production.[29]

But in Mozambique the household gendered division of labour was not confronted and the family remained the most fundamental oppressive unit for women. Exhorting women to accept their position in the sex division of labour, Machel asserted:

> Keeping the city clean is mainly the task for women. Are we going to take men out of the factories to come and sweep?"[30]

In short, and reflective of the extent to which the guiding ideology of OMM was predominantly patriarchal, the campaign never challenged the subjugation of women within the family. Consequently, though they had not waited passively for the state to transform their position, many peasant women began to view the OMM's activities with suspicion, and even hostility.

For some women, as for a twenty-three year old rural woman who was married at about thirteen and never went to school, the OMM was just another structure with no relevance to their lives. As she puts it:

> In Macate, yes *they* (OMM women) are there. But we only see *them* when we are called for meetings. *They* sing for the *chefes* and sweep the place where meetings are held (emphasis added).

The use of the terms 'they' and 'them' seems to suggest the absence of a consciousness of belonging to or a common agenda with the organization. The way she described how they were called to meetings gave the impression that to her it was a rather unwelcome interruption of her private life.

Many other women, like Gilda Sazero, a single mother aged thirty and illiterate, did not even know about the OMM, and had never attended its meetings. Another woman, a grandmother of nearly one hundred years old said that she used to see the OMM secretaries (leaders) totter/pass by but was never helped and did not know their function. Yet another single twenty-three year old woman, then going to night secondary school, attacked the OMM for corruption. Complaining at the failure of the organization to help her secure a court order for a fair distribution of property she owned with her now estranged husband she said: "In the past they (the OMM) used to resolve marital problems. But now they want to be bought".

Unlike the other two illiterate women, this woman was aware of the OMM and its activities, and this seems to be a function of her education. It is worthy pointing out here that education, an area that Frelimo deserves credit for its (limited) success, as well as the participation of women in the

217

independence war, are some of the major forces that led to the changes in women's position and perspectives. But ironically, those who acquired education under Frelimo have become, though not exclusively, the most vocal critics of it's liberation project.

In fact for some women, the OMM and its campaign were not only unnecessary, but have been the main cause for the collapse of the family and the values and norms that had kept society stable. According to a 23-year old mother of two, who had not finished primary education because her father believed that 'only boys should go to school':

> They (the OMM) go around teaching people to wash plates, cleaning houses and encouraging women to attend meetings. But their talk of 'equal rights' causes confusion. For example, because in OMM we don't work and/or walk separately as women, it is easier for me to go out with another woman's husband. Meanwhile, my husband gets involved in affairs while I am away on OMM business... It was quite common then seeing women boasting about having a nice time and dinning with the *chefes* (officials).

Thus for her, the 'equality' that the OMM promoted had been the main cause of the collapse of the family; it allowed women to rival men in all their vices.

Though uneducated, the question she raised about what 'equal rights' between the sexes should mean is vitally important. The question has dogged feminists and politicians alike. Some feminists (in general) have talked of 'equality in difference' (or right to be different'), whilst others have emphasized 'equal opportunity', and yet others still want 'total equality'.

In addition to such critical discourses against the hegemonic ideologies, the surprisingly low turn-out at the International Women's Day celebrations spoke much about the popularity of OMM's campaign.[31] In Beira, only a small group of women dressed in *capulanas* (bearing the party's emblem) attended the ceremonies while the rest of the population went on with their daily activities. The main event was a women's traditional dance, with a few men playing the drums. Of note was the fact that all the proceedings at the meeting were directed by men. Thus it appears, in defending their privileges men have either, as in this case, simply hijacked the women's movement, or overtly resisted women's advances, especially by recourse to myths of traditional heritage.

Men whose traditional privileges were most threatened tended, though not exclusively, to blame the OMM's activities for the collapse of the family and rising social decadence. For example, according to two men, one in his early twenties and the other middle-aged:

> Notions of equality promoted by Machel are bankrupt and do not work...There should be only one cock [head] in a household.

In a similar vein, and justifying his polygamous relationship, a thirty-five year old man separated from his three wives by the war and living with another woman, declared: "It is our tradition".

Not all men were against equality with women, however. On the contrary some believed, as one middle-aged man put it, that since women had fought side by side with men in the independence war, they deserved equal rights. A few even cited Biblical teachings that since woman was created from the rib of man, she was neither above (head) nor below (feet), but equal.[32] However, the general trend seems to be the exaltation of the most retrogressive elements of patriarchy, and a down-playing of the potentialities of women.

As is clear from these political discourses, not only did Frelimo's campaign for the liberation of women fail to achieve its stated objectives; it also generated many contradictions and different responses from different categories of people. This seems to be a result of a combination of factors the most important of which are: the limited capacity of the state, inevitable given its weak penetration of civil society, to effect changes in social attitudes and values; underlying assumptions about the nature of women's problems; the way in which the policy was implemented; and the resistance from various segments of society.

Thus the outcome of the revolution for women was far from the officially stated objectives. After initial success, the campaign failed to gain momentum, and this was largely because it was imposed from above, instead of growing spontaneously from women's initiatives, as seems to be the case now. More often than not the OMM, itself a bureaucratic organisation, was reduced to a mere mouthpiece for (male) official ideology. The unintended effect was to stifle initiative among its supposed beneficiaries.

Nonetheless, despite the campaign's own shortcomings and the counter-tendencies that it generated, women did make some limited gains under the revolution, especially in the spheres of education and health care. Apart from that, by merely raising the question of gender Frelimo played a crucial role in raising women's consciousness about their rights. It was this consciousness, constantly changing as it were, that formed the launching pad for the current upsurge in attempts at feminisation of the social. Catalysing this process have been two major variables, viz war and liberalization, to whose impact on women we now turn.

Women in the face of change: War, liberalization and the disintegration of the family

The current gender struggles have been conditioned by the exigencies of surviving in a war situation. The fundamental impact of war on women has been through its undermining of the patriarchal family, the creation of economic opportunities and forced politicisation/militancy. The economic demands of the war itself have forced social changes, that in turn have enabled women to break out of strictly defined gender roles. In addition, the war has undercut the state's capacity, forcing it to relinquish monopoly of control of public life and hence opening up space for women to take the initiative. Finally, the liberalisation programme, whose key component is the enhancement of the role of the individual in society, has provided further impetus to the historically contested process of women's emancipation.

The reforms are geared towards shifting state responsibility for socialisation on to the family with the mother at the centre. Effectively, they amount to replacement of class reductionism with market reductionism. In the latter, as in the former, the family remains the prime site both for women's oppression and for the socialisation of children. The overall effect of the interaction of war and reform has been a radical change in the family structure and gender relations.

The erosion and, in some cases, the breakdown of public institutions has affected the interrelations between kin, friends and neighbours. New forms of family and association are replacing kinship and extended family ties. For example, and showing the demise of the extended family, out of the fifty-nine households interviewed, only 6 per cent lived with four or more relatives, while about two thirds lived with none. Also 5 per cent were headed by widowed mothers, 12.5 per cent by divorced or separated parents and 17.5 per cent constituted simple or complex co-habitation. As in Uganda, kinship as a determinant of material relations has remained important as the public climate of opportunities has deteriorated, but kinship as "a metaphor that united people through social sentiments designating lines of autonomy has been greatly eroded".[33]

One cause of these changes in family structure and form, whose most visible manifestation is the rise in single female-headed households, is that many men have been tied down in fighting the war. Some men have fled to

220

neighbouring countries, and as a result the ratio of women to men is skewed. As Rodriguez, a member of the OMM national secretariat pointed out; "In some areas we find 1 750 women and only 300 men. How can we combat polygamy in this situation?"[34] This has not only entrenched and legitimated polygamy; it has also given rise to the collapse of the institution of marriage as men can easily divorce and find another woman. Remarking on the high rate of divorce or separation, one old timer put it thus: "Nowadays they wed to divorce [meaning that marriages no longer last and that weddings are largely for a show of wealth]".[35] Another important factor which accounts for increased marital instability is women's involvement in the informal sector, whose demands often conflict with family obligations.

Unemployment, women's entrepreneurial activities and marital instability

The combined effect of war and privatisation has caused a number of companies to close down in Manica Province. As a result unemployment has risen. The lack of employment opportunities has driven women into the informal sector. Women, especially those who have been uprooted from the rural areas have been the most disadvantaged group in getting formal employment. Sex discrimination against women, apart from lack of relevant skills on the part of women, is due to the perceived unprofitability of employing women by the new owners of the privatised companies. Frelimo's laws on maternity leave, which granted two months paid leave and 30 minutes every four hours for breast-feeding at work, have been incompatible with the interests of the new capitalist entrepreneurs. As the Provincial Director of Labour pointed out:

> We encourage companies to give first priority to single women and disabled men in their recruitment. But the problem is that these companies view this sub-category as the least economically productive and they don't want to employ them. There is nothing we can do. We can't force them.

Consequently it is only in companies still owned by the state, most of which are facing grave financial problems, that the policy of first priority to women and the disabled is still pursued.

Not surprisingly therefore, for example, only 175 women as compared to 2, 904 men were formally employed in the whole Province during the period 1988-92.[36] Even the number of formally registered unemployed women was far less than that of men, 1,907 as compared to 6,656, and this bears out the pervasiveness of patriarchal assumptions about women's rightful place. Women are not only systematically discriminated against in the formal sector:

221

they are even encouraged to think of their unemployment as a private affair rather than a state responsibility. Caught between the hammer of the war and the anvil of reform, women have had no alternative other than to enter the informal sector (as in innumerable other countries where there is no war).

Women entrepreneurs in the informal sector, as was shown in Chapter Three, engaged in various activities that range from vegetable vending and selling cooked food to 'big business' that more often than not involved under-hand practices. In the process of production and reproduction - work and parenting - women have confronted changes and conflicting demands. Depending on their specific needs and structural constraints, women have incorporated or rejected these changes and tried to reconcile their conflicting demands. In extreme cases in which business demands and marital obligations could not be reconciled, the latter was often the casualty.

Facing the economic crisis: Women's life histories

An examination of the lives and beliefs of individual women, through life histories, can provide some insights on ideas about women's position. Life histories, located in the context of personal discourse can unveil the kinds of politics that different women engage in according to their image or sense of self, their place in society and their rapport with the researcher.[37] As Werbner argues, only through knowledge of the sensitive, "sometimes petty, personal discourses among family members can we understand the moral argument resonating in each life history and between all the life histories".[38]

The main problem with this approach lies in its failure to transcend the subjectivities of both the narrators and the interpreter. In a context of dire misery, most narratives are bound to be tainted by or fed on a quaint nostalgic feeling of the past (imagined?) golden days. Nonetheless, because the 'personal' is also 'political' or at least a constitutive element of it, its analysis can provide the basis for thinking through wider issues about progress, development, individualism, collectivity, the state and the individual.

One life story that captures the impact of war and change on women is that of a middle-aged woman, separated from a polygamous marriage and now supporting her family by brewing and selling traditional 'opaque' beer. Explaining how she got separated she began:

> In the past everything was alright. My husband used to support all of us (the four wives) well, but later things started getting bad. He [could] no longer support all of us equally. He was favouring the youngest wife - I was the third.

222

Jealousy ensued and in one of the fights, which had become a characteristic feature of the family, she lost a finger (it was bitten off by her opponent). As she added:

> I said to myself I can't die for a man. So I packed all my belongings and left with all my five children and came to Chimoio (from Beira). When I came here my brother and his family welcomed me. With his support, I started brewing and selling beer.
>
> But now he is no more - he was murdered while going to work as a night-shift watchman. The person who brought his corpse said he was beaten to death by local people after being caught trying to steal chicken.

Now, with the bread winner in that family dead, leaving six young children and a wife, life has become increasingly difficult. As she puts it:

> My brother's wife is ill. How can I support two families - my brother's and my own? For instance, right now the malt [sprouting grain for beer brewing] is already rotting in the river because I don't have the money to buy sugar [an essential ingredient in beer brewing].

She was so overwhelmed by her problems that she resigned herself to drinking. In response to the question whether or not she had any question she replied; "I want to know whether or not my brother and my son, who was run over by a car while going to school, will be compensated?" Evidently, the loss of her loved ones, and whether or not some justice will be effected is the main burden of her heart, while immediate survival needs are a persistent concern. She had in fact tried several times, but in vain, to seek justice through the courts. Frustration and desperation led to militancy when, after sharing her experiences with other women, they decided to get organized politically. In July 1992, with some women in a similar situation, she went to the streets of Chimoio demonstrating against the government for failure to end the war, lack of protection for women and lack of jobs. Although their immediate demands were not met, this confrontation with the state marked a crucial phase in the contested relationship between the patriarchal state and women. In the case of individual women involved, it was a conscientising experience in which they discovered the potential of collective action in the struggle for a fair distribution of power. In these conditions women's specific demands are not a luxury but a precondition for their active involvement in the movement for social change.

Clearly, for this woman, as for many others, the war has meant family breakdown, increased suffering, forced innovativeness and a critical outlook. The economic hardships caused by the war partly explain the intense rivalry among the wives, which in turn resulted in this particular woman's decision to leave her husband, after having lost a finger. As explained, her marital status was vital in determining her access to income: before separation her situation was slightly better than after. Whether or not her brother was killed actually trying to steal a chicken, the point remains that, because they were people surviving on thieving, his death is explicable by reference to the generalised economic crisis.

Finally, it appears from this woman's case that family size, the age structure of the members, as well as skills or lack of them are crucial variables determining the options open to women. For instance, because none of her children or her brother's, eleven in all, was old enough to work or engage in independent entrepreneurship, the meagre returns she got from beer could hardly be re-invested: it all went to feeding the family. Lack of skills, and failure to quickly adapt (due to her age), resulted in her engaging in the most labour intensive but least numerative economic activity.[39]

Unlike this woman whose divorce has entailed more hardships, the case of Mariana Simao illustrates a situation in which a woman's access to income can alter her marital relationship. Mariana, a twenty-four year old mother of one, had been married to a primary school teacher, but initiated a divorce which she did not regret. According to her, since separating she has "been making much more progress than before". In her words:

> My husband was a drunkard and irresponsible. He never brought money home - he spent it all on drinking. In fact when he had finished drinking his money, he would steal mine which I got from vegetable vending. Even when our son was ill, he never bothered to look at him nor take him to hospital. We used to fight a lot. I finally decided I could not take it any more - I could not live with a *bandido* (bandit) - and I left him three years ago.
>
> When I left him I went to live with my brother who later helped me build a house for myself. Meanwhile I continued selling vegetables at the market. My business - because I had good relationships with my customers (selling on credit) - was so successful that I managed to keep myself and my child happy. I bought clothes, food and furniture and, am now building a bigger house.

As this case indicates, male violence and irresponsibility, which are associated with the frustration of a worsening economic situation, have been the main reason for women to seek divorce or separation.[40] Free from dependence on an irresponsible husband, this woman, like many others, has been able to live an autonomous life making decisions on how to use her labour and control the products therefrom. Unrestrained by the strict morals pertaining to married women she has a greater opportunity to explore her sexuality and express her needs.

Another example of a woman gaining some economic and political autonomy through separation is that of a twenty-four year old woman, who is now a successful cooked-food vendor in Gondola town. According to her, before he left for South Africa her husband had been a tailor and the breadwinner of the family, while she was primarily responsible for housework. For reasons unknown to her - he might have been pressed-ganged into Renamo or even died - he never came or wrote back. With the family (herself and two young children) facing increasing financial difficulties and relatives unable to help, she decided to start selling vegetables in order to raise some income. As she recounts:

> Before my husband left we lived quite well. But when he left, things started getting difficult. I had no money to buy food or clothes for my children. My husband's relatives could not help and mine are too far away in Maputo. A friend suggested to me that if I buy vegetables from the 'green zones' [farming areas around the city] and sell them in town - as she was doing - I could get some money to feed my children. I borrowed some money and did as she had said. After a while it started paying off. Later another friend suggested that I could make much more money if I cooked and sold food.

By selling cooked rice and chicken, tea and bread etc, she has managed to build herself a three roomed house. Her first born is going to school, a privilege which many cannot afford: many children do not go to school because they have to help their parents raise some income or because their parents cannot afford to pay a bribe to get a school place. As evidence of success and a sign of status, she has employed a young housemaid to assist her and take care of the children when she is at work, and finally to top it all, she was planning to build a bigger house.

Like many other cases, economic necessity was the mother of creative enterprise for this woman, which in turn has been rewarded by increasing economic independence and political autonomy. Many women have managed to earn enough and thereby make important changes in their relationships.[41] Also, like their counter-parts in Ghana and elsewhere in sub-Saharan Africa[42], a relatively high proportion of women in this category desired to acquire houses of their own. As a matter of fact, those who became prosperous did establish their own households over which they would exercise full control. Thus, security and freedom, seem to be the most pressing needs for most women, but many women have found it difficult to reconcile the two.

225

In some instances, women have ventured into areas that have been the domain of men such as large-scale entrepreneurial activities, commercial farming, trading and smuggling as well as ownership of small shops. For example, some of the most popular and prosperous unlicensed houses selling beer in the city were owned by independent women. In Sussundenga district one of the few productive farms is owned by a woman. The bulk of goods from Zimbabwe is imported or smuggled by women. Increasingly women are taking on men's roles, such as physically building their own houses.

Much has been written about this group of women who engage in petty-trading[43], but little or no attention has been devoted to the study of important adjustments such women make when income generating activities conflict with marital obligations. Although the majority of women reported marriage was important to them, they were not prepared to give up their businesses or work for the sake of marriage. This finding is consistent, for example, with that of Aborampah in the Ghanaian town of Techiman, where women traders would "in most cases, not fall on their husbands for financial assistance, neither would they abandon their trades to concentrate on their marriages even though marriage is very important to them'.[44]

As Aborampah correctly points out, because most of these women "make their daily living from their trade, they tend to be more concerned about their prospects in this area".[45] In Chimoio, as in many other African cities[46] the ever expanding markets in food, cloth and imported goods (see Chapter Three) has afforded market woman "a much stronger basis for adjustment to an emancipated status than is available elsewhere".[47] Of note here, as in Ghana, is the small or non-existence of husbands in the business of their spouses. Instead women relied more on the extended family, kin and mutual aid associations, and more often than not their adult children assisted them.

This non-involvement of husbands in women's businesses is due to a combination of factors. First, as in the case of the above cited woman whose husband 'stole' her money to get drunk, women are reluctant to let their spouses tamper with their profits lest that endangers their future capacity to trade advantageously. Second, the relatively low incomes, if any, of their husbands make women's demands for financial assistance from their spouses unrealistic. Finally, as already pointed out, women tend to prefer economic independence from their husbands and husbands' relatives.

Through action around production and consumption, and primarily in the informal sector, women have thus laid claim to rights and citizenship and expanded their political space. In doing so, they have carried forward the 'revolution' initiated by Frelimo, but stifled by its bureaucratic and patriarchal ideology. However not all women have been able to transform their misfortune into opportunities. Others have actually degenerated into more poverty and misery and in some cases are forced to resort to crime and prostitution, and this is related to class position and age.

Women, social differentiation and marginalization

As already pointed out elsewhere in the book, the operation of the grass-roots war economy has generated a polarisation of wealth and power. Many single mothers, especially middle-aged ones whose children are still too young to help, have become increasingly marginalised in this process. Of the many such examples, the story of a middle-aged mother of a seven year- old beggar is most illustrative. After the death of her husband, and being illiterate and unskilled, the 36 year old rural woman could not cope with the hardships on her own. No-one could re-thatch the hut, buy food and cloth and ensure the general security of the family. One day she was arrested, allegedly trying to steal a blanket, and sent to prison for six months. Meanwhile her son became a full-time beggar. When she was released, all their few belongings had disappeared and the hut had collapsed. Forced to start from scratch, she said she had no option other than to join the ranks of the ever expanding sex workers in order to build her life. But for her, prostitution was only a means for immediate survival, and as she pointed out, she wanted to be re-married.

Like another single mother in a similar situation, who said she was "looking for a man, any man who can look after me and my son", financial and security considerations seem to be her main reason for desire to be re-married. This need for 'any man' to depend on, contrasts with the appreciation of freedom that separation entailed exhibited by many divorced and enterprising younger women. Thus, while there is a relationship between marital status and access to income, the nature of the link is not clear. It seems to vary with the age of the women concerned, the size of their families and the class of the spouse. In other words, women occupying different positions in society will always want different things and have different beliefs and attitudes.

Women's changing needs and wants, aspirations and attitudes

The needs, wants and attitudes of women are not static. Instead they are constantly changing, with the satisfaction of some needs leading to other needs, and this generally reflects changes in the material and social culture. Thus women's perspectives on questions of marriage or re-marriage, and the family as well as societal change are ambivalent. This ambivalence, as shown below, is a manifestation of their contradictory situation, and the varied social positions they occupy in society.

The most surprising thing to emerge from most of the life history narratives by women, especially young women, was that virtually none made a direct reference to the impact of war on their lives. They only mentioned the war in passing or when specifically asked. Instead most young women's narratives tended to concentrate more on their romantic or married life, their aspirations and problems, economic dislocations and impacts thereof. This perhaps reflects the fact that for many young women, war is all they have ever known and as such they take it for granted as a daily fact of life. More important, it bears testimony to the resilience of Mozambican women to live through and with violence. Apart from that, and as a few examples given below suggest, the emphasis on socio-economic relations shows that women's prime concerns centre on their personal lives. This leads us to the question of the interface of the private and public spheres: to what extent does personal experience shape the public realm and vice-versa?

The personal as political

Amply demonstrating the degree to which the personal can also be political is the story of Rosilina Leia, a twenty-four year old separated young woman. Forced into a marriage to a man nearly three times her age at the age of twelve, she adapted to the new situation, but after eight years the marriage broke down. Now, a mother of two - both the children live with the husband -and an independent woman she looks back at her past and present situation with ambivalence, but is determined to build herself a future. She could not forgive her father for forcing her into the marriage. In her words:

> My father greatly offended me. He was bought off with beer by the man - a prosperous builder. When they first told me about it, I ran away from the rural areas and went to Beira. There I was arrested and returned home by the police who had been instructed to do so by my father. He lied to them that I had run away from home in order to become a prostitute. But that was not true because then I was living with some Roman Catholic sisters at the mission where I had been studying for the previous two years.

Her mother, however had no say in the marriage proceedings. After initial revulsion and trauma at being abused she later began to enjoy the marriage. In her own words:

> At first I did not like it and it was painful. But the man lavished me so much with presents, fashionable clothes, good food. He built a big four

228

bed-roomed house for me. I did not do much work. The maids took care of that. I made my hair and prepared 'special dinners' for my husband only. I was living like a white person. I enjoyed it and even forgot that I had been forced into it.

Obviously she had every reason to enjoy life and forget the past: a poor peasant daughter suddenly catapulted to a middle-class wife, living in a finely furnished house in the beautiful city of Manica and attended to by maids. But this was to be a short-lived bliss. As she continued:

When we started living with his young brother's wife, who was much younger than me, things started changing. They were having an affair, and when I discovered it I smashed her head with a bottle in a fight. He chased me away after that incident.

The husband, using his economic power to divide women and abuse them, was eager to enjoy his patriarchal rights. According to her, it was wealth that attracted the younger woman to her husband. When this incident happened, for instance, the younger woman's husband had gone to Zimbabwe where, in order to raise money for bride-wealth, he was working in the rural areas herding cattle.

Reflecting the prevalence in beliefs in witchcraft and superstition, she concluded that her husband had been given a love potion by the younger woman. More important, touching on the contested issue of power within the household and cultural conflict, she added:

He felt threatened by me because I was a bit more educated than him and, as I had lived with whites at the mission, I knew many things he and his relatives did not know. His relatives also did not like me, because they said I was too *murungu* [literally white person, but here meaning upper class].

As in many other cases where women's increased economic power compromised their marriage relationships, this woman's relative power, based on education, partly caused her divorce. Her husband's rural relatives' dislike of her high class life-style, seems to be reflective of the conflict of values between the countryside and the urban areas. As noted in Chapter Four, in Chimoio there was a marked difference in attitudes and behaviours between rural and urban women.

Demonstrating a preference for her new found freedom to an unequal relationship, she has rejected her repentant husband's repeated calls for a reconciliation. His new wife, she claimed, has ruined him financially and that is why he wanted her back. Rejecting his pleas, she has set her eyes on the future, and seems to be managing to make it her way. At the time of the interview she was working as a shop keeper, having worked at Infloma (a timber factory in Manica Province) and attending night secondary school. Her main dream, she pointed out, was to build a good house for herself and get her children back, a desire that almost every women expressed. But the problem is:

> I don't have the money to buy the place, the materials and bribe the officials. The OMM has been unable to help me get a fair distribution of property - two houses, a car, a tractor and furniture - we acquired while living together. It is also corrupt, they (the officials) want to be bought ... but where can I get the money from?...Also his relatives will kill me when they see me get some of our property.

Consequently she has had to try to make ends meet on her own, and in doing so has attained a certain level of autonomy in her life style, the ways in which she uses her income and leisure time. But as she admits, this is not a perfectly satisfactory state of affairs: "Ideally I would want to be married again, but I don't have the luck".

Clearly, this woman's sad story brings out the needs, constraints and the resilience of women, and how the personal merges with the political. Patriarchal ideology both legitimated her forced marriage and her subservience within that marriage. Now political corruption and the patriarchal belief that family property belongs to the husband have combined to shatter her hopes for retribution. Finally, because of the persistence of conservative patriarchal ideas, she cannot find a suitable man to settle down with and establish a family in which power is fairly distributed.

She is not alone in deciding that if marriage brings nothing positive and does not bring happiness (to women), then it should be avoided and is dispensable. She has joined the ranks of the pioneers, single women with or without children who have shown sufficient proof of their ability to manage their own affairs without the oppressive tutelage of men. In fact, in many cases, because of the happiness they draw from their freedom, they are envied by unhappily married women.

Nonetheless, although single mothers are immensely strong - they have to be because circumstances demand it - this way of living is actually forced upon them. It is a response to a less-than-perfect real life where the man has disappeared or is irresponsible, leaving the women to cope on their own - often in hard, unhappy circumstances. While there is a great deal of scope for expanding the boundaries of women's newly found freedoms, the ways in which they sought pleasure and leisure has thrown up dilemmas as to whether it is repressive or liberating development.

The issue of pleasure and leisure maximisation, seems to be among the upper most concerns of contemporary young urban women of Chimoio. War and liberalisation have brought a sexual revolution and/or "sexploitation"[48], in which young women seek to explore their own sexuality and pleasure. This phenomenon raises important questions about the place of sexuality and changing self-images of women in both their oppression and their project for liberation. In the following section the analysis addresses itself to these questions.

Changing values, sexuality and permissiveness: 'Sex revolution or sexploitation'?

The combined effect of war, structural adjustment, the erosion of Marxist morality, western penetration, foreign troops (then mainly from Zimbabwe) and urbanisation has functioned as a decoder for erotic experiences, both reinforcing and subverting expected sexual behaviours. The sudden mushrooming of sexual images - western films, videos and music as well as pornographic magazines - and the rapid fads in fashion-wear have been accompanied by a spread in sexual permissiveness, especially amongst young women. This has also been related to both the spread of prostitution and the increasingly prevalent practice of young men of abandoning responsibility for their children. This scenario is a far cry from the strict morals of the supportive community of extended families, where uncles, aunts and grandparents worked together for social harmony.

In Chimoio, the clash of two cultures, African traditional and assimilated elite western/'luso-tropical' culture, in the context of poverty has increased the emphasis upon material things among young women. Western influence is increasingly becoming widespread upon Mozambican culture, and women amply reflect it. Contrary to the stereotyped African women suffocating under the burden of tradition, the middle-class young women of Chimoio projected in their dress and street manners more liberty and boldness. Many would want to catch up with the latest fashion in vogue. But many families can hardly provide their daughters with fashionable clothes, cosmetics and an elegant life-style, through the consumption of which the 'new' feminine identity is seen (by young women) to be constructed.

Young women have therefore turned to prostitution to achieve the identity they desire.[49] As a sixteen year old school girl, a part-time prostitute painfully, but frankly put it:

Here in Mozambique everything is difficult. At school you need money to buy ball-points, books and food all of which are very expensive. My father is dead and my mother works at Textafrika, but she does not get enough to support us. In the past, when I was younger it was better because I did not need much. Now I am grown up and I need many things - fashionable clothes and cosmetics - but my mother cannot afford it. That is why I am doing it (prostituting). I know it is bad, but I need the money.

Prostitution has steadily been increasing in Mozambique, and since the arrival of United Nations Operation in Mozambique (ONUMOZ) personnel in large numbers "the quality of urban life" has been "negatively affected".[50] An investigation ordered by the United Nations (UN) representative in Mozambique in February 1994 found out that "some Onumoz personnel have fermented prostitution, and in some cases have apparently used child prostitutes.[51]

The point is, while prostitution has existed as an established social phenomenon before the arrival of foreign troops and workers, their relative wealth compared to most of Mozambican society exert a strong influence on the supply of young women willing to serve as prostitutes: it is the demand that leads to supply. Forced sex labour of this nature is therefore a necessary survival strategy, the microcosm of a society where exploitation is a general rule. Despite the rising epidemic of AIDS, prostitution is increasing, and especially in larger cities where it is linked to the expanding tourist industry.

Far from being accepted, this phenomenon is something that worries a substantial section of the population, with many in despair over the problem. This new cultural pattern, or youth sub-culture to be precise, like the break up of the patriarchal family and the emergence of single female headed families, has evoked deep despair among the elder members of the community. Men are often quick to point out that, the 'social decadence' - teenage pregnancy, juvenile delinquency, women's more public profile in places of leisure etc - is due to women's failure to perform their traditional duties of socialising children within the family.

The war is also blamed for under-cutting families' self-sufficiency, thereby causing wives and daughters to supplement or raise income through prostitution. The despaired desperately hope that with the end of the war, this social malaise will die a natural death when people are self-sufficient. Men also hope to re-assert their hegemony. In short, while elder members of the community generally view the changing behaviours, attitudes and roles of young women as a social deviation from the norm, for the latter it is freedom worth fighting for and/or necessary survival strategy. These contesting perspectives lead us to our final observation that, running through and

232

between all the women's narratives is a moral argument of self-justification and moral reflection.

Moral and counter-moral arguments: Self-justification and blame

Within the broader unifying themes of power and sexuality, family break-down has been the most recurring theme. Though offering some relief that at last women would be in control of their lives, the collapse of the family has been a cause of anxiety and a matter of blame. Male violence, within the household in particular, has been cited as the main cause of this situation with wronged women opting for separation or divorce. (In one extreme case, a twenty year old single young woman went even further to assert that: "I don't want Mozambican men ... because they are backward". As in all the other narratives, this woman's position is not without a moral basis, indeed it is based on a perceived injustice which justifies certain positions and behaviours: her extreme dislike of Mozambican men is partly the result of bad treatment by lovers and partly due to the fact that her father had abandoned them because her mother gave birth to girls only - five daughters). It appears the woman, a victim of psychological violence, sex and racial domination, by adopting such a negative attitude against local man, is increasingly becoming an 'alienated person', a stranger to herself.

Such 'psychic alienation', Fanon argues prevents its victim from achieving self-realization:

In the [people] of color there is a constant effort to run away from [their] own individuality, to annihilate [their] own presence.[52]

The point is, as Fanon stresses, racial and sex domination is a "systematic negation of the other person and a furious determination to deny the other person".[53] The defensive attitudes created by violent up-bringing, such as this woman's, form a structure which shapes the victim's personality. Men, victims of colonial and racial domination, have also exhibited similar tendencies; they, as Fanon would put it, 'wear white masks, ape the language and mannerisms of the colonizer[54], in their defence of patriarchal privilege.

Advancing counter-moral arguments, men have actually blamed women for the perceived social degeneration, juvenile delinquency and prostitution in particular. Citing women's perceived 'untrustworthiness' and 'materialism', and changing behaviours, men justify their multiple affairs and their refusal to settle down. Some have even went further to argue that natural disasters such as drought and famine are due to women's 'excesses' - their new found freedoms. This supposed link between cause and effect, whether correct or not, demonstrates the perceived connections between the personal and

233

public/political in women's lives. Such moral and counter-moral arguments are only one aspect of the always emerging, already distorted arena of women's struggle.

The unifying themes of power, domination and sexuality confound definitional distinctions, providing evidence of permeability of boundaries. For instance, the images young women portray suggest that they are rejecting the coarseness, hardness and masculinity of their mothers' generation and desire a more glamorous and feminine identity. On the other hand, elder women are 'ready to give the lesson of experience'. But what experience? As Machel pointed out, the most common advice is on how to look after the house, how to be obedient, and never to fight with a husband.[55]

While women-headed households are on the rise, single mothers carry much less status than either widows or those who are married. At the risk of over-generalisation, the married seem to envy the apparent freedoms of the single women, while the latter envy the former's security, and yet both categories are contemptuous of each other. Mozambican feminism has thus to confront, in addition to resistance from populist patriarchs, the divisions amongst women themselves. As is shown below, the diversity of women's immediate priorities threatens to undermine the women's movement and to play into the hands of their enemies.

Women, class and politics: Conflicts in feminism

As is implicit from the foregoing accounts by women, women are not an homogenous empirical category. They are neither revolutionary nor conservative as a group. The image of the conservative traditional women guided by the oppressive ideology of 'proper femininity' cannot be replaced by an equally simplistic vision of a militant woman with a coherently articulated liberation project. Women's activities have been localised and sporadic and this makes the community, rather than class, more appropriate for organization and consciousness raising. But since the community is also divided over other issues of age and ethnicity, the reality seems to lie somewhat in between.

There is the difficulty in mobilizing women from different class positions for a common project. Elite women of Chimoio, in their tastes, life styles and priorities, are a world apart from the women in the slums around the city without basic amenities. Inevitably, their priorities are different. In fact women from the rural areas complained about the apparent egotism of urban women who were in their opinion, condescending and excessively concerned with individualistic issues of sexual pleasure and fashionable dressing.

234

This serves to remind us that, patriarchal domination notwithstanding, class division and struggle persists. For instance, professional or middle-class women, often with other women as their housemaids, are likely to resist the demand for better working conditions and wages by the latter, as this would undercut on their financial base. As a matter of fact, in these difficult times, many middle-class women have shifted the burden to their house-servants by resorting to super-exploitative strategies such as paying in kind - second hand clothes and food - and occasional employment. (In the former, the servants stand to lose as it is difficult, for instance, to assess the exact worth of rugs/tattered clothes, while in the latter there is no security of tenure and hence no bargaining power). In short, class (and culture) is a crucial variable in shaping the problems and opportunities confronting women, and in dividing and uniting them.

The fact is that women's fate is bound up with that of exploited males; both are victims of an exploitative class system. But this must not cause us to lose sight of the specific reality of the woman's situation. As Penvenne pointed out with reference to single working women in Maputo, women shared important day-to-day experiences as women and mothers which cut across their diverse class and ethnic identities.[56] These experiences are conditioned by relations embedded in the cultural institutions of society, and are mediated by class and age.

The age factor

Age difference among women could be both a unifying and divisive force. For instance, from my observations it appeared the strongest family relationship was that between mothers and their daughters, in particular, and mothers and their children in general. But when the focus shifted away from the family cleavages based on age started appearing among women.

As Machel pointed out in an address to a women's meeting in 1986; "Ages of women, ... can be a problem.... For women they indicate wisdom".[57] Identifying four age groups - old women; young brides; young (teenage) mothers; and mature mothers - he correctly pointed out that there could be a difficulty in having a serious debate between women of such diverse age groups. The elders, he continued "the ones who know it all: who understand life and "don't talk to women still child-bearing ... cannot debate with the other women."[58] The point is, in a genealogical lineage system elder women, by virtue of their age, are presumed to have acquired wisdom through experience, a wisdom that cannot be questioned. Questioning it is considered a disrespect of tradition, and this has been one major obstacle confronting women who wish to break out from the restrictive grip of traditional society. But in the contemporary struggles, such established rules

235

and norms, already disrupted by the war, are increasingly getting eroded as older women are economically and politically marginalised.

Thus age difference could potentially be a divisive issue. Interestingly, many more younger women, particularly those within the 18-29 age group, seem to have been able to adapt much better than older women. A significant proportion of those between 18 and 22 seem to be adapting via sex work, and most of them have never been married and are hence in greater demand, especially by foreign workers and NGOs personnel. Those within the 23-29 age group seem to be coping largely through successful enterprising, and it was amongst this group that many gave more attention to their business than their marriages.

Part of the reason for elder single women's failure to adapt quickly, lies in the fact that they lack skills, are illiterate and usually have large families. Having grown up during the colonial era most women in this age group, like Blacks in general, did not have access to education. This has disadvantaged them. Their large families, especially when the children were not yet old enough to help, meant that there was little investible surplus even if they were involved in business. The different impact of war on these different age groups of women and their different coping strategies has given rise to problems within the women's struggles for emancipation.

The specific responses of individual women to change, their survival strategies and their achievement have been conditioned by a number of factors, the most important of which are class, education, age and marital status. These, and the general ideology of patriarchy, which is manifest in all aspects of social life and which elder women have unconsciously supported[59], have all combined in defining the limits of women's emancipation in Mozambique. Consequently, there seems to be no simple answer to the question 'what do women want?', let alone that of how they can struggle for change. Instead there is a perplexing and contradictory multitude of ideas, emotions and actions which have given contemporary gender struggles their defining characteristic, a tantalising combination of radicalism and conservatism.

Summary: Issues in engendering democracy and development

At independence Frelimo inherited a weak state starved of resources, both financial and human. This placed considerable constraints on its capacity to translate principles into practical policy. Second, the women's liberation campaign was based on false assumptions about the nature of women's problems and needs. Women's problems were reduced to "complexes - complexes that destroy her capacity for initiative"[60] - and the victims were blamed for their problems. Third, part of the problem was the instrumentalist conception of women's emancipation, evident in Machel's emphasis on the 'priority' or 'essential' task, as the destruction of "the colonialist and capitalist structures".[61] While the development exigencies of the new state called for the incorporation of women into the labour force, it failed to re-define men's roles in a manner comparable to the redefinition of women's roles. Finally, the campaign also encountered resistance not only from men, but from women as well who felt that the security that traditional kinship ties offered them was being eroded. Other social movements, such as churches, were also propagating counter-hegemonic ideas about the proper place of women in society.

As we have seen, the combined effects of war and liberalisation have substantially altered the position of women vis-a-vis men, accelerating, in a different direction though, a process that had been initiated by Frelimo. While women made significant gains from the 'revolution', these gains were limited to those compatible with the drive for national construction. The pursuit of broader feminist objectives was regarded as a distraction from furtherance of the main revolutionary goals. Lately challenges to women's subordination have been contained within an over-arching nationalist rhetoric to end the war, which positions woman at the heart of the family in her idealised role as wife and mother. More seriously, the male political leadership entrenched the pre-eminence of the state over the individual via interventionist policies. In the statist development project, women were viewed simply as another segment of society to be fully mobilised as a pre-condition for the success of the revolution. Consequently a dual role model of women's emancipation was adopted as state policy: on the one hand, women were encouraged, and in line with Marxist-Leninist principles, to get 'proletarianised' by working in state farms and collectives, while on the other hand they were also encouraged to remain primarily responsible for the private sphere - the home.

The freezing of gendered identities in the post-revolutionary period remained unchallenged. On the contrary, these gendered identities were re-entrenched through the re-invention of the mythologised women's 'rightful place', and this presented serious problems to a gendered re-thinking of the relationship between democracy and development, the state and the individual. The result was a promotion of the patriarchal family, with the wife expected to be submissive to men.

Clearly, immediate male interests dictated the continued subordination of women, but certainly the long term developmental needs of the country, even for men, are impossible against the interests of half the population. Therefore patriarchal statism can only be fought by a feminism that places women's needs and individuality above the hierarchy of priorities. Since the changing

237

nature of patriarchy itself can only be relatively autonomous from its socio-economic base - but never totally autonomous from it - the main thrust should be on altering this socio-economic base.

The war and liberalization, have offered unprecedented opportunities for this to happen, and for women to break free from patriarchal control and statism. But the narrow economic base of women's expanding power in the informal economy does not, at least in the short-term, present a very formidable challenge to statism and patriarchy. More worrying is the shift towards strategic expedience, rather than moral considerations, that is central to the logic of global capitalism and structural adjustment. This, as we have seen, is entrenching 'sexploitation' and social cleavages and tension among women, as actors, subjects and objects. The definitive or total liberation of women can therefore only be achieved when the logic of patriarchal capitalism is checked and when women are empowered and allowed to develop their potential. Whether or not this can be achieved depends on the nature of the post-peace state and, more important, on the actions of women themselves.

Conclusion

In pre-war Shona communities men and women inhabited different spheres in the complementary social duality. This situation had begun to change after independence as the OMM set women on the move for new identities and new relations. With the post-independence orientation of the state towards bureaucratic authoritarianism, marked by the transformation of the Liberation Front into a Vanguard Party, the support to women's struggles disappeared. Although the women continued fighting, now it was a defensive gender struggle, aiming to maintain at least their traditional rights and the sources of power they had in the past.[62]

The civil-war and liberalisation have forced the state to roll back, undercut the patriarchal family and replaced it with new family forms. Within the limited possibilities thrown up by the war, wartime women made varied choices and felt in certain ways about war and about how they should live. With established social rules about ways to live, ways to be, how to respond to each other collapsing under the weight of their contradictions in the face of change, women have been forced to develop new ideas about themselves and about appropriate behaviour between them and men. However progress has been limited and this underscores the fact that women's options are shaped by the dominant structures of the time, material as well as cultural.

In conclusion, the gains and losses of the war have been spread unevenly, leaving an ambiguous legacy for women. While there is space now for a separate woman's voice, no single 'woman's consciousness' has emerged. Nonetheless, it is vital to recognise that women have not been mere passive victims: on the contrary they have actively shaped the course of their lives, politics, and even the course of the war itself. Financial independence, as elsewhere in Africa[63] has become the principal goal for many women in Chimoio, and when this conflicts with their marital obligations, the latter have often been the casualty. The legacy of war for women has therefore been ambiguous at best, and a source of conflict at worst.

Notes

1. See M. Davies (editor), *Third World Second Sex: Women's Struggles and National Liberation*, London, Zed Books, 1983.

2. Audrey Wipper, "Riot and Rebellion Among Africa Women: Three Examples of Women' Political Clout", in J. O'Barr (editor) *Perspectives on Power: Women in Africa, Asia and Latin America*, New York, Dules University Press, 1982.

3. Signe Armfred, "Women in Mozambique: Gender Struggle and Gender Politics", in *Review of Africa Political Economy*, Number 41, 1988, pp. 5-16.

4. Carolyn Nordstrom, "Women and War: Observations from the field", in *Minerva Quarterly Report on Women and the Military*, Volume ix, Number 1, Spring 1991, pp. 1-15, p. 1, and Chris Johnson, *Women on the Frontline: Voices from Southern Africa*, London, Macmillan, 1992.

5. Refugee Assistance, "Repatriation and Development: A Gender Analysis", paper presented at the Conference on First Country of Asylum and Development Aid in Malawi, April 1982, pp. 5-6.

6. Ibid., p. 7.

7. Cited by Shanon, "Women as Active Agents in the Resettlement Process", a Proposal for Research, Refugee Studies Programme, Oxford University, 1994, in C. Hannan-Anderson, "Integrating, not Separating, Women in Development", in J. Kerr (editor), *Ours By Right*, London, Zed and the North Institute, 1993, p. 121.

8. Karen Sacks, "An Overview of Women and Power in Africa", in J. O'Barr (editor) op. cit., p. 1.

9. See among others, E. Dora Earthy, *Valenge Women: the Social and Economic Life of Valenge Women of Portuguese East Africa: an Ethnographic Study*, London, Oxford University Press, 1933, Sonia Kruks and Ben Wisner, "The State, the Party and the Female Peasantry in Mozambique", in *Journal of Southern African Studies*, Volume ii, Number 1, October 1984, pp. 116-127, and Jeanne Penvenne, "Making Our Own way: Women Working in Lourenco Marques, 1900-1933", Boston, Boston University African Study Centre Working Papers, Number 114.

10. See for example, Osei Mensah Aborampah, "Economic Achievement and Marriage Patterns of Techiman Market Women", paper presented at the 36th Annual meeting of the African Studies Association, Boston, MA, December 4-7, 1993.

11. Kenneth Blakemore and Brian Cooksey, *A Sociology of Education for Africa*, London, Unwin, 1980, pp. 16-17.

12. Cited in A Mumouni, *Education in Africa*, London, Deutsch by Ibid p. 17.

13. Ibid., p. 17.

14. Comment by Ken Wilson on earlier draft.

15. Cited by C. Oboo, "Women's Autonomy, Children and Kinship: A Case Study of Uganda", in *Dalhousie Review*, Dalhousie University Press, October 1989, p. 70.

16. According to one young women, a first born in a family of five girls, their father abandoned their mother because she only gave birth to girls, and was then living with another woman (see below).

17. See Karen Sacks, op. cit., p. 3.

18. Karen Sacks, op. cit., p. 2.

19. Comment on earlier draft by Ken Wilson.

20. Oft quoted statement of Frelimo's late president Samora Machel, and found among the slogans inscribed on the walls of buildings. Cited in Stephanie Urdang, *And Still They Dance: Women War and the Struggle for Change in Mozambique*, London, Earthscan Publications, 1989, p. 22.

21. Signe Armfred, op. cit., p. 5.

22. Ibid., p. 7.

23. Ibid., p. 7.

24. Ibid., p. 7.

25. Ibid., p. 7.

26. See *Mulher Mozambicana: Boletim da OMM (Mozambican Women: Bulletin of the OMM)*.

27. Stephanie Urdang has characterised the period 1980-1983 as "the period of hope", Stephanie Urdang, op. cit., p. 23.

28. There was an almost general consensus on this issue from most interviewees.

29. Stephanie Urdang, op. cit., p., 25.

30. Barry Munslow, *Mozambique: the Revolution and its Origins,* London, Longman, 1983,
p. 178.

31. Many women see the day simply as an anniversary of the death of Machel's first wife, and this is largely because the date for International Women's Day celebrations has been moved to coincide with of the death of Machel's wife.

32. Interview with Assembly of God pastor.

33. C. Obbo, "Women's Autonomy, Children and Kinship: A Case Study of Uganda, *Dalhousie Review*, Dalhousie University Press, October 1989, p. 70.

34. Cited in Anabella Rodriguez, "Mozambican Women After the Revolution", in M. Davies (editor), *Third World Second Sex: Women's Struggles and National Liberation*, London, Zed Books, 1983, p. 134.

35. Remark made at a wedding ceremony.

36. In some 27 companies only 94 out of 838 workers were women. Statistics obtained from Provincial Department of Labour.

37. Richard Werbner, *Tears of the Dead: The Social Biography of an African Family*, London, Edinburgh University Press, 1991, p. 3.

38. Ibid., p. 3.

39. Traditional opaque beer is considered much inferior to bottled beer, and therefore sells cheaply.

40. Primary teachers' wages, like most of the non-professional workers, at about 60 000Mt (then about 20 US dollars), are worthless, and inadequate for basic necessities.

41. See T. Baker and M. Bird, "Urbanization and the Position of Women", *Sociological Review*, Volume 7, Number 1, pp. 99-122.

42. See Audrey Whipper, op. cit.

43. See among others, R Sanjek and L. Sanjek, "Notes on Women and Work in Adabraka", in *Africa Urban Notes*, Volume 2, Number 2, 1976, pp. 1-27, Margerett Peil, "Urban Women in the Labour Force", *Sociology of Work and Occupations*, Volume 6, pp. 482-501, and Jeanne Penvenne, op. cit.

44. Osei Mensah Aborampah, "Economic Achievement and Marriage Patterns of Techiman Market Women", Paper presented at the 36th Annual meeting of the African Studies Association, Boston, MA, December 4-7, 1993, p. 13.

45. Ibid., p. 10.

46. Janet Macgaffey, *The Real Economy of Zaire: The Contribution of Smuggling and Other Unofficial Activities to National Wealth*, London, James Currey, 1991.

47. Osei Mensah Aborampah, op. cit., p. 13.

48. The term is borrowed from Rosamund Shreeves, Sexual Revolution or 'sexploitation'? The Pornography and Erotica in the Soviet Union", in Shirin Ral et al, (editors), *Women in the Face of Change: The Soviet Union, Eastern Europe and China*, London, Routledge, 1992, pp. 130-146.

49. See Hilary Pilkington, "Whose Space is it Anyway: Youth, Gender and the Civil Society in the Soviet Union", in Shirin Rai et al (editors), ibid., pp. 130-146.

50. "Onumoz Troops Encouraging Prostitution", in *Mozambique News Agency*, Report Number 28, 4 March 1994, p. 3.

51. Ibid., p. 3.

52. Frantz Fanon, *Black Skin, White Masks,* New York, Grove Press, 1967, p. 60.

53. Frantz Fanon, *The Wretched of the Earth: The handbook for the Black Revolution that is Changing the Shape of the World*, New York, Grove Press, 1968, p. 250.

54. Frantz Fanon, op. cit. p. 60.

55. Barry Munslow, op. cit., p. 172.

56. See Jeanne Penvenne, op. cit.

57. Barry Munslow, op. cit., p. 172.

58. Ibid., p.172.

59. Some writers argue that women before and after menopause can cooperate because there is no sexual competition, unlike men of all ages.

60. Ibid., p. 171.

61. Ibid., p. 172.

62. Signe Armfred, op. cit., p.9.

63. See T. Baker and M. Bird, op. cit., p. 104.

7 Elements of a critical social theory of state, violence and development

Introduction

In the preceding chapters we saw how the destructive impact of the war on the economy has resulted in the increasing role of international aid, the 'internationalisation' of the economy, the acceleration of social differentiation, the polarisation of power and wealth and the break-down of moral bindings of the traditional society. Indeed, the unfolding situation is a concentration of many determinations, a unity of the diverse; resistance to change imposed from above and the quest for more spontaneous change, conflicts between generations and the sexes, class struggles, and the economic crisis as well as the impact of global factors all combined to fuel the war, and shape its consequences. The war redirected Mozambican society in many important respects; to get things really in perspective we need to look at the broader canvas. Specifying the dynamics of such change is essential to the effective understanding of war and its relation to society.

This theoretical and historical chapter explores new ways of uniting such different strands of historical experience, and it ends by affirming the importance of studying change and movement in history. It contents that the contested history and consequences of the war in Mozambique provide many a basis for the construction of a critical framework of analysis in which it is possible to identify the dynamics of the interrelationship between the state, violence and development, and to debate the future of Southern Africa. Most scholars, across the ideological divide, have focused too much on the tragic aspects of the conflict. Consequently, insufficient attention has been paid to the social consequences of the war, in particular its impact on the state and social and economic organization. But if we are to anticipate the future, then it is vital to understand the dynamics of these unintended consequences of war, and place its simultaneous fascination and repulsion in a dynamic world

244

historical framework. In this chapter an attempt is made to develop such an analytical framework - which links war to social change - and to delineate the main elements of a critical theory of war, society and change.

Mitchell and Russell warn us, with respect to South Africa, that there is a need to reorient state-society-and-war theory and research. Emphasising that war - both inter-state conflict and internal war - can result in the militarisation of the state and society, they argue for: a transcendence of 'internalist' or society-centred conception of the state "which fails to recognise that states are also influenced by a variety of international forces which help to shape the internal organisation of the state"; an appreciation of the significance of 'the repressive state apparatus', and not just a focus upon the 'problem of consent' or the 'manufacture of consent'; and for a recognition that the level of institutional coherence within any state is always a highly contingent matter rather than a simple assumption of a high degree of internal organisational unity.[1]

This means that the analysis of state-civil society relations must not start from abstract notions of 'an overdeveloped state', 'a relatively autonomous state' or Hyden's thesis of a state with no structural roots in society, suspended 'as a balloon' in mid-air[2]. Instead it must start from what has constituted the state historically at the level of civil society, in particular, an examination of the manner in which "forces within society penetrate the state differentially, just as the state power reinforces certain interests and undermines others".[3] Put differently, the important question to ask in trying to understand the relationship between social processes and state power is: What are the demands that society has made on the state and how has the state developed 'as a state' in response?

In analyzing relations between the state, war and the emergence of capitalism in the West, Hall makes a distinction between two types of states, the 'capstone' and 'organic' state.[4] He argues that the type of state determines the state's capacity to respond to societal demands, and the implications of its pursuit of war for development. According to his model, which is partially illuminating with respect to Mozambique, the capstone state is by definition a weak state in which an "elite sat atop a series of separate 'societies', which it did not wish to penetrate or mobilise; (and) perhaps the key to its behaviour was fear that horizontal linkages it could not see would get out of control".[5] The capstone state, of which the Chinese empire - itself created by the military - was a typical example, "blocked the fully fledged emergence of intensive capitalist relationships".[6]

For Hall, whilst the capstone state's pursuit of war is predatory in nature, for example in the Chinese, Muslim and Hindu societies, the organic state's "type of warfare that characterised its activities actually *help* economic progress".[7] The organic quality of this state, as it manifested itself in

245

Western Europe, arose from its having "to accept and co-operate with other elements in civil society if it was to survive in a social society of state competition".[8] Hall argues that, in European societies, political fragmentation was a necessary condition for the autonomy of the market, whereas in the Indian and Islamic cases, such fragmentation was not "sufficient by itself to encourage economic dynamism".[9] The ambiguous legacy of war in Mozambique tends to confirm as well as refute some of Hall's arguments.

The state, war and society in Mozambique: A brief history

The Portuguese colonial state, being a conquest state imposing itself on, but lacking infrastructural penetration of, local communities, was essentially a capstone state; this partly accounted for its weakness and perpetual recourse to warfare in its pursuit of capital accumulation. Indeed, for the five centuries that the Portuguese were in Mozambique war had been a central feature of their policy of conquest. As Newit points out:

> Of the last century of their presence in Africa the Portuguese spent half in trying to pacify their various territories. Almost every year from 1875 to 1924 saw military expeditions undertaken in all three of their mainland colonies (Angola, Guinea Bissau, and Mozambique), and 'police' operations were still needed in the years that followed.[10]

As with the post-colonial state, this struggle to enforce, through institutional structures, some degree of control and unequal cohesion, not only altered the internal organisation and class structure of the country's political economy, but it also unleashed forces that challenged its hegemony, and later to reform. (For instance, it was in response to the war that the Portuguese started industrial investment in Mozambique during the early 1970s). As a result of this resistance and challenge, at the end of the colonial era Africans were in "control of the overwhelming proportion of the land, and urbanisation was less developed than anywhere in Africa".[11]

The failure to effectively suppress the indegenes and establish a vibrant capitalist colonial economy was as much a result of the weakness of the Portuguese state itself as of the ability of the indigenous populations to mobilise resources to resist a seemingly invincible colonial state. In fact, since dialectically tendency begets counter-tendency and force counterforce, Portuguese military action might actually have "cause[d] traditional African societies to survive longer than would otherwise have been the case, [and] their cohesion strengthened by the demands of armed resistance".[12] In fact, and contrary to the objectives of 'imperial divide and rule' strategy, the

246

colonial state acted as the factor of cohesion and the focus of the contradictions in capitalism's articulation with indigenous modes of production.[13]Thus, rather than destroy pre-colonial societies - which were dynamic and changing - the colonial order managed *only* to immobilise populations, reinforced ethnicity and a greater rigidity of social definition.[14]

Local communities, through participation in the dialectic of control, not only resisted the state but also made new sets of demands on the state which it sought to manage through a combination of promotion, co-optation and coercion, especially during the height of the independence war. Overall, however, and precisely because of lack of capital, the Portuguese were forced to adopt what Anderson calls 'ultra-colonialism'.[15] This involved subcontracting the governance of the colony to Concession Companies (the Mozambique Company, the Niassa Company, the Zambesi Prazos and the Mocamedes Company), introduction of forced labour and compulsory crop growing. The contradictions of this articulation of colonial capitalism with pre-capitalist modes of production provided the dynamic for the anti-colonial resistance which resulted in independence in 1975.

The post-colonial state and revolution-counterrevolution dialectic

The contradictions of the colonial economy gave rise to the war of independence, which erupted in 1964. For strategic and historical reasons (FRELIMO was operating from Tanzania), the war was fought in a few northern provinces and lasted barely a decade, and consequently, its impact on the whole society was limited. This had fundamental implications for the relationship between post-colonial state and civil society. At independence FRELIMO inherited a capstone colonial state almost intact. The rural communities, though participating in the nascent market economy, were still largely untouched by colonial capitalism. Civil society was still struggling to be born. The fluidity of social structures and (ethnic) identity, and the exodus of Portuguese entrepreneurs and skilled personnel convinced FRELIMO of the need for a statist development strategy to achieve rapid industrialization.

Accordingly, FRELIMO embarked on a massive rural collectivisation campaign and a 'proletarianisation' of the peasantry via work in large-scale state farms. The project was based on the assumption that the organization of traditional peasant societies was archaic and hence economically counter-productive, and that their cultures and ideologies were repressive as well as obscuntarist. The haphazard and often casual violence (see Chapter Two) with which the state tried to channel, control and contain future development had the unintended effect of alienating some disaffected sections of the population, whose discontent was galvanised into an anti-state insurgency led by Renamo.

Further, the development process itself generated its contradictions and conflict as the benefits were unevenly distributed, and this created a conducive environment for anti-state sentiment to flourish.

As in most of sub-Saharan Africa, the post-colonial state in Mozambique has exhibited a paradox in which both strong and weak components simultaneously co-exist. On the one hand, as the testimonies of ordinary people documented in the previous chapters suggest, in its authoritarian modernisation project the state became the dominant power over civil society. In the construction of this hegemonic project Frelimo established a centralised bureaucracy that intervened in nearly all facets of economic, social and political life. The civic arena was delimited and legitimacy was achieved through order, cooptation/assimilation and/or punishment of dissenters. While the state appeared strong, in another sense it was also a weak state.

The state's weakness was manifested in its inability to translate policy into practice, and later, to defeat the rebels. This weakness was partly due to the lack of administrative capacity and financial resources, and to the permeation of the state by societal interests, domestic or foreign. In short, the relationship between the state and society was complex: as an actor the state had its own strengths and preferences, yet it was also contextually bound by specific issue areas that prevailed at one time in its relation to societal actors.[16] The added dimension of war has complicated this situation, simultaneously amplifying the weakness of the state and strengthening some of its institutions.

The requirements of fighting a war has been such that the state's power to produce violence increased disproportionately to that of productive activity. As state survival itself was at stake, security, and not development, became the overriding policy concern and the maxim that 'production is the best defence' was ignored. Resources were diverted to the war effort resulting in considerable stagnation, at least of the official economy. This has meant that the state's power to produce violence increased disproportionately to that of productive activity. However, this persistent concern with security, manifested in for example the recent introduction of a special unit of armed mobile police, has exacerbated the financial difficulties. In turn this contributed to the erosion of the power base of the state and fuelled the break-up of its legitimacy and its ruling ideology in the eyes of the ruled. Consequently, with demoralisation rising high, even among sections of the state apparatus, and resources diminishing the Frelimo regime could not win the war.

Like its predecessor, the post-colonial state tried to impose itself on society by promoting some forces of civil society while undermining others. For instance, while religion and tradition were undermined and discredited, some new forces such as women, workers and youth movements were encouraged (though within statist limits). Similarly, until the reforms in the mid 1980s when peasant agriculture was starved of capital, the state farm sector continued to receive the lion's share of agricultural investment. This was also the case with the service and productive sectors, in which the former, for example health and education, witnessed a boost in investment, while the later was neglected In other words, the state intervened in the economy and civil society, and in so doing shaped both the nature of the conflict and balance of forces within civil society, as well as the relationship of the state to civil society itself.

The steady expansion of state power and bureaucratic centralization simply reflected its growing difficulties in managing the crisis of its articulation with civil society. Class, age and gender contradictions within civil society ultimately found expression at the level of the state both in the constant changes in policy at the various Party Congresses held since independence, and, with disastrous consequences, in the Renamo anti-state insurgency itself. The post-independence populist authoritarian state that Frelimo built, insofar as it attempted to suppress the creative potential of civil society, constituted a counterrevolution. In other words, by attempting to impose homogeneity on the diverse and to bureaucratically control society or, in the popular euphemism of the time 'to kill the tribe in order to build the nation', Frelimo was negating and undermining the revolutionary potentials of the ordinary people. The overarching bureaucratic system that it built and its legitimating ideology were not only an oppressive burden on society, but more seriously, had a demobilising effect on the people.

The MNR anti-state insurgency, backed by white racist capital, has been the negative avatar of this post-independence counterrevolution. By undermining state power and through many other 'unintended social consequences', the war has opened up *possibilities* for revolutionary change. All this has altered the balance of forces between the state and civil society and within civil society itself. But this is not to say the MNR is a revolutionary political movement: far from that, it is an opportunistic counterrevolutionary movement led by elites exploiting quasi-nationalist ideology and ethnic and religious loyalties for their own parochial ends of personal aggrandizement. At one level the war was essentially an old fashioned struggle for power between and among the elites. Nonetheless, the social and political disintegration engendered by the war seems to have been a necessary condition for the autonomy of the market and civil society, and for an alteration in the overall distribution of power.

As Halls' captstone thesis predicts, it seems war induced political fragmentation, the break-down of moral bindings of society and the weakening of the state, as well as increased the 'autonomy of the (informal) market'. But unanticipated by this thesis, war also seems to have been the midwife for the delivery of a new dispensation in which traditional norms, privileges and ideologies have been caste aside, if not renounced, as a dynamic informal economy and civil society takes root. The paradox is that, in waging the war, the state itself has undergone profound transformation in both its nature and role. Both the colonial and post-colonial states' claim to a monopoly of violence - like all other states - generated anti-state violence, which not only almost undermined state power, but also set in motion a multidimensional process of social change, characterized by what Gramsci called the 'crisis of hegemony', changing 'war of positions', and the increasing role of local 'organic intellectuals'.

According to Gramsci, hegemony is the ideological predominance of the values and norms of the dominant groups over subordinate groups.[17] The crisis of hegemony occurs when the ruled no longer recognize the rulers as their legitimate representatives:

> When this happens violent solutions can occur, and the traditional means of using the State to maintain dominant-class hegemony deteriorates. In this moment, those elements of the society-bureaucracy, Church, high finance, and other institutions - that are independent of public opinion increase their power and autonomy.[18]

In Mozambique, the crisis of hegemony initially manifested itself in rural discontent with Frelimo policies which later facilitated the escalation of the military conflict. The consequent disintegration of the state, accompanied by the increased role of non-governmental organisations, and international financial institutions, notably the International Monetary Fund (IMF) and the World Bank as it were, has exacerbated the crisis of hegemony.

Gramsci's concept of 'war of position', which is based on the idea of surrounding the state apparatus with a counterhegemony is crucial to the understanding of the 'alternative politics' of the dispossessed.[19] For Gramsci, consciousness is the key ingredient in the process of change, and the 'war of position' is a struggle to raise that consciousness.[20] In Chimoio the dispossessed are developing a counterhegemony by creating their own alternative arrangements and institutions (mainly religious), articulating a new morality and new ways of living which oppose the dominant group's vision of existence.

Finally, 'organic intellectuals', mainly in the form of religious leaders or prophets, have also played an important role in social change. As shown in Chapter 5, they have performed the function of directing the ideas and aspirations of the social groups to which they 'organically' belong. In a nutshell, and to oversimplify, the paradox is that Renamo counterrevolution against Frelimo counterrevolution has given rise to a potential revolutionary situation, in which the idea of the state managing society, playing an extensive role in delivering solutions and services is being superseded by a number of contradictory developments, which constitute a fundamental crisis of hegemony and legitimacy.

The weakening of the state and the breakdown of censorship allowed the expansion of politics through society, thereby transforming the nature and role of the state. Traditional and religious authorities have attempted to consolidate their power by filling in the power vacuum created by the erosion of state power. The establishment of effective political and religious toleration let loose a flood of speculation that hitherto had only been muttered in secret. This protest and revolt in ideas, values and behaviours took many forms: innovative economic enterprising; increased political activism and militancy; religious revivalism; unorthodox feminine politics and youth sub-culture(s). Most of these groups have asked sceptical questions about all the institutions and beliefs of their society. The interaction of these movements, which on the surface are apparently spontaneous and unrelated, have produced the dynamic of, and for, the 'movement of the social whole'. Such changing parameters of political and social life point to the development and potential existence of a civil society in Mozambique.

The emergent civil society: Academic hallucination or contested space?

The contradictions of political economy manifested themselves at a superstructural level in the emergence of the new hegemony, which advocates for the liberation of civil society' from the suffocating grip of the state. In the new hegemonic discourses on the state and civil society in Africa "the contradiction between state and civil society is propagated as the dominant one".[21] In the literature the state/civil society relationship has indeed been a contested one. With respect to Mozambique in particular, and Southern Africa in general, the debate has centred on whether or not civil society actually exists. Central to this debate is the question of the separation and/or synthesis of the state and civil society.

Hegel posited that the state mediated between conflicts in civil society by means of corporations and bureaucracy:

> the former grouped individual private interests in order to bring pressure to bear upon the state; the latter mediated between the state and private interests thus expressed.[22]

In this formal state/civil society unity, the latter organised the economic, professional and cultural life. For Hegel the state was the highest form of

251

social organisation, "the reality of concrete liberty ... capable of synthesising particular rights and universal reason into the final stage of the evolution of objective spirit".[23] In short, for Hegel there was a potential harmony between the state and civil society. The state promoted, rather than curtailed, people's natural freedom. Unlike Hegel, Kant did not see the state as "embodying a higher good above and beyond that of the good of the individuals composing it" nor did he "envisage the particular claims of individuals being transformed, under the guidance of the state, into collective general claims".[24] Marx saw the distinction between civil society and the state in an entirely different light from both Kant and Hegel.

For Marx, "the division of roles between the individual as citizen - whose loyalty is owed to the State - and the individual as *bourgeois* - who owes no loyalty to anyone other himself, is inherent in modern capitalist society".[25] Marx denounced the supposed harmony between the state and civil society because, he claims, the capitalist economic system inevitably puts the individual's particular interest into conflict with the general social interest. Contrary to Hegel, he argued instead that the state and civil society were locked in a historically determined opposition; "the individual *bourgeois* in pursuing his private economic interests must inevitably jeopardize the well-being of society as a whole".[26] In other words, as we have seen in the case of Manica, there is an unavoidable tension between the economic level and the political level in an emergent capitalist society, and the two levels of organization will continue to exist, and be in conflict, so long as the fundamental basis of that society remains unaltered. The supposed synthesis between the state and civil society, in fact, presupposes the separation of the state and civil society: "the separation of the political state from civil society appears necessarily as a separation of political man - the citizen - from civil society".[27]

This aspect of the relation between civil society and the state comes out clearly in Kant's political theory. For him, since the state is primarily an external, restraining influence on the life of the individual, it is important to draw a distinction between a historical, factual account of the origins of the state and the ethical justification and analysis of the institution. The need for the state, he stressed, can only be derived from an analysis of the *apriori* ideas of Reason, that is "from a moral point of view".[28] As he suggests, it seems one of the major concern of political theory in changing societies such as Mozambique, is to "sort out the problem of the most appropriate type of social organization entirely normatively[29]", and imaginatively. Marx, however, could no more agree with Kant's insufficient distinction between civil life and the life of the state than with Hegel's view.

For Marx, if the state and civil society continued to be separate, then the people could not fully participate in their governance except through representation, which is itself an "expression of the separation and merely a dualistic unity".[30] The realization of real democracy, for Marx, therefore consists in reconciling the two. This is achieved by making civil society's political existence actual or politicizing the civil society such that it becomes political society. But, by making its political existence as its true universal and essential existence, "civil society also makes its civil existence unessential in contrast to its political existence".[31] This Marxian conception of civil society as the structural moment, that is as a phase towards the emergence of a political society proper, sharply contrasts with the Gramscian conception. For Gramsci, according to Carnoy, civil society does not belong to the structural moment, but to the *superstructural* one.[32] In other words, civil society is a product of voluntary political engagement, rather than merely a result of structural contradictions.

Current conceptions commonly applied to Africa often tend to treat civil society in a negative sense as the "realm of social relations not regulated by the state"[33] and in struggle against the state. What is not taken into account, however, is the fact that the state plays a central role in the constitution of civil society, and vice versa. In Mozambique, for example, the state's intervention in society, supporting some agents of society while disorganizing others, has certainly influenced the nature of the emergent civil society. The demands along the public service nexus, notably food, health, education and other social services, have been central in shaping the state as well as the construction of civil society. The notion of 'liberation of civil society' from the state must therefore not lead to an exaggeration of the distinctiveness of civil society and the state to the extent that their development and kind of values they embody might be considered mutually exclusive.

On the contrary, it could be argued that, given the amorphousness of the social structure in societies like Mozambique, the idea of a civil society independent of the state or a civil society struggling against the state has little relevance. The point is, as Beckman notes, the evolving state-civil society relationship is "linked to the restructuring of class relations in these societies and the related disintegration of state-centred development coalitions".[34] In Mozambique, both state and civil society are being formed in the process of this contestation: on the one hand the construction of civil society is based on state rules that regulate relations between competing interests, and on the other it is in its management of these contradictions that the state develops. The weakening of the state by the war, however, resulted in a redefinition of the terms of this contestation.

The result has been a remarkable increase in tolerance of difference and the expansion of the political space, which has allowed other agents of society, such as religious, women and youth organizations, to take the initiative and contribute to the on-going processes of the re-invention of the future. It is interesting to note that, although some traditional institutions are based on coercion or even connected to the state, in general terms their activities seem to expand the sphere of civil society. Global processes, such as the collapse of the Stalinist bureaucracies in Eastern Europe (which contained Mozambique's major allies), the weak performance of statist and nationalist strategies in much of Africa, the crisis of the welfare state in the West, and the world-wide crisis of the nation-state have also given an impetus to the continued expansion of civil society and its evolving relationship with the state.

Thus, the fact that both the colonial and post-colonial states were imposed from 'above' on society does not make them anymore 'cut off from society' than any other state. There is no doubt, for instance, that the weakness of both the colonial and post-colonial states, and their consequent arbitrariness, resulted in the implementation of unpopular policies. In turn this fuelled the independence and civil wars respectively. But, contrary to Hall's assertions, the weakness of the state actually facilitated its rapid disintegration when confronted with an anti-state insurgency. This collapse also speeded up the emergence of civil society and mercantile capitalism. This means that the relationship of the state to war and social change is historically and dialectically contingent. There is a diversity of possible trajectories.

Although the post-colonial state was a colonial inheritance - and hence a 'capstone state' -its character was derived from the productive logic of the peasant social organization and the conflict of interests that threaten to challenge it. Consequently, no simple view of 'the state' is of much use in understanding state-civil society relations in Mozambique: there have been different types of states in different historical periods.[35] Therefore, without underplaying the retrogressiveness of the state in terms of its relation to civil society, it is possible to conceive of a situation in which the development of a civil society could be fostered by a strong, but not necessarily totalitarian, state.[36] The point is, as Bobbio observes, it is not possible to fix the meaning and extension of the term civil society without doing the same for the state itself.[37]

The state, as the struggles in Mozambique suggest, should not only be viewed solely as an apparatus of class domination, but also as an arena of struggle in which contending ideologies about civil society confront each other. Further, as Renamo's relentless attempts to capture and control state power, and Frelimo's resistance to it testifies, the state is also an effective weapon worthy fighting for in this struggle for the definition of civil society. Although civil society is located outside the institutional framework of the state, it is not disconnected from it.[38] In a nutshell, the state plays a crucial role in the constitution of civil society, and vice versa; but as we have seen, the weakening of the state by the war altered this balance in favour of civil

254

society. In short, the precise relationship of the state with civil society remains a matter of debate both for analytical and practical purposes. What seems more important, however, is the *form* this (imagined?) civil society is taking.

Civil society and democracy

While there is no doubt of the emergence of embryonic elements of civil society, or at least the formation of a 'political society', the important question is what *form* is it taking. In the literature there has been a tendency to romanticise civil society and, in some cases, to equate it with democracy.[39] The evidence from Chimoio suggests, however, that the existence of a civil society does not necessarily mean that of democracy. On the contrary, some emergent organisations of civil society are based on hierarchical and authoritarian structures and tend to foster dependent patron-client relations. For example, as with traditional authorities, the religious challenge to the state has not necessarily resulted in a democratic alternative. Often it has resulted in a concentration of wealth and power and the intensification of struggles for hegemony within and between the religious groups.

The existence of conflict between and among forces of civil society warrants caution against the romanticisation of civil society implicit in the 'liberation of civil society' discourses, in which civil society is equated with democracy. First, it should be recognised that civil society is not a homogenous category, but is instead a heterogenous and contested social space. Second, it should also be emphasised that, some of the elements or institutions - churches, non-governmental organisations as well as families - of civil society are indeed organised on authoritarian principles and their political practices are anti-democratic.

To sum up, the idea of civil society has been subject to considerable variation and used in a variety of contexts. In Africa the debate has centred on whether or not civil society actually exists.[40] The evidence from Chimoio seems to suggest that embryonic elements of a civil society are gradually emerging on the ruins of the war: by weakening the state, the war has facilitated development and reconstitution of civil society. Private associations, churches, women's organisations and youths groups have emerged and are occupying the social space created by the disintegration of the state. With the removal of censorship, the media (newspapers, radios, and Tvs), and in particular the 'voice of the street', are also increasingly becoming effective in disseminating information. Their role in challenging state and cultural authoritarianism and establishment of democracy seems to be growing. But the question still remains as to how the apparently

255

'powerless' can alter unequal power relationships. How precisely do the subordinate social groups overcome the hegemony of the dominant social groups? What are the dynamics of change? Or, as Lonsdale put it, "Why do the weak get powerful?"[41]

Social change in war political economy: Why do the weak get powerful?

When discussing social change in Mozambique during the war, we should begin with the very important fact that there were, inspite of the near million deaths caused by the war, far more Mozambican people in the 1990s than there had been a century earlier. Although the rate of demographic growth may have slowed during the war period - to be followed by a post-war baby boom - its structure continues to be skewed in favour of youth. For example, population projections for the year 2000, put the figure of the under 15s at 44.83 per cent and that of the over 65s at 3.41 per cent (see Table 7.1 below).

A social revolution has indeed been going on in homes throughout Mozambique, and this has increased pressures on land to feed more mouths; changes in the structure of the family; attitudes to health and child rearing. The strain which such demographic change imposed upon society provided a major impetus for rapid social change. For instance, the projected increase in population density by nearly 30 per cent, will certainly intensify the political contradictions over the land issue; as Hermele shows in his study of Chokwe in southern Mozambique, "land distribution [will become] the crucial question".[42] In this regard, Frelimo deserves credit for "unambiguously prohibit[ing] any private ownership of land" in Article 69 of the 1990 constitution[43]; private ownership of such a vital natural resource would constitute theft from the people. The point is, in a context of a growing population, and as many a Mozambican feared, land alienation to foreigners could easily well become a recipe for another wave of violent land struggles. In fact, one area of social history and change which requires further research concerns the symbiotic relationship between rural and urban areas.

Change which, according to Hobbes, stimulates mental activity,[44] has been the most vital element in defining the uneven development of political consciousness and varied forms of resistance adopted by different people. The dispossessed have not been against change per se, nor have they been captives of localised loyalties[45] or intransigent defenders of their political autonomy against all forms of political domination.[46] Neither have they voluntarily surrendered their self-interest and allowed themselves to be swept up in a political drama machinated by their structural opponents. Instead, they have

256

Table 7.1
Projected population data for 2000

Year	1987	2000
Total population ('000)	13.7	18,703
Males ('000)	not available (na)	9,262
Females ('000)	na	9,441
Total fertility rate	na	5.67
Life expectancy	41 years	56 years
Life expectancy (male)	na	54.2 years
Life expectancy (female)	na	57.8 years
Crude birth rate	na	41.9
Crude death rate	na	12.2
Annual growth rate	na	2.9%
Under 15s	na	44.83%
Over 65s	na	3.41%
Women aged 15-49	na	22.54%
Doubling time	na	24 years
Population density	17 per sq.km.	23 per sq.km.
Urban population	20%	18.1%

Source: Jens E. Torp, L. M. Deny and Donald I. Ray (1989), *Mozambique, Sao Tome and Principe: Politics, Economics and Society*, London, Pinter Publishers, p. 7.

seen in the anarchy and change caused by the war an unprecedented opportunity to carve out a political space for themselves and, in the process, change society. Their actions have been contingent upon other factors and the possibilities, from their own perspectives, given their specific situations. Indeed, it was their daily struggles to survive which provided the main dynamic of the movement of the social whole during the period under consideration.

The dialectic of change and continuity has been such that contemporary actors are subject to a plurality of historic cultural influences which affect the way in which they see the world. Indigenous, Christian and Western cultural ideologies all co-exist in dynamic tension in the contemporary actor's mind. Though the hegemonic culture (itself consisting of various forms) of the dominant social groups constitutes one pole, and the counter-culture of the dispossessed the other, there are a variety of ideologies in between these.[47] For instance, many people constantly straddled the arbitrary circumscribed sectors of tradition and modernity. In the search of healing, for example, one would consult a doctor at Chimoio hospital, a spiritual/faith healer and a traditional healer one after another. Many urban dwellers have a strong attachment to their original rural background and, as a corollary, there is more and more 'ruralisation' of Chimoio as the intermediate situations of urbanisation in the peri-urban slums make it significantly difficult to identify a geographical sphere of tradition. In addition, the dispossessed's political constructions have been made with a cross-fertilisation of ideas borrowed from the dominant groups.

Though most of the dispossessed seem to recognize a structural opposition of interest and status as between themselves and the dominant social groups,"most of the time, in everyday life, for most practical purposes, they are not faced with such issues, and commonly operate with less societal views".[48] The poor have maintained patron-client relations based on kinship with the rich, who in turn have acquired western values and culture. The international agency personnel, foreign armies (and researchers), foreign traders and dealers, have brought material culture as well as values and norms which have been actively re-appropriated by Mozambicans. The result has been a cultural hybridisation, with a thin line dividing 'tradition' from 'modernity', and the 'radical' from the 'conservative'.

These are specific lines of continuity and discontinuity, precise procedures for the invention of politics in the context of social disintegration and re-integration. The multiplicity of survival strategies and other forms of engagement put into practice concurrently by the actors indicates the heterogeneity and stratification of the Chimoio communities. Amongst Chimoio's denizens, the social area is constantly being redefined by the contradictory enunciation that actors make of 'disorder' or 'power vacuum' in contemporary political production. As Balandier pointed out with respect to Africa in general, "the relationship of social agents to society reveals the continuous creation to which society is subjected".[49] What is emerging is therefore not total catastrophe, but contested alternative socio-economic and political arrangements with diverse trajectories. However, the exact nature of the relationship between agency and structure in these processes remains blurred and contested.

Sociological discussions about processes of change tend to divide into two broad camps. On the one hand, there are theories which posit that the crucial element in understanding human society is "not the conscious activities of the human subject, but the unconscious structure which these activities presupposed".[50] Althusser, for instance rejects the notion of individuals as free agents of history, arguing instead that they are the 'supports' or 'bearers' of the structural relations in which they are situated.[51] Poulantzas used these structuralist elements to develop a theory of the state.[52] On the other hand, there are theorists, classically represented by Gramsci, who exalt human agency and political action as central to social change and human progress. For him, the superstructure plays a crucial role in perpetuating classes and preventing the development of class consciousness: politics is the central human activity by means of which change can be brought about.[53] The relationship between agency and structure in social change remains a contested issue.

The situation unfolding in Chimoio suggests the need to transcend such fruitless polarisation of positions: war, as an extreme form of human action, has both been shaped by and has altered the structures. As 'the highest form of resolving contradictions between antagonistic forces'[54], it has generated and amplified social and structural contradictions. The complex war experience, as "a moment of primary concern", cut through all aspects of social life.[55] The exigences of fighting a war as well as surviving in a war situation demanded an unusual innovativeness on the part of human agents and adaptation of institutional structures of society.

The demand for a theory of war and social change therefore need to break with the rigid polarisation of structure and agency, and view them instead as mutually reinforcing. As West points out:

> structure and behaviour are inseparable ... institutions and values go hand in hand. How people act and live are - though in no way dictated or determined - by the larger circumstances in which they find themselves.[56]

These circumstances or material conditions "can be changed, their limits attenuated" by conscious or unconscious human activity. In the investigation of social change and political movement it is necessary neither to overlook the objective nature of relationships nor explain everything from the will of the person acting.

Giddens develops this argument in his 'theory of structuration.'[57] He argues that neither subject nor object should be regarded as having primacy:

Each is constituted in and through recurrent practices. The notion of human 'action' presupposes that of 'institution', and vice versa. Explication of this relation thus comprises the core of an account of how it is that the structuration (production and reproduction across time and space) of social practices takes place.[58]

He also criticizes subjectivist conceptions for not offering "an explication of the origins of subjectivity" and structuralist thought for dissolving "subjectivity into abstract structures of language" or reducing human agents into 'cultural dopes'.

In short, as Giddens argues following Kant[59], agency and structure, subject and object are mutually defining phenomena. To attempt to ascertain which is determinant is not only setting ourselves an impossible task, but also diverts attention from addressing the dynamics of change - change affecting both agents and structure.

It is this 'logical relationship between agency and structure', in particular the power of the weak to reconstruct from below, that is central to the argument of this thesis. The dispossessed, apparently powerless, have in many ways been able to influence the activities of those who control the institution of war as well as of those who hold economic and traditional power over them. In a nutshell power relations are 'relations of dependence and autonomy' and can be transformed by participation in 'the dialectic of control'. As Giddens puts it in his 'theory of action':

> [I]n any relationship which may be involved in a social system, the most seemingly 'powerless' individuals are able to mobilise resources whereby they carve out 'spaces of control' in respect of their day-to-day lives and in respect of the activities of the more powerful.[60]

Central to this participation in 'the dialectic of control' are the actions of the dispossessed who have transformed themselves from being, as Egero aptly puts it, "the wretched of the earth into agents of their own fate".[61]

However, the overall outcome of the action of individuals pursuing their own interests has been at variance with what each single individual wills. This leads us to another central concept of this thesis, namely, the 'unintended social consequences' of the war. As we have seen, unintended consequences arise precisely because, when human beings act and interact, there are so many variables or '*unacknowledged conditions* of action' that come into play in shaping the outcome. In a war situation, especially because of "the play of probabilities and chance"[62], these variables acquire a particular significance. Thus, the knowledgeability of human agents and their actions, in specific historical circumstances, is always bounded "by the unacknowledged

260

conditions of action on 'one side', and its unintended consequences on the other". [63]Consequently, agents make their own history, but not as they will it or in conditions of their own choosing.

Finally, and perhaps more important, the unintended social consequences are crucial to the understanding of the dynamics of change in so far as they become the basis of further action and change. In Chimoio, unintended consequences of war were systematically involved in social reproduction, and they became conditions of action also. For example, the consequences of war such as displacement, the disruption of the social fabric of society and the collapse of the state, have become objective conditions in which the dispossessed have continued to make their histories. In a nutshell, for an understanding of the relation of war to social change, it is important to transcend the agency/structure dichotomy, as both are constituted in and through the other; to recognise that through their participation in the 'dialectic of control' the seemingly powerless can actually develop a 'counterhegemony' and mobilise resources against the strong; and finally to appreciate the significance of 'unintended social consequences' as a basis for further change and action. The most pressing question is whether or not the conditions and combination of forces that led to the creation of this new possibility of a civil society are sufficient and comprehensive enough to sustain the more constructive project of democratisation.

Focusing on the relationship between war and society in Israel, Ehrlich made some very interesting observations which are similar to the conclusions of this study.[64] As with Israel, the Mozambique case may serve as an example of the contention that "conflict and war bring about creation, modification and change, transformation or destruction of social formations".[65] It seems probable that, as Ehrlich argues, "the longer lasting, the more comprehensive and intensive the conflict, the more salient will be its effects upon the social structure".[66] The relevance of this observation becomes clearer if a comparison is made with neighbouring Zimbabwe which had a shorter guerrilla war and where consequently the social changes were less profound than in Mozambique. Below, in the hope of throwing some light on the limits, and implications, of the dispossessed's innovative spontaneity, I will look briefly at Zimbabwe's war of independence and some of its consequences.

Spontaneity and prospects for the future: A comparison with Zimbabwe

Fanon, in a consideration of violence and spontaneity, noted the "frequent existence of a time lag, or a difference of rhythm, between the leaders of a nationalist party and the mass of the people".[67] In every political or trade-union organization, he argues, there is "a traditional gap between the rank-and-file, who demand the total and immediate bettering of their lot, and the leaders, who, since they are aware of the difficulties which may be made by the employers [or imperialists], seek to limit and restrain the workers' demands".[68] This gap, as both the cases of Mozambique and Zimbabwe suggest, partly explains why revolutions always tend to disappoint their followers. In other words, this gap presents a major obstacle to the sustenance of the new spontaneous rhythm of life that the dispossessed developed during the war period. In both countries, the root of the problem is the fundamental importance the elite attach to organization, "so much so that the fetish of organization will often take precedence over a reasoned study of ... society".[69]

Like Mozambique, Zimbabwe won its independence after a protracted armed struggle in 1980. In a striking similarity with the Mozambican peace process. Soon after independence, as with Mozambique, Zimbabwe entered into a civil-war which almost approximated the proportions of ethnic genocide and pitted the Shonas against the minority Ndebeles.[70] Both the wars in Zimbabwe were shorter in duration, and the extent of displacement as well as consequences of war much less visible, than those in Mozambique. One area that highlights both the strengths and weaknesses of spontaneity, and the gap between rulers and the ruled, is the case of women and youth.

In Zimbabwe, as in Mozambique, some women and youth, and other rural under-classes, were empowered by their participation in the liberation struggle. In some cases, they found unprecedented opportunities in the war to challenge dominant structures.[71] However, in the power equation that emerged after independence, as Samupindi vividly shows in his novel *Pawns*, the masses were a weaker political actor vulnerable to manipulation by powerful political entrepreneurs.[72] According to Kriger, it was the legacy of guerrilla coercion that 'inhibited' them from exerting a radicalizing influence on nationalist leaders in post-independence Zimbabwe.[73] For example, women who had played a major role in the armed struggle were, under the de-radicalisation campaign euphemistically dubbed 'de-bushing', encouraged to assume their traditional roles within the family. Similarly, traditional and religious, who had provided a link between the guerrillas and the ancestors, as well as the youth who had become powerful as guerrilla auxiliaries, found their new found power dissipate in the post-independence dispensation; some ex-combatants and ex-refugees who failed to 'de-bush' were also abandoned by the movement by either being expelled from school or from the army, and as Samupindi shows, it is some of these people who are now part of the army of beggars that roam Harare city.[74] The marginalization of these groups in the post-war order highlights the limits of spontaneity, and it was inevitable given the fact that the alternative politics and survival strategies of these under-classes tended to subvert the power of the dominant groups. Like in contemporary Mozambique, there was a divergence of priorities between many groups in society, and it was the interests of the powerful groups that prevailed.

If the lessons from Zimbabwe are anything to go by, another war is over, but another one of a different kind, a war of positions has just begun. In Chimoio, for instance, what is a source of hope and inspiration for some is simultaneously 'new times' for others.[75] The new forms of social organisation and economic arrangements that the dispossessed have developed threaten to undermine the power base of former dominant groups, who in response have deployed the full force of mystifying ideological discourses (eg the myth that women's new behaviours have caused natural disasters such as drought - as punishment by God or ancestors) in combination with economic enterprising and political corruption to defend their privileges. Women in particular, and other subordinate groups in general, have confronted resistance from the exponents of dominant traditional and religious ideology in their efforts to expand their political space. Another related dilemma revolves around whether the post-war re-construction programme should be informed by moral ethics or triage. Morality dictates that the poorest should get first priority. But the logic of the 'free market' embodied in the structural adjustment programme is such that the rich will get richer and the poor poorer.

However, if as Ehrlich argues, "the longer lasting, the more comprehensive and intensive the conflict, the more salient will be its effects upon the social structure",[76] then the comparison with Zimbabwe has to be qualified. As already noted, both the wars in Zimbabwe were shorter than those in Mozambique, and their impact on the economy and society was therefore less extensive. During the Rhodesian (Zimbabwe after independence in 1980) war the economy, for instance, under the import substitution industrialisation programme adapted to counter the effects of sanctions, and witnessed its fastest growth rate in history. The economy remained largely intact and most basic commodities were available in rural shops which were still accessible. The need for intensive innovative enterprising did therefore not arise. It was in fact after the collapse of the post-colonial economy that Zimbabweans were forced to increasingly seek sustenance in the informal sector.

In contrast, in Mozambique the official economy collapsed under the impact of war, forcing people to devise their own strategies for survival. The socio-economic re-organisation and power configurations engendered by the civil-war also seem more profound than those that occurred in Zimbabwe. This reality leads us to two observations which are of significance for this study: first, it appears that the extent of the socio-economic and political transformation is a function of the duration and intensity of the war; and

263

second, economic crisis, in this case exacerbated by war, plays an important role in inducing economic 'initiative'. For instance, while many urban Zimbabwean women and young children spend long hours waiting in queues for bread, their counterparts in Chimoio compete with each other in trying to sell their home-made bread.[77] In other words, some of the changes caused by the war in Mozambique may be irreversible; a whole generation has known nothing but violent turmoil, and this has a profound influence on their overall personalities, worldly perspectives and actions.

To sum up, one war is over but enormous hardships are imminent as latent tensions and conflicts hitherto overshadowed by the war become apparent. While obviously peace creates opportunities for addressing or confronting some of these complex problems, there should be no illusions about the future. For as one Provincial official said:

> Peace will be a shame. It will expose all our weaknesses [and differences]. For example, right now we are failing to manage with just a fraction of the population, what more when all the refugees return?

Paradoxically, the cease-fire agreement seems to have been an agreement to continue war by other means: since the ceasefire the 'war of position' has been characterised by continuous mud-slinging between Frelimo and Renamo amidst attempts to consolidate their positions.

Nonetheless, the resilience and innovativeness of the dispossessed in response to the crisis provides compelling reasons for reworking proposals that can show how human beings can make a better society. Their attempts to impose their own solutions to problems caused by the war in opposition to the wishes of the dominant groups show that the dispossessed are not mere victims of the war. They are active agents of change shaping the course of their history, within the constrains of given historical structures. This reality, especially the vitality of social life in Chimoio and the dynamism of the alternative economy, has profound implications for the theorisation of the relationship between war, society and change.

Summary: Implications for theory

A historical theory of war, society and change should identify the principal discursive genres of politics and their structural determinants. As should be clear from the preceding discussion, these are necessarily disparate and fragmentary, and should be examined in the specific context of their enunciation. Consequently, although illuminating, neither of the polarised approaches represented by Hanlon and Geffray mentioned in the Introduction are wholly satisfactory. The problem is that, in the 'destabilzationist' thesis, the local and people are in danger of vanishing within the global structures of domination and become quite insignificant. Similarly, in the 'bona fide civil war thesis' the local is viewed in isolation from its global context as if it exits in a vacuum. White warns us thus:

> It is important to avoid two common tendencies: on the one hand, to overestimate the 'socialist' nature of such societies and view 'full' socialism as merely a future extrapolation of current realities; on the other hand, to minimise the difficulties involved in realising socialist goals in current Third World conditions and engage in critiques which are empty because unrealistic.[78]

The 're-integrationist' approach, as we saw, does not sufficiently problematize the social changes that are unfolding. As we have seen, the struggle for power lies at the core of the dialectic of change and continuity in Mozambique, and in an attempt to capture and control state power, politics has been militarised. As Foucault points out, 'power is action over action':

> It is a total structure of actions brought to bear upon actions; it incites, it induces, it seduces, it makes easier or more difficult; in the extreme constrains or forbids absolutely; it is nevertheless always a way of acting upon an acting subject or acting subjects by virtue of their acting or being capable of action.[79]

Seen from this perspective, the grass-roots economy is a challenge to centralised economic planning; the dispossessed's anti-politics a critique of power; religious revivalism a critique of state power; and finally feminist resurgence a critique of patriarchy. Of course the concept of domination still keeps its meaning, but it should not be dissociated from the concept of autonomy as "all subjections are in themselves actions".[80]

For instance, "by virtue of their acting or being capable of action", the dispossessed have curtailed the state's omnipresence in the civil society, creating a power vacuum which has been filled by ever increasing social organisations. Similarly, the agents of political change have become more diverse and complex with religious, women, youth etc movements organising directly around the politics of real life, the politics of real issues as people confront them. Their activities speak directly to us about the 'creative destruction' of war, their changing society and their role as history-makers in this process: they have not dabbled in 'high politics' as the art of the possible: they have not changed what was possible, and in the process opened up new possibilities for alternative social arrangements. Before the war undermined the power base of the state, such actions would have been unthinkable. One wonders how any scholar can sustain the argument that the war was, *only* a political event, machinated by outside forces, with social consequences.

At the heart of the war lay the social conflict which, for five centuries of Portuguese conquest, had pitted the dispossessed against an inequitable market system. Far from ending conflict in the countryside, Frelimo's introduction of a new agrarian system based on collectivization and state farms, was bound to increase antagonism between peasants seeking more land and the wealthy agrarian bourgeoisie, the rural kulaks, as well as with urban dwellers over the terms of trade/exchange between agricultural and manufactured goods. Renamo violence aggravated and politicized these long-standing, festering conflicts between rich and poor, of both rural and urban areas. Once again, war, as well as the general political situation in Southern Africa, helped to resolve the problem *not* in favour of the dispossessed peasants. What is the basis of these festering conflicts, and hence of change?

Hegel's concept of the 'dialectic', developed by Marx into 'dialectical materialism', seems to offer an effective entry point to understanding such contested processes of social change. Hegel argued that it is the 'dialectic of negativity' which is 'the moving and creating principle' that fills the gap between what is and what might be or ought to be.[81] Central to the notion of the 'dialectic of negativity' - or 'negation of the negation' - is the contradiction between reality and the ideal.[82] This contradiction, based as it were on unequal power relationships and domination in society, is resolved by recourse to political struggle: "without parties there is no development, without division, no progress".[83]

In Mozambique, it was through fighting out this conflict, the permanently incomplete resolution of this contradiction between dominant and subordinate social groups, humankind and nature, that social change occurred, and continues to. Wars, and civil wars in particular, being the "highest form of resolving conflicts between antagonistic parties", represent (as the case of Mozambique amply demonstrates) "crucial moments in the historical development of many states and societies".[84] In fact, in Manica experience, the war was also fought at various levels of society by different individuals, with many different means, and for many different purposes.

War, as Giddens observes, is therefore not a negation of the state, nor inimical to human progress, but rather "a constituent factor".[85] The state itself, in the process of waging the war, has undergone profound transformation, resulting in a redefinition of its relationship with civil society. When Frelimo's traditional approach to the politics of the state became inadequate to meet the demands of a war economy, as the economic and social conditions it was designed to address had been transformed, it 'revolutionized' itself in response. Similarly, the dispossessed have not been the passive objects of violence and war. Neither has war completely weakened their ability to pursue their own strategies to reproduce their lives and society. Instead they have been active agents in the transformation of their societies, sometimes opposing authority and at other times obeying it.

This means that, and implicit in Hall's analysis in "War and the Rise of the West", a theory of war is simultaneously a theory of the state. The content of the unintended consequences of war are a function of many variables, the most important of which seems to be the relationship between the mode of production and the mode of warfare; in China, Hall notes, war did help create the empire, but that form proved inimical to the autonomy of the market; in Islam and India war was wholly destructive[86]; in Zimbabwe it left many expectations unfulfilled and many structures unaltered; and in Mozambique it was both destructive and regenerative. The most remarkable regenerative aspects of the Mozambican war are first, the increased autonomy of the market and expansion of the grass-roots war economy and second, the widespread rise in political activism, which has in turn enabled the hitherto disenfranchised to express and organise themselves. These developments arguably carry new implications for the nature of the relationship between the state and civil society.

A critical theory of the state and violent change should therefore not seek the development of deterministic models, such as the popular view represented by Nef who argued that war is inimical to human progress[87], or its antithesis, advanced by Hall and more recently by Bayart, which posits that war is catalyst for growth and modernity.[88] What is needed instead is the constant refinement of naunced and subtle analyses of historical processes in which global and local social forces interact to produce contingent and often idiosyncratic trajectories of change. This by definition, is an endless practical and theoretical process which expresses the inevitable and essential dialectic of ideas and reality.

As Berman points out following Tilly, '[s]uch non-deterministic analysis of history cannot be written backwards or retrospectively, but only ... projectively by beginning "with a particular historical condition and search[ing] forward to the alternative outcomes of that condition, with a specification of the paths leading to each of the outcomes."[89] As attempted here through the analysis of individual life-histories, this also requires giving full weight to the subjective experience and intentionality of historical actors. This, Berman further elaborates;

> does not mean replacing determinism with equally arid instrumentalism, but rather giving theoretical recognition to the reflection of objective structural forces in subjective experience, as well as the reciprocal

influence of human will on those structures, while at the same time allowing for the impact of accident, failure and unforeseen and unintended consequences.

Since historical truth is relative rather than absolute, there is a need for such a non-determinist, but not necessarily a non-ideological approach to the study of the state, society and violent change; it can only be hoped that a synthesis will emerge from the dialectical struggle, if not 'rat race', between the ever increasing ranks of researchers on Mozambique.

The foregoing discussion has outlined a theoretical and historical framework for understanding the political economy of war. The framework emphasises the centrality of the 'crisis of hegemony', participation in the 'dialectic of control' and unintended consequences in shaping the trajectory of the struggles between the dominant groups and the dominated. In this model, structure and agency, the state and civil society, are viewed as mutually redefining and constituted and through the other. The question of primacy does not arise. As we have seen, the Mozambican civil-war amplified pre-existing contradictions, and in the process generated its own unintended consequences and contradictions; these have become the basis for further action and change.

Through their participation in the dialectic of control, the weak of Chimoio have been able to alter the distribution of power, and this was precisely because the powerful are also dependent on the weak, and vice versa. More often than not, their survival strategies have not only been in opposition to the wishes of the dominant groups who control the institution of war, but have also exacerbated the rising disorganization of the state's legitimacy in the eyes of the ruled, a development which partly led Frelimo to abandon one-party statism and to introduce wide ranging political and economic reforms. Thus rather than viewing the unfolding situation as "[a] dream undone"[90], it is perhaps more fruitful to look at it as the redefinition of a new dream and vision. This is not to underestimate the destruction of the war nor the difficulties of rebuilding on its ruins. Indeed, as at independence, post-socialist and post-war Mozambique faces a delicate economic and politico-military situation, characterized by conflicting priorities about how to meet diverse needs with scarce means, and in the last instance, the dilemma will be resolved by the balance of forces at both a local and global level.

Notes

1. Mark Mitchell and Dave Russel, "Militarism and the South African State", in Colin Creighton and Martin Shaw (editors), *The Sociology of War and Peace*, London, Macmillan Press, 1987, p. 99.

2. See among others, Mahmood Mamdani, "State and Civil Society in Contemporary Africa: Reconceptualising the Birth of State Nationalism and the Defeat of Popular Movements", in *Africa Development*, Volume XV, Number 3/4, 1990.

3. Mahmood Mamdani, " A glimpse at African Studies, made in USA", *CODESRIA Bulletin*, Number 2, 1990.

4. John A. Hall, "War and the Rise of the West", in Collin Creighton and Martin Shaw (editors), op. cit., pp. 37-53.

5. Ibid., p. 40.

6. Ibid., p. 40.

7. Ibid., p. 46.

8. Ibid., p. 51.

9. Ibid., p. 48.

10. Malyn Newitt, *Portugal and Africa: The Last Hundred Years*, London, C. Hurst and Company, 1981, p. 49.

11. Ibid., p. 49.

12. Ibid., p. 49.

13. For a detailed analysis of the articulation of the state and society in Africa, see among others Bruce Berman and John Lonsdale, *Unhappy Valley: Conflict in Kenya and Africa, Book One: State and Class*, London, James Currey, 1992.

14. Cited in Marcia Wright, "Women in Peril", *African Social Research*, December 1975, by Bruce J. Berman, "Declining Economies, Collapsing States, Falling Paradigms: Development Theory and the African Crisis", paper prepared for the annual meeting of the African Studies Association, Boston, Mass, December 3-7, 1993.

15. Perry Anderson, "Portugal and the end of Ultra-colonialism", in *New Left Review*, Number 15, 1962, pp. 83-102.

16. See Howard P. Lehman, "The Paradox of State Power in Africa: Debt

Management policies in Kenya and Zimbabwe", in *African Studies Review*, Volume 35, Number 1, September 1992, pp. 1-34.

17. See Antonio Gramsci's, *Selections from Prison Notebooks*, New York, International Publishers, 1971, *The Modern Prince and Other Writings*, New York, International Publishers, 1975, and *Selections from Political Writings, 1921-1926*, London, Lawrence and Wishart, 1978.

18. Martin Carnoy, *The State and Political Theory*, New Jersey, Princeton University Press, 1984, p. 78.

19. Ibid.

20. Ibid., p. 83.

21. Bjorn Beckman, "The Liberation of Civil Society: Neo-Liberal Ideology and Political Theory", in *Review of African Political Economy*, 1993, Number 58, p. 23.

22. As McLellan point out:
By bureaucracy Hegel meant a body of higher civil servants who were recruited by competition from the middle classes. To them were entrusted the formulation of common interests and the task of maintaining the unity of the state. Their decisions were prevented from being arbitrary by the monarch above them and the pressure of the corporations from below.
See D. McLellan (editor), *Karl Marx: The Early Texts*, Oxford, Oxford University Press, 1971, p. 71.

23. Ibid., p. 69.

24. Howard Williams, *Kant's Political Philosophy*, Oxford, Blackwell, 1983, pp. 164-5.

25. Ibid., p. 165.

26. Ibid., p. 166.

27. Cited by D. McLellan, op. cit., p. 73.

28. Howard Williams, op. cit., p. 166.

29. Ibid.

30. Ibid., p. 74.

31. Ibid., p. 75.

32. Martin Carnoy, op. cit . 67.

33. Cited from N. Bobbio, *Democracy and Dictatorship*, Cambridge, Polity Press, 1989, by Paul G. Lewis, op. cit. p. 4.

34. Ibid., p. 20.

35. Thus for instance, the Frelimo state of 1975, before the transformation of the front into a vanguard party, is significantly different from the post-reform and beleaguered state of the 1990s.

36. In fact as Lewis points out, in Eastern Europe it was actually in the face of the apparently strongest and most tightly organised form of state power, totalitarian dictatorship, that civil society increased its resources and seemed to grow in stature sufficiently to pose a critical challenge to the exercise and very existence of that dictatorship. See Paul G. Lewis (editor), *Democracy and Civil Society in Eastern Europe*, London, MacMillan Press, 1992, p. 6.

37. Ibid., p. 4.

38. Ibid., p. 4.

39. Ibid. See also Keith Tester, *Civil Society*, London, Routledge, 1992.

40. See Jean-Francois Bayart, "Civil Society in Africa: Academic Hallucination or Contested Space", paper presented at the African Studies Association (ASA) Conference, 3-7 December 1993, Boston, and John W. Harbeson, "Civil Society and Democratisation in Africa: Some Preliminary Notes From The Field", in *African Voices*, Volume 2, Number 3, Fall/Winter,1993, pp. 1-3.

41. Commentary note on earlier draft by John Lonsdale (Professor of African History, Cambridge University, and co-author of *Unhappy Valley*, op. cit.).

42. Kenneth Hermele, *Land Struggles and Social Differentiation in Southern Mozambique: a Case Study of Chokwe, Limpopo 1950-1987*, Uppsala, Scandinavian Institute of African Studies, Research Report Number 82, p. 52.

43. See David Hoile, (review of) *Conspicuous Destruction: War, Famine and the Reform Process in Mozambique, The 1992 Africa Watch Report on Mozambique: Disappointing, Stereotyped and Fragmentary*, London, Mozambique Institute Occasional Paper Number 2.

44. Hobbes, cited from A. Wolf, *A History of Science, Technology and Philosophy in the Sixteenth and Seventeenth Centuries*, 1935, by Christopher Hill, *The World Upside Down: Radical Ideas During the English Revolution*, London, Penguin Books, 1984, p. 361.

45. For a similar view see, Goran Hyden's, *Beyond Ujama in Tanzania: Underdevelopment and an Uncaptured Peasantry*, London, Heinemann, 1980, and *No ShortCuts To Progress*, London, Heinemann, 1986.

46. See J.C. Scott, *Weapons of the Weak: Everyday Forms of Peasant Resistance*, New Haven, Yale University Press, 1980.

47. See Jean-Francois Bayart, op. cit.

48. Peter Worsley, *The Three Worlds: Culture and World Development*, London, Weidenfield and Nicolson, 1984, p. 58.

49. Cited in G. Balandier, *Sens et puissance. Les dynamics sociales*, Paris, PUF, 1971, by Jean-Fracois Bayart, op. cit, p. 37.

50. See David Mclellan, *Marxism After Marx: An Introduction*, New York, Harper and Row, 1979.

51. Althusser's structural determinism rejected economic determinism and argued instead for the relative autonomy of politics and ideology from the economic base: although economic structure is always 'determinant in the last instance', any of the three structures can be the 'structure in dominance' in a particular mode of production. See Louis Althusser, *For Marx*, London, Penguin, 1971, and his *Lenin and Philosophy and Other Essays*, New york, monthly Review Press, 1971.

52. See Nico Poulantzas, "The Problem of the Capitalist State", *New Left Review*, Number 58, 1969, pp. 67-78 and his *Political Power and Social Classes*, London, New Left Books, 1974.

53. See Antonio Gramsci, op. cit.

54. Mao Tse Tung, *Selected Works*, London, Penguin, 1970.

55. Anna Bravo, "Italian Peasant Women and the First World War", in Clive Emsely et. al. (editors), *War, Peace and Social Change in Twentieth Century Europe*, Suffolk, Open University, 1989, p. 102.

56. Cornel West, "Race Matters", in Cornel West and bell hooks, *Breaking Bread: Black Insurgent Intellectual Life*, Boston (MA), Common Courage Press, 1992.

57. Anthony Giddens, *Profiles and Critiques in Social Theory*, Berkeley and Los Angels, University of California Press, 1982, p. 8.

58. Ibid., p. 8.

59. See Howard Williams, op. cit.

60. Ibid., pp. 197-198.

61. Bertil Egero, *Mozambique: A Dream Undone, the Political Economy of Democracy, 1975-1984*, Uppsala, Nordiska afrikainstitutet, 1987, p. 11.

62. See Carl Von Clausewitz, *On War*, London, 1971.

63. Anthony Giddens, op. cit., p. 32.

64. Avishai Ehrlich, "Israel: Conflict, War and Social Change", Collin Creighton and Martin Shaw, op. cit., pp. 121-142.

65. Ibid., p. 121.

66. Ibid., p. 121.

67. Frantz Fanon, *The Wretched of the Earth: The Handbook for the Black Revolution that is Changing the Shape of the World*, New York, Grove Press, 1968, p. 107.

68. Ibid., p. 107.

69. Ibid., p. 108.

70. See Richard Webner, *Tears of the Dead: The Social Biography of an African Family*, London, Edinburgh University Press, 1991.

71. See Norma Kriger, *Zimbabwe's Guerrilla War: Peasant Voices*, Cambridge, Cambridge University Press, 1992.

72. Charles Samupindi, *Pawns,* Harare, Baobab Books, 1992.

73. See Norma Kriger, op. cit.

74. Charles Samupindi, op. cit.

75. Thus, for example, while for two middle-aged lower middle men 'everything is spoiled' and the 'whole society ill', for an eighteen young woman, "everywhere in the world things are changing. It is new times, and we must change".

76. Avishai Ehrlich, op. cit., p. 121.

77. Interestingly, when Harare women demonstrated against the rising price of bread towards the end of 1993, the government responded by asking them to form their own cooperative bakeries if they wanted the price of bread to go down, as in Mozambique.

78. Gordon White, *et al, Revolutionary Socialist Development in the Third World*, Sussex, Wheatsheaf Books 1983.

79. Cited in Michael Foucault, "Le pouvoir, comments' exerce-t-il?", in H.L. Dreyfus and P. Rabinow, Michael Foucault, un parcours philosophique, Paris, Gallimard, 1984, by Jean-Francois Bayart, op. cit., p. 27.

80. Jean-Francois Bayart, op. cit., p. 27.

81. D. Mclellan, *Karl Marx: His Life and Thought,* London, 1972, p. 125.

82. Hegel had tried to reconcile the ideal and the real by showing that reality was the unfolding of an idea - the 'Ideal' or the 'Spirit' - and was thus rational. See Hegel's Phenomenology and, The Philosophy of Right, Oxford, Oxford University Press, 1967. Marx criticised this idealistic element of Hegelian philosophy - 'Hegel standing on his head' - but accepted and developed, by borrowing from Feuerbachian materialism, his dialectical method. In contrast to Hegel, Marx emphasised the opposition between ideals and reality in the secular world and categorised Hegel's whole enterprise as speculative

83. Cited in D. McLellan op. cit., p. 51.

84. Collin Creighton and Martin Shaw (editors), op. cit., p. 6.

85. Cited in Anthony Giddens, *The Nation-State and Violence*, Berkely, University of California Press, 1987 by Jean-Francois Bayart, *The State in Africa: The Politics of the Belly*, London, Longman, 1993, p. xiv.

86. Ibid., p 52.

87. John U. Nef, *War and Human Progress*, Cambridge, Harvard University Press, 1950.

88. John A. Hall, "War and the Rise of the West", in Colin Creighton and Martin Shaw (editors), op. cit.

89. Bruce Berman and John Lonsdale, op. cit.

90. Bertil Egero, *Mozambique: A Dream Undone, The Political Economy of Democracy, 1975-84*, Uppsala, Nordiska afrikainstitutet, 1987.

Conclusion

Introduction

Throughout these pages we have seen Mozambicans, as individuals and in their collectivity, forge their own destiny, painting the fresco of their political engagement in a context of violent change. Anarchy and disorder has changed, and continues to change, the character of politics, and how it is conducted, what it is about, and where it takes place. Inevitably, in the long-run this will undermine the current consensus, both locally and globally. For instance, there has been a significant transformation of what is 'political', with sexuality, religion, private associations all setting the agenda for the new times. In addition, the syncretic articulation of these forces has been an intensely contested process characterised by a 'revolution-counterrevolution' dialectic between the forces of change and conservatism. War has thus, in addition to its more visible negative impact on society, actually made society more dynamic and vibrant.

The war was a product of the revolution-counterrevolution dialectic in Mozambique, which dates back to the upheavals of the mid nineteenth century when the Southern Africa sub-region was integrated into the periphery of the global capitalist system. In that period the Portuguese colonial state, which was struggling to impose itself on the indigenous communities, set in motion a revolutionary process which manifested itself in the form of the latter's resistance and struggle. The post Second World War global revolution, characterised by the disintegration of the European empire in Africa and in the rest of the 'Third World' promised to set free an emancipatory vision. That was never to be. Instead it was immediately followed by another global counterrevolution epitomised by the rise of Stalinism in Eastern Europe and its extension to the Third World, including Mozambique. The US-led global counterrevolutionary crusade, characterized by support for dictatorial regimes in the Third World, has further shattered this vision.

In Mozambique, as discussed in Chapter Two, this revolution-counterrevolution dialectic took a new turn when Renamo, backed by white supremacist racist capital, appeared on the stage. The immediate roots of this phase of the revolution-counterrevolution dialectic can be traced back to both the protracted war of independence waged by Frelimo, and to the contradictions of the Southern African political economies. The unresolved ideological questions of the independence struggle and the national interests of the states in the sub-region, as well as the 'Cold war' rivalry, all combined in shaping the course and nature of the war. The ideological disputes over the nature of the society to be created that almost tore FRELIMO apart in the mid-1960s have also been central to the civil war (and of course Renamo is led by ex-Frelimo members), providing it with an internal dynamic. At one level, and as is evidenced by the current squabbles between the rebels and the government over administration of territory, the war had been an old fashioned struggle for power between and among the elites.

This internal dynamic has been conditioned by the geo-politics of the region and the changes in the global political economy. Relations with the west, as elsewhere in Africa, have been crucial in local power struggles.[1] Backed by South African white racist capital, the MNR anti-state insurgency became the negative avatar of the post-independence authoritarian modernisation. But the MNR itself seems to be an opportunistic counterrevolutionary movement led by elites exploiting quasi-nationalist ideology, ethnic loyalties and people's legitimate grievances against the state for their own parochial interests. Thus, although external interference constitutes a key experience for Mozambique, it should be regarded only as a partial explanation which can throw some light on the history of the country. In this phase of the change-continuity dialectic, as in earlier ones, agency and structure have been intermeshed. Through participation in the dialectic of control the dominated have challenged the status quo. The outcomes have been far from the intentions of the actors involved. As a contingent outcome of the war, it appears the stage has been set for the regeneration of society. More specifically by undermining the oppressive structures of the state and society, MNR violence has opened up possibilities for radical change. It has altered the power relationship between the state and civil society. It has also accelerated processes of social and political re-alignment and economic re-organisation as well as power configurations within civil society itself. These 'unintended social consequence' of war seem to carry new implications for the understanding of the relationship between war, society and change as it has evolved in Southern Africa in general, and Mozambique in particular. Would it be naive to hope that, given the balance of forces in the post-Cold War international disorder, Mozambique is on the verge of a revolution?

Managing this volatile transition and elections process was the United Nations mission in Mozambique (UNUMOZ). Events abroad, for example in Angola, confirm the significance of this modern 'byzantine' bureaucratic machine and that it would be quite wrong to dismiss it as an ineffective and unproductive body. However, in Mozambique its task of supervising the elections, in a context of global 'market triumphalism' and wide consensus about multi-partyism as a universal panacea to the world's failing democracies, was essentially applying the *coupe de grace* to an antiquated bureaucratic system, already mortally wounded by the war. After the elections of December 1994, squabbling over the rich spoils of war became the order of the day; here again, the dispossessed are reluctant to go away empty-handed. However, the collapse of the 'new consensus', which is central to an understanding of the subsequent course of the unfolding processes, is imminent; all over the world, cracks are appearing in the political systems based on a 'free market' consensus, as it increasingly fails to deliver its promises.

As everywhere in the world, but in vain, the people of privilege, politicians, the petit bourgeoisie, men of the cloth, traditional patriarchs and feudo-bureaucrats close their eyes to the revolution from below that war, time and the force of things has brought about; it is real none the less.[2] Formerly, the politicians were respectable *chefs,* with the last word on everything noble and revolutionary. Today, as 'fat cats' of market fundamentalism, they are objects of disdain and contempt by all but their few dependents. But, backed by other nationalists of other nation-states, the local nationalist politicians, and through the influence of false belief in the sanctity of the nation-state, still tenuously hold unto power; but the people have every reason not to trust politicians, and the upper-class in general.

From the point of view of the dominant groups, the most dangerous development is the view, repeated by many prophetic preachers, that the ordinary people have a very special role to play in this crisis, that they are somehow more chosen than the rich and powerful. As shown in Chapter Five, for example, many locally rooted religious groups have depicted dominant groups as arrant traitors and rebels against God. Brother Elijah, a heretic prophet teaches: "There has been too much sinning. Don't alert the sinners [rich people and politicians]. They must die". This position, based on millenarian hopes as it were, is not new nor unique to such groups. It is indeed latently ubiquitous in all social movements, including women and youth organisations.

As shown in Chapter Three, this latent struggle has been most intense within the sphere of production, exchange and consumption. The intensity of the struggle within this sphere of civil society is primarily due to the fact that the economic opportunities of war have been unevenly distributed.[3] Although some of the dispossessed have become relatively established entrepreneurs, the majority are starved of capital and are unable to consolidate their position against big local and international capital. Also, the emerging labour, exchange and social relations have altered the balance of political power among and between the new economic elites, their employees and the state. The different impact of war on different groups of people has had a great deal of influence on their attitudes and on how they have positioned themselves politically and economically. This diversity in their responses raises difficulties in identifying and distinguishing between 'radical' and 'conservative' elements and/or forces.

To oversimplify, there have been two interrelated revolts, the MNR anti-state insurgency and a latent 'social revolt'. The immense destructiveness of the war has tended to overshadow the latter, a revolt whose success might form the basis for a strengthened civil society. This development, 'the quiet revolution' in a famous Mozambican journalist's words, discredits the one-sided pessimistic view of war as solely a negative or destructive force. Although a painful experience, war is an immensely creative force capable of multiple consequences, good and bad for different groups of people: the subversion of the old order has been accompanied by a fascinating flood of radical ideas and alternative arrangements. But the emerging civil society is not necessarily democratic nor is it completely independent from the state. Instead it is an intensely contested social space, and its specific forms are mediated by its interrelation with the state. The exact nature of the relationship between the state and the civil society will be ultimately related to both these fundamental economic and political struggles, both at a local and global level.

Conclusion

To recapitulate, the main proposition of this book is that the war has been a most unusual catalyst of social change, change which has shaped both the course of the war itself and the social system. In the anarchy created by the war the hitherto disenfranchised have found unprecedented opportunities to carve out a social and political space for themselves and to demand more freedom. This has intensified the struggle for dominance among and between the emergent social forces, in which political alliances are shifting and/or disintegrating. These shifting alliances, the accompanying reconfiguration of power relations, the redistribution of wealth (albeit unevenly) and changes in norms and attitudes, are characterized by numerous intersections of

279

conflicting forces and processes, and by cultural hybridisation in the forms of political engagement and construction. Indeed, the unfolding reality in Chimoio is a motley mixture of contradictions and paradoxes. Contradictory impulses co-exist in dynamic tension as bitter change has given rise to inflated expectations. There is hope and disillusionment, extreme wealth and absolute poverty, regeneration and ossification, and radical and conservative ideas.

As we have seen, the war, building on pre-existent tensions, generated its own contradictions, and caused so much damage whose effects would be felt for years afterwards; some of these effects are permanent and cannot be reversed. Some of the survival strategies adopted by the dispossessed have often conflicted with each other, and the outcome of these social processes, in particular the quest to expand the scope of politics, is most uncertain. What is certain, however, is that the idea of the state managing society, playing an extensive role in delivering solutions and services is being superseded by two contradictory developments. First, there is a widespread desire for a state which is capable of taking determined, strategic action to sort out the problems. This desire is matched by another - exhibited in the dispossessed's innovative enterprising -- for a less embracing, intrusive, paternalistic state, an enabling state which helps people reach their own solutions to problems. But in reality, the state is either unable to deliver the goods or to protect the ordinary people, forcing people in response to invent the grass-roots war economy. Therefore, the starting point for understanding the war-society interface should be the concept of power: how it manifests itself in various systems of control and domination, and how it is challenged and subverted.

In conclusion, war, as an historical process, has accelerated the process of social change. Its impact on hegemonic structures, state and traditional, has shaped the forms in which the dialectic of control manifested itself, as well as the nature of the multiple unintended consequences. No doubt from a statistical and even a structural standpoint (the expansion of the grass-roots war economy, for example), the war did not produce a miraculous development, such as a modern, urban, industrialized society. However, to deny the importance of the economic, political, social legal and juridical changes which were precipitated by the war, all of which did mark an important stage in the evolution of Mozambican society, is to barter historical truth for ideological advantage. As we have seen in Chimoio, the people, who are all the time adding to their knowledge in the light of war experience, have shown themselves capable of directing their struggle, "[a]nd still they dance".[4] Having survived the holocaust of slavery, the catastrophe of colonialism and lately the duplicities of those who control the institution of violence and war, Mozambicans in particular, and the people of Southern Africa in general, seem well placed to continue the invisible "revolution that is changing the shape of the world"[5], and that is the legitimate inheritor of the anti-colonial revolution.

Notes

1. See Jean-Francois Bayart, *The State in Africa: The Politics of the Belly*, London, Longman, 1983, p. 29.

2. See Andrew Marr, "The Rise of do-it-yourself democracy", *The Independent*, London, 18 January 1996.

3. The new economic opportunities engendered by the war in Mozambique are most reflected by the number of Zimbabweans who cross the border, both legally and illegally, to sell goods from Zimbabwe and to buy goods for re-sale in Zimbabwe. In fact, a racket in fake Mozambican identity papers is apparently thriving along the eastern border areas, as economic refugees and criminal fugitives from Zimbabwe try a new life in Mozambique. See, Rodrick Chinodakufa, "Zimbabwean fugitives buy fake IDs to settle in Mozambique", in *Moto*, (Harare), July 1993. Also it is rumoured that Zimbabwean commercial farmers, worried about Mugabe's continued radical/nationalist rhetoric about land re-distribution, are buying farms in Mozambique.

4. Stephanie Urdang, *And Still They Dance: Women, war and the Struggle for Change in Mozambique*, London, Earthscan Publications, 1989.

5. Frantz Fanon, *The Wretched of the Earth: The Handbook for the Black Revolution that is Changing the Shape of the World*, New York, Grove, Press, 1968.

Selected bibliography

Adam, Y. "War, Hunger, Drought and Development: Lessons from Changara, Mozambique", paper for the Workshop, Mozambique: Contemporary Issues and Current Research, 23 February, 1991.

Alpers, A. Edward, "The Struggle for Socialism in Mozambique, 1966-72", in Roseberg and Callaghy (editors), *Socialism in Sub-Saharan Africa: A New Assessment*, California, University of California Press, 1979.

Anderson, N., *Mozambique: A War Against the People*, London, MacMillan, 1992.

Berry-Koch, A. "Refugee Women in Malawi: Their Role in Household Food Security", paper for the Expert Group Meeting on Refugee and Displaced Women and Children, 2-6th July, Vienna,1990.

Birmingham, David, *Frontline Nationalism in Angola and Mozambique*, London, James Currey, 1992.

Boeder, R.B. *Silent Majority: A History of the Lomwe in Malawi*, African Institute of South Africa, Pretoria, 1984.

Boothby, N. P. Upton and A. Sultan, *Children of Mozambique: The Cost of Survival*, Institute for Policy Studies and Public Affairs, Duke University, USA 1991.

de Braganca, Aquino and Wallerstein Immanuel, *An African Liberation Reader*, London, Zed Books, 1982.

Brennan, T.O. "Refugees from Mozambique: Shattered Land, Fragile Asylum", United States Committee for Refugees Year Book, USA, 1986.

Brennan, T.O. "Mozambicans: A People at Risk", World Refugee Survey, 1987, p.41-47, USA 1987.

Brett, E.A., *The World Economy Since the War: The Politics of Uneven Development*, London, Macmillan Press, 1985.

Brochmann, G. and A. Ofstad, *Mozambique: Norwegian Assistance in the Context of Crisis,* Chr. Michelen institute, Norway, 1990.

Cain, Edward, "Mozambique's Hidden War" in Moser, Charles (editor), *Combat on Communist Territory*, Regenery Gateway, 1985.

Callaway, H. "Women Refugees: Their Specific Needs and Untapped Resources", Refugee Studies Programme, Oxford 1985.

Chilcote, H. Richard, *Emerging Nationalism in Portuguese Africa: Documents*, California, Hoover Institute Press, 1972.

Chilcote, H. Richard, (editor), *Dependency and Marxism: Toward a Resolution of the Debate*, Colorado, Westview, Press, 1981.

Davison, Basil, "The Politics of Armed Struggle: National Liberation in the African Colonies of Portugal" in Davison, Basil et al, *Southern Africa: The New Politics of Revolution*, London, Longman, 1988.

Department of Ideological Work FRELIMO, *A History of FRELIMO*. Maputo, 1982.

Derrick, Knight, *Mozambique Caught in a Trap*, London, Christian Aid, 1988.

Duncan, Graeme, *Marx and Mill: Two Views of Social Conflict*, Cambridge, Cambridge University Press, 1978.

D'Souza, F. "Background Paper on Mozambique National Resistance (MNR), Frelimo and the Civil War", unpublished paper, Pretoria 1986.

Eisenstein, Hester, *Contemporary Feminist Thought*, London, Unwin Paperbacks, 1984.

Frazer, Elizabeth, et. al., (editors), *Ethics: A Feminist Reader*, Oxford, Blackwell Publications, 1992.

Finnegan, W. *A Complicated War: The Harrowing of Mozambique*, University of California Press, USA, 1992.

First, Ruth, *The Mozambican Miner: Study in the Export of Labour*, Maputo, Eduardo Mondlane University, 1977.

Frelimo, *On Underdevelopment to Socialism*, Report of the Party Central Committee, 1983.

Gersony, R. *Summary of Mozambican Refugee Accounts of Principally Conflict-related Experience in Mozambique*, Report to Ambassador J. Moore and Dr. C.A. Crocker, Bureau for Refugee Programs, Department of State, USA, 1988.

Gibboin, Peter, "The World Bank and African Poverty, 1973-91", in the Journal of Modern African Studies 30,2 (1992): 193-220.

Government of Mozambique and the United Nations, *The Emergency Situation in Mozambique: Priority Requirements for the Period 1990-1991*. New York: United Nations Publications, 1990.

Hall, M. "The Mozambican National Resistance Movement(Renamo Study in the Destruction of an African Country", in *Africa*, Volume 60, Number 1, 39-68, 1990.

Hammond, R.J., *Portugal and Africa, 1815-1910: A Study in Uneconomic Imperialism*, Stanford, Stanford University Press, 1966.

Hansen, A. "Once the Running Stops: Assimilation of Angolan Refugees into Zambian Border Villages", in *Disasters* Volume 31, Number 4, 1979.

Harrel-Bond, B.E. *Imposing Aid: Humanitarian Assistance to Refugees*, Oxford University Press, 1986.

Henriksen, H. Thomas, "Marxism and Mozambique", in *African Affairs*, Volume 77, Number 309, October, 1978.

Hermele, K. *Migration and Starvation: An Essay on Southern Mozambique*, AKUT, No.34, Sweden, 1984.

Hermele, K. Mozambican Crossroads: Economics and Politics in the Era of Structural Adjustment, Chr. Michelson Institute, Norway, 1990.

Holborn,L.W. *Refugees: A Problem of Our Time. The Work of UNHCR, 1957-72*, Volume 2 (Chapter 41,pp 1167-81), Scarecrow Press, UK, 1975.

Hoogvelt, M.M. Ankie, *The Third World in Global Development*, London, Macmillan, 1985.

Ian, Bray, *Chicualacuala: Life on the Front-line*, Oxford, Oxfam, 1981.

Ibeanu, O. "Apartheid, Destabilisation and Displacement: The Dynamics of the Refugee Crisis in Southern Africa", in *Journal of Refugee Studies*, Volume 3, Number 1, 1990, pp. 47-63.

Jessop Bob et al, *Marxism and Democracy*, London, Lawrence and Wishart, 1980.

Johnson, Phyllis, and David Martin, (editors). *Frontline Southern Africa*, Peterborough, Ryan Publishing, 1989.

Kanji, N. "War and Children in Mozambique: Is International Aid Strengthening or Eroding Community-Based Policies?" in *Community Development Journal*, Volume 25, Number 2, 102-112, 1990.

Kibreab, G. *Refugees and Development in Africa: The Case of Eritrea*, Red Sea Press, Trenton, USA, 1987.

Kibreab, G. *The State of the Art Review of Refugee Studies in Africa*, Uppsala Papers in Economic History, Research Report Number 26.,Uppsala, 1991.

Knight, D., *Mozambique: Caught in the Trap*, London, Christian Aid, 1988.

Korner, Peter, et al, *The IMF and the Debt Crisis*, London, Zed Books, 1987.

Le Scour, J.P. "The Snake of Fire, Memorandum on the Electric Fence Between Mozambique and South Africa", for the Bureau for Refugees, South Africa Catholic Bishops Conference, South Africa, 1989.

Lewis, Gwnne, *The French Revolution: Rethinking the Debate*, London, Routledge, 1993.

Liesegang, G.J. "Famines, Epidemics, Plagues and Long Periods of Warfare: Their Effects in Mozambique 1700-1975", paper presented at the

Conference on Zimbabwean History: Progress and Development, 23-27th August, Harare,1982.

Machika, M.R.E. "Income Generation Activities Among Refugees: The Case of Muloza Camp", presented at the International Conference on First Country of Asylum and Development Aid, York University and the Malawi Government, Malawi, 1992.

Machel, Samora, *FRELIMO and the Transitional Government of Mozambique: The Lusaka Agreement*, Braamfontein, the South African Institute of International Affairs, 1974.

--------------, *The Enemy Within*. Maputo: Department of Information and Propaganda, 1982.

--------------, *Unity of Purpose*, Maputo, Reprinted Speech, 1976.

--------------, *Our Sophisticated Weapon*, Maputo, Reprinted Speech, 1977.

--------------, *Mozambique: Sowing the Seeds of Revolution*, Maputo, 1978.

Maliyamkono, T.L. and Bagachwa, M.S.D, *The Second Economy in Tanzania*, London, James Currey, 1990.

Mandala, E.C. *Work and Control in a Peasant Economy: A History of the Lower Tchiri Valley in Malawi, 1859-1960*, University of Wisconsin Press, USA, 1990.

Manor, James, *Rethinking Third World Politics*, London, Longman, 1991.

Mazur, R., "The Political Economy of Refugee Creation in Southern Africa: Micro and Macro Issues in Sociological Perspective", in *Journal of Refugee Studies,* Volume 2, Number 4, 1989, pp. 441-67.

McKibbin, S. "Mozambican Victims of Slave Trade in South Africa", unpublished report for the Anti-Slavery Society International, London, 1992.

Mead, Margaret, *War: An Invention, Not a Biological Necessity*, London, Basic Books, 1964.

Mondlane, Eduardo, *The Struggle for Mozambique*, Baltimore: Penguin Books, 1969.

Munslow, Barry. "Refugees and Migrants in Mozambique: An Historical Overview", paper presented at African Studies Association Meeting, 13-14 September 1979, School of Oriental and African Studies, London, 1979.

Museveni, T. Yoweri, *Fanon's Theory on Violence: Its Verification in Liberated Mozambique*, Dar as Salaam, Tanzania Publishing House, 1975.

Negrao, J. *Mulheres em Situacao Dificil*, Maputo, UNICEF, 1991. Newitt, Malyn. *Portugal in Africa: The Last Hundred Years*, London, C.Hurst and Company, 1981.

Nilsson, A. "War and Displacement in Homoine District,Inhambane", Verbal presentation at Mozambique: Contemporary Issues and Current Research, Refugee Studies Programme Workshop, Oxford, February 1991.

Nunes, Jovito, "Pilot Study to Investigate the Problem of Social Organisation Within Displaced Communities: Preliminary Report", Mozambique Community Contact Group, Project Report, Maputo, Mozambique,1990.

Nunes, Jovito, "Peasants and Survival: The Social Consequences of Displacement", unpublished report for SIDA, Maputo, Mozambique, 1992.

Ohadike O. Patrick, *Development in Africa*, Legon, University of Ghana Publications.

O'Keefe, P. et al. "Mozambican Environmental Problems: Myths and Realities", in *the Journal of Public Administration and Development, Volume* 11, Number 4, 1991, pp. 307-24.

Ottaway, Marine, "The Theory and Practice of Marxism-Leninism in Mozambique and Ethiopia", in Albert, David (editor), *Africa and International Communism*, London, Macmillan, 1980.

Plank, David N. "Aid, Debt, and the End of Sovereignty:Mozambique and its Donors." in the *Journal of Modern African Studies*, Volume 31, Number 3, 1993, pp. 407-430.

Quan, J. *Mozambique: A Cry for Peace*, Oxford, Oxfam, 1987. Ratilal, P. *Mozambique: Using Aid to End Emergency*, United Nations Development Programme (UNDP), New York, 1990.

Richman, N. "Reconciliation and Revenge? The Legacies of War", unpublished paper, Maputo, 1991.

Ruiz, H. *Peace or Terror: A Crossroads for Southern Africa's Uprooted*, United States Committee for Refugees, Washington, USA, 1989.

Rutherford, G.W. and A.E. Mahanjane. " Morbidity and Mortality in the Mozambican Famine of 1983: Prevalence of Malnutrition and Causes and Rates of Death and Illness Amongst Dislocated Persons in Gaza and Inhambane Provinces", in the *Journal of Tropical Paediatric*, Number 31, 1985, pp. 143-9.

Sachs, A. "Apartheid, Destabilisation and Refugees", in the *Journal of Refugee Studies*, Volume 2, Number 4, 1989, pp. 491-503.

Schoffedeers, M. and Bindeger W., *Theoretical Explorations in African Religion*, London, 1986.

Serapiao, Luis B. and Mohammed A. El-Khawas, *Mozambique in the Twentieth Century, From Colonialism to Independence.* Washington DC, University Press of America. 1979.

Sidaway, J.D. "Contested Terrain: Transformation and Continuity of the Territorial Organisation in Post-Independence Mozambique", in *Tijdschrift Voor Economische en Sociale Geografie*, Volume 82, Number 5, 1991, pp. 367-76.

Sidaway, J.D. "Mozambique: Destabilisation, State, Society and Space", in *Political Geography*, Volume 11, Number 3, 1992, pp. 239-258.

Smith, S. *Frontline Africa: The Right to a Future: Oxfam Report on Conflict and Poverty in Southern Africa*, Oxford, Oxfam, 1990.

Sykes, John, *Portugal and Africa: The People and the War*, London, Hutchinson, 1971.

Thomas, S. and A. Hallam "Associations as a Means of Organising Small Enterprises in War-Affected areas of Mozambique - Reflections after four years of Working with Displaced People", in *Small Enterprise Development*, ITDG, September, 1992.

Tickner, Vincent, "Military Attacks, Drought and Hunger in Mozambique", in the *Review of African Political Economies*, Number 33, August 1985, pp. 89-91.

Vail, L. and L. White, *Capitalism and Colonialism in Mozambique: A Study of Quelimane District*, Heinemann Educational Books, London, 1980.

Walter Rodney, "The Year 1895 in Southern Mozambique: African Resistance to the Imposition of European Colonial Rule", in the *Journal of the Historical Society of Nigeria*, Volume 5, Number 4, June 1971.

------------, *How Europe Underdeveloped Africa*, London, Bogle, 1972.

White, L. "Review Article: The Revolutions Ten Years On", in the *Journal of Southern African Studies*, Volume 11, Number 2, 1985.

White, L. *Magomero: A Potrait of an African Village*, Cambridge University Press, 1987.

Wilson, K.B., Linking Returning Home with Development in Northern Mozambique: Some Preliminary Suggestions, unpublished Report, Refugee Studies Programme, Oxford, 1991a.

Wilson, K.B., "The Re-emergent Patroes and Economic Development in Zambesia: Some Comments, unpublished report, Refugee Studies Programme, Oxford, 1991b.

The World Bank, "Demobilization and Reintegration of Military Personnel in Africa: The Evidence from Seven Country Case Studies", Discussion paper, Africa Regional Series, October 1993.

Yanane, Y. Aguibou Mouke, "Peace, Peacemaking and Peacekeeping: The Theory Revisited and its Relevance to Security, Stability and Economic development in South Africa and Southern Africa", paper presented at the Conference on "Revamping and Rebuilding the Security Forces to Achieve and Sustain a Democratic South Africa", Harare, Zimbabwe, January 26-28, 1994.

Appendix

Table I
Impact of insecurity on population distribution

Province	Population (millions)	% displaced	% affected (1989)	Total % displaced and affected (1989)	Total % displaced and affected (1985)
Maputo	1.85	9.37	12.11	12.43	15.46
Gaza	1.20	3.21	54.82	58.00	29.38
Inhambanhe	1.31	14.34	32.44	47.79	34.66
Sofala	1.24	10.08	15.70	25.78	48.57
Manica	0.75	12.19	19.31	31.49	24.18
Tete	1.01	0.60	12.38	21.98	47.69
Zambezia	3.08	17.51	11.85	29.38	29.40
Nampula	2.94	6.81	18.21	25.02	n.a.
Niassa	0.64	31.39	18.79	50.17	73.72
Cabo Delgado	1.13	3.21	7.00	10.21	n.a.
Total	15.17	11.14	18.95	30.10	24.57

Source: Ministry of Commerce and the United Nations, Priority Emergence Assistance Requirements, 14 March 1989.

Table II
Data on displaced and affected populations in Manica Province

District	Displaced population	Affected population	Total
Tambara	8,275	-	8,275
Guro	5,499	36,094	41,593
Barue	11,971	8,425	20,396
Mossurize	2,945	11,893	14,838
Sussudega	11,274	27,722	38,996
Machaze	3,023	22,851	25,874
Maica	11,050	2,060	13,110
Gondola	11,344	80,016	91,360
Total	65,381	189,061	254,442

Source: Courtesy, Provincial Department of Planning, Chimoio.

Name index

Africa   1-4, 6-8, 12, 16, 20,
  25-27, 29, 31-35, 45, 46, 48,
  49, 54, 57, 58, 73, 74, 76,
  78, 79, 86, 98, 101, 103,
  107-113, 116, 128, 134, 137,
  144, 146, 209, 210, 212-214,
  225, 226, 239, 276, 277, 280
ANC   31

Bairro   89, 92, 96, 97, 100,
  108, 131-133, 135, 136
Barwe   131
Beira   15, 17, 30, 47, 48, 51,
  73, 74, 86, 88-90, 97, 99,
  102, 103, 112, 119, 131, 138,
  150, 153, 218, 223, 228
Brother Elijah   278

Caetano   39
Chimoio   13-17, 30, 33, 43, 47,
  48, 52, 54, 59, 72, 74, 86-89,
  92, 95, 97-99, 102, 103, 105,
  106, 108, 110, 118, 129-138,
  142, 145-147, 151, 152, 154,
  155, 223, 226, 229, 231, 234,
  239, 280
Chissano   143, 148, 149, 151

Christianity 59, 214
Cold War   32, 101, 277, 278

Dandaro   133
Dhlakama   30, 140, 146, 147,
  149-151

Fepom   133, 134
FLS   32
FRELIMO   1-4, 8-11, 16, 19,
  25-28,   30-38,   41-44,   46,
  48-50, 54-58, 72, 74-78, 111,
  112, 114, 116, 130, 136, 137,
  140, 142-147, 149-151, 155,
  214-216, 218, 219, 221, 226,
  236, 237, 277

Gaza   3, 16, 54
God   54, 87, 133, 141, 143,
  148, 157, 219, 278
Gondola   16, 39, 42, 46, 54, 86,
  99, 135, 138, 155, 225

ILO   101
Inhambane   16

Kenya   45

Macate 89, 92, 93, 137, 217
Machel 3, 9, 31, 34, 37-41, 49,
   57, 88, 138, 142, 144, 148,
   149, 151, 155, 214, 217-219,
   234, 235, 237
Machipanda 15, 84, 88, 89, 99,
   102, 103, 105, 131
Malawi 51, 71, 77, 136, 210
Manica Province 8, 10, 15, 16,
   30, 35-37, 39, 42, 46-48, 52,
   54, 72-74, 77, 78, 80, 84, 86,
   99, 101, 103, 112, 119, 137,
   221, 230
Manica Town 74, 103, 146
MANU 33
Maputo 3, 12, 16, 37, 47, 48,
   73-75, 103, 106, 107, 130,
   131, 144, 149, 151, 225, 235
Marforga Mission 135, 155
MNR 1-4, 19, 25, 26, 28-31,
   41, 44, 49, 51, 56, 58, 92,
   93, 105, 133, 137, 153, 277,
   279

Nampula 4, 26, 47, 106, 130
Ndau 16, 30, 43, 48, 131
NGOs 87, 107, 155, 236
Niassa 47

OMM 135, 145, 153, 214-219,
   221, 230, 238

Renamo 1-4, 6, 9, 11, 16, 17,
   26, 27, 29-31, 33, 35, 36, 38,
   40-46, 48, 50-58, 75-78, 86,
   88, 90, 92, 93, 106, 112,
   118, 133, 137-140, 142,
   144-146, 150, 151, 155, 225,
   277
Rhodesia 16, 29, 30, 33, 74,
   75, 80, 97
Roman Catholic 129, 155, 228

Sete de Abril 85, 88, 94-96,
   131
Shona 15, 106, 131, 238
Sofala 16, 47, 74, 79, 112, 142
South Africa 2, 4, 16, 29,
   31-33, 73, 74, 76, 78, 79, 86,
   103, 107, 110, 111, 134, 144,
   146, 225
Southern Africa 2-4, 7, 20,
   25-27, 29, 31, 32, 45, 46, 49,
   54, 58, 74, 109, 110, 210,
   276, 277, 280
Sussundenga 96, 226

Tanzania 79, 116, 120
Tete 47, 73, 136

UDENAMO 33
UN 4, 26, 33, 93, 155, 232
UNDP 3
UNICEF 76, 77

Zambezia 12, 53, 73
Zambia 59, 77, 103
Zimbabwe 15, 16, 18, 29-32,
   34, 37, 50, 54, 73-75, 77-80,
   86, 88-90, 96, 97, 99,
   103-106, 108, 110, 119, 132,
   141, 226, 229, 231, 279